Career Guidance in Communities

At best, daily life, like art, is revolutionary.
At worst it is a prison house. At worst reflection,
like criticism, is reactionary. At best it creates plans
for escape. Taking part in detailed life in order
to reflect can be to combine the worst of both.
It takes the innocence of the former to congeal
the latter with guilt.

Paul Willis, 1981

To Michael
You can add up the parts,
you won't have the sum.

RIE THOMSEN

Career Guidance in Communities

Career Guidance in Communities

© The author and Aarhus University Press 2012
Original title: *Vejledning i fællesskaber*. Danish language edition published in 2009 by Studie og Erhverv A.S., Schultz information, Annexstræde 5, DK 2500 Valby, www.schultz.dk © Rie Thomsen and Studie og Erhverv A.S.

Graphic design and layout: Carl H.K. Zakrisson & Tod Alan Spoerl
Cover design: Camilla Jørgensen, Trefold
Printed in Denmark by Narayana Press, 2012

ISBN 978 87 7124 012 2

Distributed by:

Aarhus University Press
Langelandsgade 177
8200 Aarhus N
Denmark
www.unipress.dk

Gazelle Book Services Ltd.
White Cross Mills
Hightown, Lancaster, LA1 4XS
United Kingdom
www.gazellebookservices.co.uk

ISD
70 Enterprise Drive
Bristol, CT 06010
USA
www.isdistribution.com

Financial support for the publication of this book
was kindly provided by Soransk Samfunds Legater and
Aarhus University Research Foundation.

Contents

Preface

The goal of *Career Guidance in Communities* is to help further develop the field of career guidance through a discussion of the following points:

- Career guidance is often thought of and organised in the form of individual interviews, a practice which has been criticised for contributing to individualisation.
- Career guidance is described as having a basic dilemma in which the interests and needs of the individual are contrasted with the interests and needs of society.
- Career choices are linked to concrete participation in communities as well as to interventions aiming at reflection.

The empirical basis of the analysis and discussion presented in this book comprises a study of career guidance at a Danish folk high school (*højskole*[1]) and a Danish factory. The factory was in the process of closing down and dismissing its production staff. In both cases the career guidance provided was characterised by the fact that it took place in existing communities.

The theoretical basis of this book is located in categories of critical psychology such as conditions, reason and meaning, participation, personal conduct in everyday life and self-understanding. These categories are based on a dialectical understanding of the individual and society. People act on the basis of the meaning they ascribe to these conditions; through their actions they modify, change and create these conditions and those of others, while the new conditions create further possibilities for action.

The methodology used is that of practice research. This means that the research was carried out in cooperation with folk high school students, teachers, employees at the factory and career guidance practitioners. Practice research is based on the ideal of a democratic research process in which participants are perceived as co-researchers with a shared problem: how to organise career guidance so that it can be useful and relevant for the participants. Two cases of career guidance were studied intensively through participatory observation over a period of time; 15 participants including students, teachers, staff and career guidance practitioners were each observed over a two-day period ending in a semi-structured interview.

This book takes on a decentred perspective on career guidance, and consequently an interest in how career guidance interacts with the everyday lives of its participants. The meaning and relevance of participation in career guidance is illustrated through:

- Analysis of the situations of participants at the two study settings, and the various ways in which career guidance is connected to these situations.
- Analysis of the way in which the participants influence career guidance, and the influence of the place where guidance occurs.
- Analysis of the way in which the possibilities for participation are not only embedded in the individual but also strongly linked to concrete conditions in the communities in question.
- Analysis of the importance of community with regard to aspects of education, employment and career guidance.

The discussion focuses on the way in which:

- The experiences of other people can be seen as a resource in career guidance contexts.
- The fact that career guidance becomes part of the collective life of communities has an impact on ethics and confidentiality.
- The difference between understanding choices as an internal process of reflection as opposed to being connected to concrete participation in various contexts for action is important and forms the basis for how career guidance is organised.

This book conceptualises career guidance as an institutional arrangement, giving rise to a focus on how participants' encounter with career guidance is connected to the societal problems and conditions to which career guidance practices are suggested as an answer. The empirical exploration of the link between an ascribed significance to career guidance by participants and the inherent structural issues of career guidance is important, because this connection is often regarded as normative, essential and static – a fundamental dilemma for career guidance practice. This discussion leads to a renewed conceptualisation of career guidance that aims to create new possibilities for participation in education and work.

This book provides a concrete example of systematic and theoretical research into career guidance issues and considerations of practice research as a modus for developing practice and policy – a contribution of particular relevance to researchers and practitioners who work with and are interested in a collective turn in career guidance.

This book will be of interest to professionals involved in the fields of educational, vocational, and/or career guidance, or those interested in how institutional practices may be relevant to the everyday lives of its participants, as well as to politicians and other policy-makers in diliberating how career guidance can be applied to societal problems.

Acknowledgements

The publication of this book is a great delight for me. I should like to thank Professors Jenny Bimrose and Ronald Sultana for supporting me in bringing *Career Guidance in Communities*, originally written and published in Danish, to an international audience and to international colleagues.[2] I should also like to thank Nick Wrigley and Tod Alan Spoerl for sharpening my English, as well as Iben Stampe Sletten, my editor from Aarhus University Press.

A warm thanks goes also to Raimo Vurinen at the European Lifelong Guidance Policy Network (ELGPN) and my good colleagues and former supervisors Peter Plant, Aarhus University, and Charlotte Højholt, Roskilde University. And to my husband Michael Thomsen, for his love and support. Careers are collective.

The book *Career Guidance in Communities* can now lead a life of its own amongst all of us interested in career guidance. Its publication is a pat on the back for everyone who has worked together with me and supported my study on the way in which career guidance influences their lives: employees at the factory, students at the folk high school, teachers, HR consultants and career guidance practitioners. This book shows that their ideas about career guidance and everyday life are of a great interest to a great number of people.

Ring the bells that still can ring.

Rie Thomsen, Kirkebjerggaard, Slots Bjergby, September 2012

1 **Introduction**

POUL: I've helped loads of my colleagues to apply for new jobs, and it's been very rewarding to talk with them about this. We talk about it a lot. Flemming went to an interview the day before yesterday, for instance. I had a chat with him yesterday. We talk a lot about who will get a new job and who we think will fail to do so. A good deal of the day passes like that.

RIE: I see … Do you help each other with ideas about where to look?

POUL: To some extent. For instance if we spot something in the newspaper. Yesterday I told Flemming that he ought to look for a job at the driving centre – I know they're often looking for new staff. He could try at least. He likes gardening work and cutting grass, and that's how we help each other. It must be pretty sad to work somewhere where you can't talk to anyone. I wouldn't like to work at such a place.
(*Interview with employee at a factory*)

TINE: We're all walking around thinking: what are we going to do next and what's the best way of moving forward? We're all in the same boat at the moment. And some people have tried – they applied last year and had a few interviews, and some people have done a few courses at university. So we can all help each other somehow and get plenty of different angles on our situation. I actually think it's been great because otherwise you just hang out with the people you normally hang out with, discussing a few things occasionally, and you never really get anywhere. We talk about it all the time (laughs). There's lots to say about the different subjects too, and we talk about it in the lessons. When you say something, ask a question, and

1

they present you with a concrete issue: try doing X, Y or Z when you leave. I was very much in doubt about whether I should apply this year or not. I talked it over with some of the other students and some of the teachers. You must have heard us too – even at breakfast we talk about it. So actually I think it's great. There's a really relaxed attitude about it.
(*Interview with folk high school student*)

These quotations are extracts from the empirical material contained in this book, comprising a qualitative study of two different institutional arrangements for career guidance, one at a Danish folk high school and another in company with a view to discovering the influence of career guidance on individuals in these settings. 15 participants (folk high school students, teachers, employees and career guidance practitioners) were monitored for two days each using participatory observation, ending in a semi-structured interview. This cooperation took place over a two-year period.

In the extracts above Poul talks about his thoughts in relation to applying for a new job after a round of collective dismissals, and Tine talks about applying for further education. We gain insight into how they both orient themselves towards other people to help them handle the situation, using expressions such as: *"We talk about it a lot. It must be pretty sad to work somewhere where you can't talk to anyone. We can all help each other somehow."* This is what everyday life looks like for Tine and Poul. The sense of community they enjoy with their colleagues and other students is used actively as they head towards new jobs and further education; their thoughts about choosing a course or finding a new job take up a lot of space in their everyday lives. *"A good deal of the day passes like that. We talk about it all the time."*

At the same time, in our society we have set up special institutional arrangements which are referred to in general as *career guidance* to support us when we are involved in processes like these. Career guidance takes place in many different contexts, and we often connect it with individual sessions focusing on the choice of course or job, involving one person looking for career guidance and a career guidance practitioner. The Danish education sector spends 60-80 million Euro (DKK 500-600 million) per annum on education guidance (Rambøll, 2008, p. 183). This reflects a political attitude: the idea that guidance can make a difference in relation to a variety of issues. Career guidance is linked both to the thoughts of individuals regarding education and jobs, and to the societal goal that all citizens should have an education and that a high rate of employment is necessary in a welfare society. Guidance practices vary a great deal, but the types that we shall regard as forms of career guidance in this book are all organised with a view to intervening people's thoughts and actions concerning education or employment – thoughts such as those expressed by Tine and Poul: *"Where should we look? What are we going to do next and what's the best way of moving forward?"*

These interventions are often organised in the form of individual sessions carried out by career guidance practitioners using different methodological approaches, often based on socio-dynamic and Social Cognitive Career Theories. The objective declared in the legislation on guidance in education in Denmark is that the choices made based on the career guidance process should benefit both the individual concerned and society as a whole – with particular reference to the business community and labour market. (The Danish Agency for Universities and Internationalisation, 2012). In other words, career guidance is expected to do something for people's lives, and the choices made during career guidance should balance two interests: those of the individual, and those of society. This means that some potential choices do not serve these interests (deciding not to get an education, or deciding to take vocational training, but not to take supplementary training). The fact that these choices are not accepted is revealed by the fact that career guidance is targeted at the individuals who make them – thereby failing to contribute to the Danish government's goal that 95% of each young generation should gain an education that equips them for the labour market, or failing to help boost the qualifications of the Danish labour force (regarded as necessary by the Confederation of Danish Industry and the Danish prime minister in order to guarantee the future of the Danish welfare state). This objective reflects a clear wish to ensure the future of the welfare state for the benefit of all Danish citizens, and fundamentally I regard this as a praiseworthy project. The question here is what the role of career

1

guidance should be in this project. Do individuals decide against further education because they know too little about the options, or because they lack information, support or belief in their chance of completing the course of their choice? Or are there other factors at play?

The issue I discuss in this book has not been plucked from thin air. It comes from my experience of career guidance – partly as a career guidance practitioner, and partly as a researcher. In 2001 I worked as a teacher and career guidance practitioner at a school in Aalborg, where I was responsible for career guidance for 6th-grade pupils. This involved a 20-minute session with each pupil every year. They came along to my office one by one – most of them slightly confused about what they were doing there and what on earth we would talk about. We filled in their education records together and talked about how things were going at school. They left my office with a transcript of their education records to take home for their parents to sign, and it was always extremely difficult to get these records back again after they had been signed.

As a researcher I have met 9th-grade pupils who explained that career guidance was all about giving career guidance practitioners what they were looking for: in other words, it was a question of saying what the practitioners wanted them to say. I have also met career guidance practitioners who were delighted when pupils actually said (and chose) the things that they themselves had been thinking.

I have met unemployed individuals who reported that being summoned for career guidance felt like being monitored by Big Brother; and that from their point of view the main objective was to avoid being forced to take part in any more meaningless activities which they saw as simple control measures that had a negative effect on their self-esteem.

Obviously, these are all examples of situations in which career guidance seemed meaningless to the individuals concerned. In all these examples there was a career guidance practitioner on the other side of the table who felt just as frustrated about the fact that their job was meaningless in the lives of the participants (and in their own lives). These situations have been inspirational for me in writing this book, which basically focuses on how career guidance can come to have a meaningful impact on the lives of the participants.

1.1 Career guidance as an institutional arrangement

In this book, career guidance is studied as an institutional arrangement (Dreier, 2008, pp. 76 ff.) This means focusing analytically on the fact that career guidance is an answer to societal issues, an institutional practice that has been put into the world to help solve particular problems. As the former Danish Minister for Education Bertel Haarder once said: "We need to be able to say that if career guidance did not exist we would be forced to invent it" (Haarder, 2008; author's translation). If there were no such thing as career guidance, would this mean that the problems of high student drop-out rates, bottlenecks in the labour market, students delaying the completion of their studies etc. did not exist? Or would it mean that our politicians would be working on other solutions to these problems instead of offering people career guidance? When career guidance is described as an institutional arrangement, two particular characteristics of career guidance are brought into focus: (1) career guidance as a practice has institutional links, one of which is the legal basis which establishes and regulates career guidance practice; and (2) career guidance must be *arranged* in the sense that someone must act in relation to practice in order to make it work and give it meaning. An arrangement has participants who each contribute to the performance of the arrangement. Conceptualising career guidance as an institutional arrangement draws attention to practice as a societal institution which is arranged with a specific purpose, as well as to the fact that concrete meetings and activities need to be arranged by the participants to ensure that practice takes place and works.

A range of measures passed by the Danish *Folketing* in recent years mean that the field of career guidance has expanded. Some of the most extensive of these measures were the career guidance reform in 2003, the establishment of the option of competence assessment, and the establishment of the adult career guidance networks. The Danish Ministry of Education described a number of the goals of the reform of educational guidance in 2003 (often referred to as the career guidance reform of 2003). Among other things, career guidance should:

1

- Help to ensure that choices about education and career benefit
  the individuals concerned and society as much as possible.
- Be targeted at young people with a special need for career
  guidance in relation to their choices of education, vocational
  training and career.
- Take its point of departure in individual interests, personal
  qualifications and abilities, including real competences,
  previous experience of education and the labour market,
  and expectations regarding future needs for a workforce
  and entrepreneurs.
- Help to reduce the student drop-out rate.
  (*Danish Ministry of Education, 2004; author's translation*)

Clearly, different institutional arrangements for career guidance are
intended to play a role in relation to problems connected to the education system and problems connected to the composition of the
workforce and development of the labour market. But is it reasonable
to assume that career guidance can make such a big difference in relation to the way the education system works and the way the labour
market can be developed and changed? Are we as a society turning
certain issues into career guidance problems in order to tackle them
in particular ways? This extract from the goals of the career guidance
reform underlines that career guidance must take its point of departure in individual interests and personal qualifications, and that the
choices made during career guidance must be based on the individuals concerned but with due regard for the interests of society and for
the benefit of both the individual and society as a whole.

If career guidance is to solve these problems, then pupils, students,
the unemployed and others involved in career guidance must enter
into the career guidance process in such a way that it is relevant for
them, involves them, and has an effect for them. But what does a career guidance practice need to ensure that the individuals being guided perceive it as relevant and useful? This question is one of the driving forces of the work that lies behind this book, and it should be seen
in the light of a wish to contribute knowledge to the field of career
guidance which makes it possible to develop career guidance practice
in a direction which the participants perceive as relevant and useful,

and in a direction which career guidance practitioners perceive as satisfactory because they can see that their work makes a difference.

1.2 Including users in quality work

Bertel Haarder, Minister for Education in the previous Danish government, was keen to include users in the quality work involved in developing career guidance practice (Haarder, 2008); according to him, quality in career guidance is initially all about measuring effects and other results. For instance, this involved tracking the paths of the users when they moved around the career guidance and education system, and measuring the effect of career guidance. But according to Haarder, measuring effects and registering results have their limitations when it comes to developing career guidance practice. He asks "But how can quality be measured in the encounter between young people and career guidance practitioners? This is a challenge that extends beyond measurements and the registration of results" (Haarder, 2008, p. 2; author's translation); and he points out that the goal of career guidance is to make young people autonomous, making it difficult to measure the effect of career guidance. "So it is natural that the users of career guidance schemes […] should be included in quality work with a view to creating the basis for user-driven development" (Haarder, 2008, p. 2; author's translation).

This book contributes knowledge about the encounter between users and career guidance from a user perspective. A number of research traditions deal with user perspectives (or participant perspectives, which is the term I use in this book). Within the fields of practice research, social practice theory and critical psychology, people are particularly interested in exploring the dilemmas and problems facing practice seen from the perspective of participants. Consequently, this book is based on these research traditions, which are explained at greater length in chapter 6. The section below explains the way in which, via practice research, the participant perspective can generate knowledge about how career guidance can have an impact on the lives of participants.

1

1.3 **The participant perspective**

The participant perspective is one particular way of understanding the way people are in the world. Within the fields of social practice theory and practice research, which are the theoretical point of departure of this book as explained in chapter 6, participation is described as an ontological concept: we are in the world owing to our participation in it (Dreier, 1999b; Lave & Wenger, 2007). Charlotte Højholt has the following to say about practice research: "You could say that in our work we take our point of departure in a dialectic concept of structure – we are interested in the fact that people *act* and create together in and with social structures. In this way we seek to underline that structures are things which we create together in various types of human community in which we structure our possibilities for doing things when we act together" (Højholt, 2005, p. 31, emphasis in the original Danish). The participant perspective is important with regard to organising my own research process, since I appraoch two career guidance practices by studying the way people participate in them from their own perspective, with their own reasons, and in interaction with their participation elsewhere. The study is therefore decentralised in relation to the actual career guidance practice (Dreier, 2008). Centred analysis takes it point of departure in practice, focuses on career guidance practice, and remains within career guidance practice by asking questions such as: What happens in a career guidance session? How do career guidance practitioners meet the participants in career guidance? What is the apparent effect of various career guidance methods in relation to the way interventions are conducted and what is the benefit to the users? By contrast, decentred analysis is interested in focusing on the way participants lead their lives and the impact of career guidance on these lives. Decentred analysis examines how career guidance interacts with the many different ways in which people tackle vocational and educational challenges, as well as examining the interaction between career guidance and the many other contexts in which these challenges are handled (in the workplace, with friends or anywhere else where people join forces to consider their jobs, education and careers).

1.4 **Guidance – career guidance**

One of the latest definitions of guidance can be found in the EU's *Resolution on the integration of lifelong guidance in strategies for lifelong learning*, which gives "the definition of guidance as referring to a continuous process that enables citizens at any age and any point in their lives to identify their capacities, competences and interests, to make educational, training and occupational decisions and to manage their individual life trajectories in learning, work and other settings in which those capacities and competences are learned and/or used. Guidance covers a range of individual and collective activities relating to information-giving, counselling, competence assessment, support, and the teaching of decision-making and career management skills" (Council of the European Union, 2008). The resolution mentions various ways of supporting this process: information-giving, counselling, competence assessment, support and teaching people how to make decisions and plan their careers. Guidance is targeted at people of all ages and in all kinds of life situation, and it can be organised either individually or collectively.

In a Danish context educational and vocational guidance often involves young people, because in Denmark the term was originally linked solely to vocational guidance for young people (Plant, 1996)[3]. But at the moment "career guidance" is the favoured term in this country. As Plant indicates (Plant, 1998), the term "career" in Danish used to be linked solely to the labour market, and it had negative connotations (people carving out a career for themselves without considering the needs of their spouses, children or colleagues). But now the term is used in a variety of ways (see Højdal & Poulsen, 2007). An attempt has been made to abandon the understanding of a "career" as an upwardly mobile process reserved for a small minority; instead the use of the term today constitutes an attempt "to capture the complexity arising owing to the fact that people live their lives at the same time as they create the framework for their lives" (Højdal & Poulsen, 2007, p. 13; author's translation). And in this sense the concept of "career" seems also to connote a broader target group than that covered by educational and vocational guidance alone. The target group for career

21

1

guidance contains people in employment, recent graduates and un-employed people of all ages. Nowadays everyone has a career, and a career is not seen in terms of linear progress within a specific field – instead, it can involve many different fields and life contexts.

I have chosen to use the term "career guidance" instead of just "guidance" in the title of this book emphasise its focus on the form of guidance that aims to support individuals in relation to education-al or vocational thoughts and decisions – by contrast with guidance in writing assignments, guidance or supervision of colleagues, per-sonal counselling etc. At the same time, it is important to note that delimiting the themes of guidance is a problematic thing to do in the light of the fact that the aim of the book is find out how guidance af-fects the lives of participants by studying how it interacts with the ways they lead their complex lives. This is why I am more interested in focusing on interaction, connections and contexts than in defin-ing what career guidance is and what it is not. So the definitions above should not be regarded as complete in relation to the way this book perceives career guidance, but rather as examples of possible understandings of career guidance. This book also provides new un-derstandings of the term.

This book studies the meeting between participants and career guidance practice: the researcher is present at career guidance sessions with the participants and enters into, goes through or even goes past career guidance practice in order to explore the way in which it inter-acts with the everyday lives of the participants and is influenced by people's participation in different contexts. So the participant per-spective is important in relation to the selection of study settings. In order to explore a decentred perspective on career guidance, settings were chosen in which it is possible to monitor the participants for many hours as well as seeing and discussing the challenges they were facing and considering how career guidance affects them. I was given the opportunity to do this at both a Danish folk high school and a Danish company.

1.5 Study settings

The participants in career guidance in this study were: (1) individuals trying to choose a course of further education (young people at the folk high school), and (2) individuals who had lost their jobs and had to find new ones (employees at the production company). Participatory observation and interviews enabled me to follow the everyday lives of the students and employees involved. I also observed the teachers and career guidance practitioners in both settings. The company employees and the folk high school students encountered very different career guidance practices. The company organised a "career guidance corner" at the company, manned by a career guidance practitioner provided by the company to help its employees find new jobs or courses of supplementary training. At the folk high school career guidance was provided by all the teachers and present in the everyday pratice of the folk high school as an overall space for career guidance (Kofod names this the folk high school's career guidance space; Kofod, 2004). In addition various career guidance events were organised for the students in cooperation with the Regional Study Choice Centre and different institutions of education. The legal basis of the Danish folk high schools states that career guidance must be offered,[4] that cooperation with Study Choice Centres is one option, and that on their homepages folk high schools must describe the career guidance service that they provide. The career guidance offered by VUS Kontakt, who were responsible for career guidance at the company, did not relate to any specific legal basis but started life as a pilot project involving career guidance for people in work who had completed short-term training. The objective of VUS Kontakt was clearly connected to the political objectives of career guidance, in which increasing the qualifications of (and providing supplementary training for) people with short-term training behind them is placed high on the agenda (e.g. *Trepartsudvalget*, 2006). The objective is virtually the same as that of the 22 adult career guidance networks that were established in 2007.

This introduction generates a series of questions concerning career guidance. How can career guidance be organised to ensure that

1

it is perceived as relevant and useful by the participants? What are the problems that career guidance is required to solve?

The questions are linked to both the perspective of the participants and the societal expectations of career guidance. The research question outlined below explores the meaning of career guidance as connected to other contexts of action in the everyday lives of the participants.

1.6 **Research question**

— How can the meanings of career guidance seen from a participant perspective be understood on the basis of a study of two different institutional arrangements of career guidance?

The question indicates that the study must be based on a theoretical foundation that provides concepts rendering it possible to analyse connections between institutional arrangements and their societal meaning, and the meaning that individuals attribute to their participation in these arrangements. Critical psychology is a potential option, and is presented in chapter 6; thoughts regarding the methodological organisation of practice research are presented in chapter 7.

The term "meanings" is used in the plural in the research question to underline two things: first, that there may be different meanings for the same person; and second, that there may be different meanings for different individuals. These meanings are explored by using participatory observation of everyday life at the company and folk high school involved. Career guidance practice is explored in the way in which the employees and students in question encounter different career guidance activities. These observations are followed by interviews in which we jointly explore the way in which the meaning attributed by the participants to their participation in career guidance is connected to their participation elsewhere. This is why the meaning for each participant is never in the singular – there are always several often contradictory meanings existing side by side which explain their participation in (or rejection of) career guidance in various ways. So the term "meaning" is not used in the sense of assessing the meaning of career guidance practice in the long term or the meaning of career guidance from a political perspective, where the term "effect" is often used. The two latter understandings would call for a different methodological approach to the study as either longitudinal and/or comparative.

2 **Study settings**

Chapter 2 introduces the study settings. The aim of doing this at an early stage of the book is to make the settings in which career guidance is practised concrete and specific for the reader. Career guidance is then described in more general terms because it has to function in many different contexts, interacting with the everyday lives of the participants concerned. Finally, the reader is presented with a summary of the analysis themes in the material obtained from the two study settings.

2.1 **The folk high school**

The folk high school (*højskole* in Danish) where this study was carried out was founded in 1897, and now defines itself as an institution that prepares its students for further study (particularly in nursing/medicine, social pedagogy and journalism). There is an outdoor pursuits course and a travel project, and the school emphasises its Christian foundations. Students can attend for 17-19 weeks or one month, during which time the focus is placed on identifying and defining their competences. This course is called"Valuable Competencies". Most of the students take both courses. They are aged 18-25, they live in two-person dormitories, and each corridor has its own teacher dealing with corridor duties. The building is typical of Danish architecture from the 1970s, with classrooms located along long corridors and dormitories along another corridor. The dining room, gymnasium and basement recreational area are all in the same building. I met the students for the first time at morning assembly, at which there were various presentations and communal singing from the folk high school hymn book. My presence and the aim of the project had not been presented to the students yet, so I described the project briefly and underlined its anonymity and other points. Then I distributed a brief questionnaire offering the students the opportunity to take part in my research project by allowing their everyday lives to be monitored for a couple of days. A number of students said that they were happy to be involved. The next day I gathered these students together for a meeting and we decided who I should monitor. We agreed on a number of days for future meetings. Subsequently these were altered a number of times. The interviews included students from the journalism course, the nursing course and the social-pedagogy course. For practical reasons it was not possible for the students on the travel project to take part.

2.1.1 Career guidance at the folk high school

Under Danish legislation folk high schools are obliged to offer their long-term students career guidance. At this particular folk high school one of the teachers was the "Educational and Vocational Guidance Counsellor", but in principle all the teachers provided career guidance for any students who wanted it. Several of the teachers said that spontaneous discussions or informal dialogues were the best way of making a difference. In this respect this folk high school resembles many others in Denmark; other research has demonstrated that the career guidance provided by such folk high schools is characterised by the fact that it is organised informally (Kofod, 2004). The folk high school offers its students a variety of dialogues, discussions and interviews, an introductory interview and concluding discussion as well as personal dialogues in connection with the "Valuable Competencies" course, plus a number of more subject-related discussions. Even though the folk high school underlines its high degree of informality on the one hand, there are a relatively large number of planned interventions on offer.

2.2 **The company**

2

The company under question produces paint, and has done so for many years – first as a Danish company, and now as part of an international corporation. When I arrived at the company there were about ten employees in the production department. They had been with the company for an average of 18 years, and their average age was almost 50. The men in the production department had their own particular way of communicating – they described it as "rough but caring". Their jobs were physically demanding, involving lifting and moving heavy plastic containers of paint. They worked on platforms located around the production hall. Hooks suspended from the ceiling were used to lift big sacks of dye powder for mixing in the mixing tanks. I saw a number of fork-lift trucks racing around the production hall carrying raw materials for the various products. The employees belong to the union called "3F" and the shop steward works in the production hall. In the lunch room each employee has a mug with his name on it hanging on the wall. Photos of previous fishing trips and football tournaments are pinned on one wall; Ulla, the career guidance practitioner from VUS Kontakt, uses the other wall for job advertisements. The lunch room is used for smoking, breaks and dining.

Everyone in the company wears working clothes or old jumpers and T-shirts, and they recommended that I wore old clothes too – in the factory your clothes get soiled with the kind of dirt that never comes off. The employees were introduced to the project at morning coffee in the lunch room. The foreman, HR manager and VUS Kontakt career guidance practitioner had already identified the employees who would be asked whether they wanted to take part in the project before my meeting with them. The only criterion was whether people wanted to take part.

2.2.1 Career guidance by VUS Kontakt

VUS Kontakt is an organisation established jointly by Copenhagen Municipality, Copenhagen County, Frederiksberg Municipality and parties representing the labour market. "VUS" stands for "Adult

Education Service" in Danish. It was established in 1992. Information and career guidance were free in the Copenhagen region up until 2005. Today VUS Kontakt is funded by the career guidance and consultant services that they sell. It offers companies, organisations and employees information and career guidance regarding supplementary training as well as relevant financial guidance. VUS Kontakt employs a manager and a career guidance practitioner, as well as taking on extra career guidance practitioners when required. It is not a career guidance centre for individuals – you cannot walk in off the street. VUS Kontakt approaches adults through contacts with companies and trade unions. It focuses on people in employment who have a short-term education behind them; in its annual report the organisation describes its goals for 2006 as follows: "The focal points for the year will be the need of companies and organisations for career guidance when companies move or merge; efforts concerning the basic competences of people with a short-term education behind them; and the development of institution-neutral career guidance services" (VUS Kontakt, 2005, p. 10; author's translation). This objective resembles that of the 22 public adult career guidance networks that were formed in 2007.

The point of departure for the agreement with the company was that a career guidance corner should be set up in which the career guidance practitioner could provide career guidance for the company. In the analysis the use of career guidance corners is dealt with in greater detail. The company was involved in winding up its production and closing down a warehouse. Two career guidance practitioners from VUS Kontakt were hired to set up and man career guidance corners in both locations, and were available for any dialogues and discussions that were required. In their annual report, VUS Kontakt describe the task as follows: "Following an approach by 3F and the company, VUS Kontakt have provided consulting services to employees from the production departments of two companies in the same group whose employment had been discontinued. Both companies are closing down their production and warehouses in Denmark. Both are moving to Sweden, and the companies have been forced to fire 18 and 22 employees respectively. The companies wanted to provide full support for these employees in relation to their future job situation,

2

and VUS Kontakt were asked to take part in these efforts. The consulting services comprised individual interviews to identify needs, career guidance sessions, employment and career education, the establishment of career guidance corners involving notices about situations vacant, and assistance in producing CVs and applications for jobs that had not been advertised" (Annual Report 2006, VUS Kontakt 2005; author's translation).

2.3 **Analysis themes**

The analysis consists of two chapters: chapter 8 (Career guidance in the company) and chapter 9 (Career guidance at the folk high school). The analysis contains the following sections:

2.3.1 Analysis of material from the company

Section 8.2 ("Losing your job") begins the analysis of material from the company. A typical working day at the company is described, using quotations from my interviews and observations to paint a picture of the way in which the employees describe their current situation: their place of work is closing down and they have to find new jobs. This situation causes a break in the cycle of their lives and creates a new transitional situation which helps them to see their conditions in a new light – something to which I return in section 8.5 ("New possibilities for participating in education"). Section 8.3 is entitled "Career guidance in the company"; this is where I consider how the employees encounter, perceive and use the career guidance provided for them by the career guidance practitioner. This section discusses what the employees describe as career guidance and their wishes in relation to career guidance in connection with the transition to a new job or unemployment. It forms the basis for a discussion of the way in which the possibilities for participation perceived by the individual are also linked to their perception of who is responsible for finding them a new job, to their perception of and participation in career guidance, and to the organisation of career guidance. In section 8.4 ("Career guidance corners") I deal with the way in which career guidance was developed in the company, showing that career guidance is a flexible practice which is influenced by the place in which it is practised. The career guidance planned by the career guidance practitioner was changed in the course of the process at the company, and I demonstrate how these changes were also influenced by the concrete places and contexts in which career guidance took place. The analysis of material from the company is concluded in section 8.5 ("New possibilities for participating in training"), where I demonstrate that the employees' possibilities for taking part in supplementary training changed in the new situation – partly because the company offered to pay for courses other than those it had offered before, but also because the ideas of the employees about what was relevant for them changed. This section forms the basis of a discussion of the issues that need dealing with in career guidance.

2.3.2 Analysis of material from the folk high school

Section 9.2 ("The situation of the students") begins the analysis of material from the folk high school. I describe a typical day at the school, using quotations from interviews and observations to paint a picture of the current situation of the students, who need to choose a course of education and submit an application for it. In this section I deal with the reasons why students choose to study at the folk high school, and their sense of being in the same boat when it comes to making decisions about their future. I also deal with the expectations of the folk high school with regard to student participation in the life of the school. This section provides the basis for discussing the way in which understanding yourself also involves others and a "we". In section 9.3 ("Career guidance at the folk high school") I am interested in the encounter the students have with career guidance. What is their picture of career guidance? What activities do they regard as important in relation to the career guidance in which they take part? What are their wishes with regard to future career guidance? Three themes are identified. The first theme is a wish that career guidance will help them to create a link between their opportunities and their qualifications. The second theme deals with information about and perceptions of the social life at educational institution or place of employment to which it leads. And the third theme is a wish to be challenged in relation to the reasons for their educational choices. This is followed by section 9.4 ("Career guidance space at the folk high school"), in which I concentrate on the interaction between physical places at the folk high school and the possibilities provided by the contexts in relation to the organisation of career guidance. The final section in the analysis of material from the folk high school is section 9.5 ("The importance of community"). In this section I analyse the importance of community seen from two perspectives: (1) the perspective of the students (what significance do they attribute to the community of which they are part?); and (2) the perspective of the teachers (what are their ideas about the importance of community in relation to the students' ideas about choosing an education?). This section explores the opportunities available to career guidance practitioners when it comes to including the importance of community in the interaction between career guidance and the practice of the folk high school.

2.4 Two stylistic features

Two stylistic features occur in this book which I would like to account for here. One of them is that before the analyses the reader will encounter two vignettes describing a day at the folk high school and a day at the company seen from the perspective of the folk high school students and employees respectively. The second is that throughout the book the grammatical perspective alternates between the third person and the first person.

The aim of these vignettes is to give the reader a more detailed impression of the two study settings. Participatory observation means that as a researcher I have to be present in these settings for many hours and a number of days, observing a variety of individuals and processes. I am interested in the importance of the places and human interaction, which is why I wish to give the reader an impression of these places which does not only include the year the buildings were built, the number of employees/students etc. This is why I have chosen to introduce my analyses in chapters 8 and 9 with two vignettes ("Welcome to the company" and "Welcome to the folk high school"), in which I try to give an impression of everyday life at the company and folk high school from a participant perspective. These passages include individuals and their thoughts about the place in which they find themselves. The people in these vignettes are composite individuals, and the events described are typical of days at the locations in question as observed by me throughout the study period. The thoughts presented in the vignettes constitute a condensation of the thoughts, ideas and impressions communicated to me during discussions and dialogues with employees and students, observations and interviews. A similar approach can be found in Wenger's book entitled *Communities of Practice*, in which vignette I describes a working day at the insurance company Alinsu seen through the perspective and thoughts of an employee (Wenger, 2004, p. 29).

The shift in perspective becomes apparent in passages in which I switch between the third person (he, the individual or the participant) and the first person (I, me or my participation). The purpose of this grammatical shift is to make it clear how an analytical or theoretical point appears to come from a first-person perspective. This means that I do not write "the folk high school student" or "the employee" but "I" when the participant in career guidance is talking. This stylistic feature is used with the same motive by other researchers wishing to underline theoretical or analytical points from a first-person perspective. Here is an example from Ole Dreier's book *Psycho-Therapy in Everyday Life*: "Experiences are my experiences in a first-person perspective from my location in a context and my exchange with others' perspectives in it. Indeed, it is also my relation to others' experiences from my location as a particular part thereof. In understanding the experiences of others from my perspective, I am aware that, just like mine, they are having experiences from their locations in our context. The experiences we exchange share this basic quality" (Dreier, 2008, p. 35).

3 Career guidance as an institutional arrangement

In this book career guidance is conceptualised as an institutional arrangement, leading to an analytical focus on the fact that career guidance has institutional connections and that it is arranged concretely between individuals. I present institutional connections in the form of organising career guidance into various activities practitioners can, the societal objectives of guidance and the way in which guidance handles these (including the use of ethical standards for guidance). The overall idea is to provide insight into the regulated field to which career guidance, as practised in my two study settings, is linked. I demonstrate the way in which career guidance is described in Danish legislation, and how it is described in the ethical standards by actors in the field and by other researchers as having an inherent and normative basic dilemma, with "normative" denoting a naturalised and inevitable understanding. The basic dilemma consists of a double objective in relation to the fact that practice must accommodate both societal and individual interests. And in conclusion, this double objective is problematised.

3.1 The Danish career guidance system

There are about 55 Acts of Parliament and Executive Orders defining the structures of career guidance in Denmark.[5] The institutional arrangements for educational and career guidance can be found primarily in the following main areas: education, employment, the third sector (adult education, folk high schools etc.), the labour market (unemployment insurance funds, trade unions etc), and companies.

– Guidance regarding *education*. This takes place under the auspices of Youth Guidance Centres (*Ungdommens Uddan-nelsesvejledning*), of which there are 52 independent municipal centres, in the seven regional Guidance (*Studievalg*) Centres, and at all educational institutions including institutions for adult and supplementary education.
– Guidance is offered as part of the municipal *employment scheme* and focuses on educational and vocational guidance. The practitioners provide guidance for both individuals and companies about the options for competence development and supplementary training of employees, for instance.
– Guidance in *the third sector* in connection with public educa-tion obliges folk high schools and other similar organisations to offer their long-term students both educational and voca-tional guidance.
– *Guidance in unemployment insurance funds*. Under Danish legislation, unemployment insurance funds must offer guidance to their members, which focuses on job applications, effective job advertising and relevant activities capable of ensuring the unemployed person a rapid return to the labour market (VEJ15, 2007).
– 22 adult guidance networks have been set up to provide guid-ance for adults in employment who have little or no further education, with a view to identifying their competences and options for further training.
– Private-sector career guidance is available in the form of career coaching and counselling. It is not subject to legislative require-ments; the titles "supervisor", "coach" and "mentor" are not authorised titles. Private actors can also submit tenders for public-sector guidance projects.

Career guidance starts in the first grade of school in Denmark with a subject called "Information about education, vocations and the labour market" (UEA). No specific number of lessons is allocated to this subject, and it is generally taught by the class teacher (perhaps in collaboration with a career guidance practitioner from one of the Youth Guidance Centres. From the sixth grade all schoolchildren have to attend an annual meeting with a career guidance practitioner from Youth Guidance Centres; and from the eighth grade this increases to two meetings a year. This has been regulated since the study on which this book is based. For an updated overview of the Danish guidance system, see Thomsen and Plant 2012) There has been a political wish in Denmark to establish a coherent career guidance system ensuring that nobody is left behind without any career guidance at all.

In Denmark it seems to be the institution to which people are linked that determines the way in which they participate in career guidance practice. For some groups (young people and the unemployed), participation in career guidance is compulsory. For many years the possibilities for career guidance available to adults who were in employment were limited to the educational institutions that provide adult and supplementary education; 22 cross-institutional adult career guidance networks were set up in 2007 to remedy this problem. The main task of these networks is to offer career guidance to small and medium-sized enterprises employing people with little or no further education (Ministry of Education, 2007). In terms of career guidance for adults the provision is limited to one specific group: people with little or no further education. It is also worth noting that the primary target group for these adult career guidance networks is not the individuals concerned but the companies at which they work. This should be seen in the light of the fact that people with little or no further education are often described as the target groups who are least motivated for career guidance – people who rarely look for career guidance themselves (Holsbo, 2005; Jensen, 2008). As a result, career guidance for these individuals is organised proactively, for instance in the form of career guidance corners at the companies concerned. I shall return to this point in section 8.4 ("Career guidance corners").

3.2 **The societal goals of career guidance**

Professor A.G. Watts from the National Institute for Careers Education and Counselling at Derby University in the UK has worked on the societal objectives of career guidance.[6] Based on an analysis of career guidance from a socio-political perspective, Watts characterises four different angles on career guidance: *liberal, conservative, progressive* and *radical* (Watts, 1998, pp. 214 ff.) It is important to remember that the use of these terms by Watts differs from the way in which they are used in more general contexts in Denmark. *Liberal* covers career guidance as a client-centred process with reference to humanistic approaches such as the theory of psychologist Carl Rogers (Rogers, 1961), which involves helping individuals to choose options corresponding to their abilities, skills, interests and values. According to Watts sociologists often adopt a different critical angle in which the goals of career guidance are criticised because they adapt the choices of individuals to match the needs of the labour market as much as possible – a perspective categorised by Watts as *conservative*. From a third and more emancipatory angle the societal objectives of career guidance are described as having a *progressive* function, with the goal being to help individuals to break the mould. The career guidance practitioner assumes the role of the person who helps to move barriers in the path of the young person so they can perceive and pursue new opportunities. The final angle on the societal objectives of career guidance is categorised by Watts as *radical*, with the term "radical" referring to the wish to promote radical social changes by regarding society as something that is divided into groups whose interests interact with each other. As a result, changes for one group will promote or inhibit social changes in society for other groups as well. When viewed against this background, career guidance in a radical understanding will focus on group culture and the development of socio-political awareness in the participants in career guidance. Krøjer and Hutters' method, categorised as "Storytelling workshops" (see chapter 5), could therefore be regarded as radical.

3

Figure 1 shows Watts' four socio-political angles on career guidance as well as similar ideas outlined by Plant, who is often quoted in
Danish career guidance literature (Plant, 1996; Watts, 1998). Plant's
concepts are in italics.

	Main focus on society *Societal focus*	Main focus on the individual *Individual focus*
Change	Radical (social change) *Social change*	Progressive (individual change) *Individual development*
Status quo	Conservative (social control) *Social control*	Liberal (uncontrolled) *Individual adaptation*

Figure 1. The goals of career guidance in a four-field table

Watts points out that the liberal and progressive angles dominate
career guidance practice (Watts, 1998, p. 217). It is important to emphasise at this point that he is talking about career guidance practice
(the perceptions of career guidance practitioners regarding the societal goals of career guidance), and not necessarily political understandings of the function of career guidance. In Denmark the model
is often referred to as "the four-field table". It presents career guidance in a conflicting perspective in which the various main aims seem
to be separate, something which (as shown in Anders Lovén's argument below) might lead career guidance practitioners to prioritise
individual development over social adjustment, for instance, which
might in turn conceal the fact that what is involved is always an interaction between these four fields.

Knowledge of the four-field table is important with a view to understanding why the division into societal and individual interests
is so dominant in these fields. It is often used as the analytical basis
for deciding what the main emphasis of a particular practice should
be, or how career guidance practitioners perceive their tasks, or what
should be prioritised within any one method.

If we consider the Danish Act on educational and vocational guidance (LBK630, 2008) through the lens of the four-field table, various
socio-political angles also become apparent. The first section of the
Act states that career guidance should help to ensure that educational

38

and vocational choices should benefit the individual and society as much as possible, and that all young Danes should complete a course of education providing them with the competences needed to get a job. From a political point of view, career guidance clearly has a dual objective in Denmark. It is debatable whether it is possible for career guidance practitioners to predict which choices will benefit society and which will not, in light of the fact that both market conditions and individual needs change over time, and that these changes do not always benefit either society or the individual (Preisler, 2008). When career guidance is discussed in a context in which the aim is to achieve a well qualified labour force quickly in order to preserve the welfare state, career guidance practitioners are likely to provide guidance based on the current needs of society. These are the societal needs with which they are familiar and which can be easily identified. The question is whether this does not lead to the risk of promoting a conservative function for career guidance with the focus on social control and adaptation to meet current societal needs, encouraging participants in career guidance to make choices in line with the current needs of society. If this is the case, career guidance will resemble an institution that maintains or preserves the existing society. But the Danish legislation also contains a liberal angle, because young people should also make choices based on their own interests. So the Danish legislation differs from Watts' view that most career guidance can be regarded as progressive or liberal (focusing on individual change on a non-controlling basis). Instead, Danish legislation seems to promote an understanding of career guidance which is conservative and liberal (social control on a non-controlling basis), which may seem like a contradiction in terms. It seems that that the political view of career guidance in Denmark is characterised more by its focus on the status quo in relation to preserving the (welfare) state we have today than by any attempt to use career guidance as part of a societal development.

The Danish legislation is very clear in stating that the career guidance offered must meet the needs of society, and the needs of society are specifiedas the need for a future labour force. According to Watts, this kind of clarity may create problems when it comes to achieving the potential goals and benefits of career guidance. He encourages governments to adopt the position of beneficiaries in relation to financing career guidance for its citizens, thereby reducing the focus on the societal perspective (Watts, 1998). The focus on the societal perspective can be reduced if career guidance practitioners identify both practical and ethical reasons why individuals in career guidance must be the primary clients, because career guidance only works if practitioners enjoy the confidence and trust of the individuals with whom they are working (Watts, 1998; FUE, 2005). From this perspective, the fact that the societal interest in career guidance is identified so clearly may conflict with the view that career guidance practitioners should enjoy the trust of the participants. Practitioners point out that this kind of trust is very hard to achieve if the participants are uncertain about whose interests practitioners are protecting. Perhaps this is the reason why the focus of many methodological approaches to career guidance is placed on how professionals can gain the trust of the participants in career guidance (Buhl & Flindt Pedersen, 2007; Løve, 2005).

The double function of career guidance in relation to catering for both individual and societal interests leads us to problematise various aspects of career guidance practice. Two studies are presented below, each taking its point of departure in what we could call the basic problem of career guidance. Lovén asked the practitioners in his study of how they perceive the function of career guidance to place themselves in relation to Watts' four-field table. The majority saw career guidance as a practice that preserved society and were divided between the individually focused area in the field *individual adaptation* and the socially focused area in the field *social control*. None of the career guidance practitioners in Lovén's study saw the function of vocational guidance as something that could change society (Lovén, 1995, p. 110). To some extent this contrasts with the expectations that I presented in the introduction to this book (in general, career guidance is expected to contribute to the solution of societal problems such as the lack of manpower and the marginalisation of certain groups by changing the actions of the individuals).

The way in which the societal goals of career guidance are perceived by the actors involved in the field (career guidance associations, trade unions, schools and associations of employers) is illustrated in a study of the responses given by various actors in connection with the presentation of the reform of educational and vocational career guidance for young people in 2003. This analysis shows that these actors expect career guidance to help to change society. Three "voices" can then be identified, each focusing on the balance between the interests of society and the interests of the individual (Callesen, Jensen, Roesen & Thomsen, 2003).

Here is a description of the three "voices" within which the actors involved in career guidance in Denmark can be grouped:

3

THE INDIVIDUAL AS FOCUS

The personal growth of the individual participating in career guidance comes first, and using an uncontrolled basis the idea of career guidance is to help individuals to make the most of their potential. This approach challenges the idea that the needs of society should be the primary goal of career guidance. The perspective of the individual is clearest, and this voice can be contrasted with the voice called "society as focus".

SOCIETY AS FOCUS

The characteristics of this voice are: career guidance is seen as a tool for generating a labour force for occupations with good employment prospects; declarations are made regarding greater inclusion of the parties involved in the labour market; and career guidance is approached as a means of avoiding high drop-out rates. This voice is not particularly loud in the responses received by the study.

THE CONSENSUS VOICE

The interests of society and the individual coincide, and this is not regarded as a problem. What benefits society also seems to benefit the individual, and vice versa. Many of the responses expressing these views can be classified as reflecting a consensus approach in which conflicting interests between the interests of society and those of the individual are toned down.

The individual perspective and the consensus voice are the dominating voices in the responses in this study (Callesen et al., 2003).

41

The responses obtained by Callesen et al. revolve around the two poles (society and individual) mentioned above; so this is not merely a theoretical division produced by Watts and Plant – it also seems to reflect the dual goals of career guidance pursued by actors in the field.

Researchers studying a variety of issues in relation to career guidance also comment on this division. For instance, in her doctoral dissertation on career guidance interviews Gunnel Lindh writes that the goal of career guidance gives rise to a number of conflicts of a normative/ideological nature, because career guidance is expected to benefit individuals and their personal development while society makes demands for the right labour force with the right qualifications (Lindh, 2000, p. 24). Lindh deals with this issue by pointing out that career guidance can be carried out to fill the empty spaces at institutions of education or to fill specific positions in the business community – but this is not career guidance in the sense that she employs in her dissertation (Lindh, 2000, p. 27). Lindh tries to avoid the problem by acknowledging that it is normative by nature, and then by placing herself in the individual perspective. However, subsequently she explains the connection between the interests of the individual and society by developing concepts such as "adapting to reality", to which I shall return later.

In Lise Lund's dissertation, which deals with career guidance and the achievement of plans of action in a biographical perspective, she asks whether career guidance practitioners should serve as a form of control and harmonisation of the labour force for society – an allocation mechanism – or whether respect for individuals and their choices should be the deciding factor. The big (eternal) dilemma of career guidance practitioners is therefore: respect for the wishes of the individual regarding a free choice of occupation compared with the actual possibilities available to the individual concerned, which must then be combined with the fact that society needs an effective labour force for specific occupations at specific points in time (Lund, 2003, p. 85). Once again, the tendency to divide these two interests into either/or can be seen.

The idea that career guidance is something that has an inherent conflict of goals can be seen in the legislation, among the actors concerned, and in the research. This conflict of goals is apparently accepted as a basic dilemma which is not explored theoretically or empirically.

Arguments for the role of career guidance in relation to preserving the welfare state are often linked to demographic challenges: a large number of elderly people are currently leaving the labour market, which means that career guidance must help young people to complete their courses of education faster. There is also an increasing need for a qualified, specialised workforce, so career guidance needs to help increase the level of education in general: more young people must attend further education, and the competences of people with little or no further education need to be boosted. So the fact that the aim of career guidance is to create a connection between the choices of the individual and societal development is presented in normative fashion. This normativity is connected to the various career guidance clients, each of whom must put their faith in the idea that career guidance can make a difference to them.

A.G. Watts identifies three career guidance clients: the immediate clients are the individuals participating in career guidance; the intermediate clients are institutions of education and further education and employers; and the final client is society as a whole (Watts, 1998, p. 239). He points out that governments often have two objectives in mind for career guidance: the goal of economic efficiency in relation to administering the human resources of any society; and the goal of social equality in relation to gender, ethnicity and social background (Watts, 1998). But the political goals are not clear. The wish for economic efficiency can be seen as related to ideas of "the productive society", whereas goals regarding social equality in terms of gender, ethnicity and social background can be seen as related to the idea of "the good society". The Danish legislation contains no references to the goal of social equality, although this theme is perhaps implied when the target group for career guidance is identified as young people who will find it difficult to choose, start or complete a course of education or choose an occupation without intensified career guidance efforts (LBK630, 2008). However, the legislation does underline that the need for a well trained workforce must be included on an equal footing with the interests and personal qualifications of the individual, including informal competences and previous training and work experience as well as the expected need for a well trained workforce and entrepreneurs (ibid.). It seems as if the idea of "the productive society" is the dominant ideology in the legislation. But this does not mean that the idea that the goal of career guidance should be "the good society" is not to be found elsewhere in the field of career guidance, or that this idea does not influence career guidance as an institutional arrangement. In the next section we shall take a closer look at the ethical standards for career guidance and how they tackle the basic dilemma of this field.

3.3 **Ethical standards**

The Danish ethical standards for career guidance also contain a form of dualism whose two poles are whether career guidance should primarily cater for the interests of the individual or the interests of society. This is a clear dilemma – the ethical standards say that "Career guidance always takes place in a context subject to terms and conditions that often have an institutional connection and a political and social anchor. This context may represent goals and interests on a social level which are not always in accordance with the interests of citizens. The schism between the two represents one of the significant and classic fields of tension in career guidance and constitutes a basic background for the necessity of ethical principles for career guidance" (FUE, 2006; author's translation). The main points of these principles are: respect, equality, independence, openness and trust. In relation to the principle of independence the dualistic goal of career guidance is defined with extreme clarity, with the guidelines stating that "Career guidance must cater for the interests of the citizens – and it must be neutral and independent of political interests, the interests of institutions or other special interests. Career guidance always takes place in a context and will therefore always be dependent on time, place, the relationship between career guidance practitioners and citizens, the institutional context and the social terms and conditions in question. Consequently, complete neutrality and independence are not possible – but they are values which career guidance practitioners should seek to achieve by maintaining an awareness about power and context relationships between practitioners and citizens, and by keeping the interests and lives of citizens in focus" (ibid.). So career guidance should be neutral and independent, but this is an impossible ideal. An attempt is made to solve this dilemma by inserting the principle of transparency openness: "Citizens must be made aware of the context, terms and conditions in which career guidance takes place" (ibid.).

The societal perspective does not seem to be underlined to quite the same extent in the international ethical standards, but the principle of openness regarding the fact that career guidance is socially embedded is expressed in virtually the same words: "Members of IAEVG inform clients, orally or in writing, of the purposes, goals, techniques, policies and ethical standards under which educational and vocational guidance is provided, conditions in which consultation with other professionals might occur, and legal or policy constraints which relate to how services are provided" (IAEVG, 1995). Unlike in the Danish ethical standards, the conflictual position of practitioners is underlined: "Members of IAEVG avoid conflicts of interest which compromise the best interests of their clients when they engage concurrently in the career counseling of clients, serve as representatives of paid employment exchanges or as paid recruiters or intermediaries for training facilities. Where potential conflicts of interest occur, they should be made known to the client" (ibid.). In the ethical standards for career guidance, the duality between the interests of the individual and society is conceptualised as one of the significant and classic fields of tension. So the basic dilemma of career guidance is also expressed in the ethical standards for career guidance, where transparency regarding the socially embedded nature of career guidance apparently represents an ethical consideration of this dilemma.

There seems to be broad agreement in the field of career guidance that it should be perceived as being built on a basic dilemma or classic field of tension; it is characteristic that the description of the goal of career guidance is dualistic, whether the two poles are regarded as conflictual or unproblematic. My ambition in this book is to go beyond this discovery and explore the connection between the poles in this dualism, between the interests and needs of the individual and the interests and needs of society, as well as studying the significance of the fact that the goals of career guidance are described in dualistic terms.

3.4 **Problems of dualistic descriptions**

This section discusses the significance of the fact that the purpose of career guidance seems to be dualistic. The basic problem of career guidance is described as follows: career guidance must cater for both individual and societal needs. A clearly dualistic picture of the goals of practice is created in policy, research and ethical standards. This way of conceptualising a practice is not unique to career guidance – it is also seen in the field of learning research, where other binary poles are at play such as formal/informal learning, school learning/ apprenticeships, abstract knowledge/concrete knowledge, and theory/practice. In the book *Apprenticeship in Critical Ethnographic Practice*, Jean Lave explores the importance of dualistic pictures and theories. Her goal is to examine apprenticeship as a principle. Through her ethnographic studies of tailor's apprentices in Liberia, using concepts and problems anchored in previous studies of apprenticeship and learning, she finds it hard to match reality with the expectations that her concepts of learning provide. She links the discrepancy between theoretical understandings and practice with the fact that the actual concept of apprenticeship is perceived as a dualistic counterpole to "superior" school learning. Taking this as her point of departure, she seeks to use her fieldwork to disprove basic dualistic assumptions about learning, and instead to formulate a standpoint from which learning can be studied in ways that make it possible to change our perceptions.

She points out that dualistic theories and descriptions are themselves a political technology (Lave, 2011). With reference to Stallybrass and White, she writes that "They argue that dualist theories that separate subject and social world (or science and craft, or formal and informal education) are making claim that the two do not partake of one another, but instead are polar opposites. Such claims deny their interdependence, and thereby suppress their connections. This politics of binary extremism comes from and sustains social hierarchy from the locus of those in power" (Lave, 2011). I have shown a number of examples of the way in which the individual and society are contrasted with each other in the description of the basic dilemma of career guidance. In Watts' and Plant's four-field table the contrast between the individual and society is accompanied by other dualisms such as development and adaptation, and change and control. And in the ethical standards a conflictual aspect of the goals of career guidance was underlined in relation to whether career guidance practitioners focus on the interests of society or those of the individual.

According to Lave, the problem with dualistic descriptions is that they ignore the mutual dependence of the two poles and suppress the connection between them. Lave points out that dualistic descriptions can be regarded as a political strategy from the locus of power because dualisms are formulated by the people who have power and are intended to maintain the existing social hierarchy. Lave explains this point as follows: "When binary theory assumes its poles to be truly separate, it produces a rhetoric justifying marginalization or stigmatizing of the socially problematic low – rather than critique and change in the politically repressive high" (Lave, 2011).

She explains that "Furthermore, this encourages a habit of treating social phenomena representing the 'poles' only one at a time". This habit can also be found in the research on career guidance in the form of either a structure or an actor perspective (Lindh & Lundahl, 2007). Lave explains that drawing this distinction reduces the contrasts that the division produces, and allows researchers (and others) to treat them both as either good or evil. Similar tendencies can be found in the field of career guidance, where analysis of the responses provided in connection with the reform of career guidance in Denmark identified the voices designated as "society as focus" and "the individual as focus" as being in contrast with each other (Callesen et al., 2003).

Lave gives researchers a recipe for avoiding the reproduction of dualistic descriptions of problems. Take one particular abstraction, such as apprenticeship or informal learning (or competence identification). Find a place in which it would be likely to occur. Ethnographic study of this place, practice and participation will then give the researcher the basis for producing detailed descriptions of the pole that is normally suppressed. She then says that "Discrepancies between residual characterizations of 'the low' issuing from elite centers and actual examples of what they purport to describe make rigorous fieldwork a powerful tool" (Lave, 2011). Such descriptions make it possible to reject the naturalisation of polarised distinctions, as well as the idea that such distinctions are politically neutral.

Both of the study settings in this book can be said to represent the stigmatised or "the low". The folk high school students and employees are described as individuals who have a special need for career guidance. In the political rhetoric folk high school students are described as individuals who are particularly undecided about their future; and the context of which they are part is described as something of an (unwanted) intermediate position which helps to delay the start of a course of education and subsequent employment. The employees at the company belong to the group of people with little or no further education, whose work functions are being marginalised owing to developments in Danish production companies. The ambitions on their behalf focus on their acquisition of new competences equipping them to do other jobs. As a result, special institutional arrangements are organised for this group including career guidance, the identification of competences and the assessment of actual competences with a view to helping them achieve these ambitions.

3.5 **Summary**

When career guidance is examined as an institutional arrangement, we realise that the career guidance which people are recommended to use depends on the institutional connections of the individuals concerned. Career guidance is intended to be a lifelong effort performed by a variety of institutions. It is described in Danish legislation, in the ethical standards, by actors in the field and by other researchers as having an inherent and normative basic dilemma involving dual objectives which oblige career guidance practitioners to cater for the interests of both society and the individual. But this description of the problem of career guidance can also be debated: the problem is not just a basic problem. If we follow Lave's general argument concerning dualistic descriptions, the dualistic presentation of the basic problem of career guidance may come to permit the marginalisation of individuals who do not pursue the objectives; in the field of career guidance, people who are not in education or involved in the labour market are described as nedding intensified career guidance. It is not inconceivable that career guidance could be described and conceptualised in different ways, but this would require a form of research that does not simply accept and reproduce societal and individual interests as opposites. Lave recommends that researchers wishing to explore and criticise dualisms should refuse to separate these poles. She explains how this causes difficulties both conceptually and linguistically: difficulties which have also characterised my research process when trying to examine participation in career guidance as a part of everyday life and not separate from it. Along the way I have had to deal with problems involving the identification of career guidance: what is career guidance, and what is not? But the point is that by examining everyday life and considering career guidance from a decentred perspective I can pursue a research effort that looks for connections and points of contact rather than focusing on division and delimitation. This is why I examine career guidance from a decentred perspective, and in chapter 6 ("Theoretical point of departure") I explain how a critical-psychological research basis gives the opportunity to examine dualisms as connected rather than separate. This is done by focusing on connections between contexts, individuals and participation in communities in an analysis of the material presented in this book. And the concept of participation opens up the opportunity to theoretically connect aspects of career guidance that are often separated: the respective interests of the individual and society. This is explained in greater detail in chapter 6.

3

4 Contours of a field of knowledge

Chapter 4 presents career guidance as a field of study and asks the questions "What characterises research in career guidance both internationally and in Denmark? What is the significance of the fact that a majority of career guidance research can largely be characterised as commissioned research? What levels of analysis does the field of career guidance invite? And what is the knowledge that this book seeks to contribute to the field of career guidance?

4.1 Career guidance research

Sciences are constituted by their fields of study. Career guidance is an independent field of study, an area which can be examined from various scientific angles. There is no single science called "career guidance" – instead, career guidance is a field of research. This means that career guidance does not have its own philosophy of science but must draw on scientific assumptions and theories that have been developed within other scientific areas. Psychology and the social sciences constitute the more important of these; but pedagogics, philosophy and economics also contribute their own particular approaches. Career guidance as a phenomenon invites us to study it from a variety of standpoints. In an article entitled "Nordic Research in Educational and Vocational Guidance", Plant concludes that career guidance research in the Nordic countries is examined primarily from the following perspectives: historical, sociological, psychological, ethnological and philosophical – with a clear majority of studies from a sociological and psychological perspective (Plant, 2007a).

Internationally speaking the research field of career guidance is expanding, and knowledge developed within this field is published in a variety of international journals such as the *International Journal for Educational and Vocational Guidance*, the *British Journal of Guidance and Counselling*, the *NICEC Journal* and *Career Development Quarterly*. The field of career guidance research is growing, presenting a number of challenges. These challenges are expressed in several international reviews focusing on guidance in a variety of areas. Hughes et al. at the Centre for Guidance Studies at Derby University in the UK point out that "There appears to be a lack of robust quantitative studies, longitudinal research and comparative studies that focus on outcomes from career development interventions" (Hughes, 2005, p. 3). Similar arguments are put forward by researchers from the Warwick Institute for Employment Research: "Future research needs to have clear parameters and a longitudinal timeframe, be theoretically-informed and influenced by a range of research that goes beyond the consideration of what works" (Bimrose, 2005, p. ii). So even though career guidance is relatively well established internationally speaking, there is a feeling that the research should be more theoretically informed.

The goal of the research review entitled "A systematic literature review of research into Career Development Interventions for Workforce Development (Hughes, 2005) is to systematise knowledge of which career guidance interventions motivate people with a short course of further education behind them to commit to learning. In general, the review underlines that "Research findings indicate that career development activities are made available through a variety of *formal and informal* mechanisms" (Hughes, 2005, p. 3). The availability of career guidance depends on local conditions both inside and outside the workplace. In other words, it is not equally available to everyone. This creates special difficulties in connection with studies of career guidance because career guidance cannot be studied as a total system and solely in its institutionalised form. Instead, it must be studied in context, from which more general problem complexes can be focused upon. The review concludes that many studies of career guidance focus on "process" and/or "activities" rather than on what the individual gets out of career guidance interventions. This indicates that there is a need for studies of career guidance activities seen from a participant perspective.

In Denmark there are two career guidance journals, which are directed primarily at the field of practice of career guidance, career guidance practitioners, politicians and teachers. One of them is published by the Danish Ministry of Education and is entitled *Via Vejledning*. It relates primarily to career guidance practice under the auspices of the Ministry of Education. The other is called *Vejlederforum*. The Ministry of Education maintains a homepage called *vejledningsviden.dk*, comprising a bibliography of the field of career guidance. This bibliography contains everything from Danish legislation to books on method to research articles. Searching by genre is not possible, so it is dificult to gain an overview of career guidance research in Denmark or to perform an analysis or review of this research.

With a view to carrying out an analysis of Danish career guidance research, I joined forces with Mette Marie Callesen and *Studie og Erhverv* to draw up a research registry of career guidance research in Denmark.[7] The aim of this registry was to answer questions such as: What does the current career guidance research look like? What areas of research are being explored, using what methods? (Callesen & Thomsen, 2005a). On the basis of this registry we were able to conclude that in 2005 career guidance research in Denmark did not constitute a single research field but was distributed across other fields to a great extent, fields in which an interest in studying career guidance arises in connection with other studies – studies of young people, for instance (see Nielsen & Sørensen, 2004), or the motivation of people with little further education when it comes to participating in supplementary training (see Holsbo, 2005). Central research projects were selected for further analysis. The criterion of selection was that career guidance practice or participants in career guidance practice were central themes. The purpose of the analysis of the projects was to find out how researchers worked with and presented their fields of study, and the research questions were: How are central concepts such as participants in career guidance and career guidance practice itself understood and presented? What are the challenges facing career guidance research?

Callesen and Thomsen conclude:

– Career guidance research is characterised by the fact that much of it is commissioned research which can be categorised as short-term evaluations or best-practice examinations. The focus is seldom placed on theoretical analyses.
– The issues researched are often expressed based on a political perspective, such as: the wish to reduce drop-out rates, the wish to break traditional gender-based choices by young people and the difficulties of defining young people with special needs. The solutions proposed often involve young people making different choices based on improved methods used by career guidance practitioners or on the fact that sufficient focus is directed at the issues in question.
– Career guidance research does not include consideration of the limitations of career guidance, something which could be used to define when career guidance is relevant and when other solutions are required. As a result, the idea that career guidance can influence individuals to act differently becomes almost omnipotent in relation to solving many different educational and vocational problems in society.
– The assumption on which career guidance research is based is that it is possible to influence individual choices by career guidance; it is assumed that career guidance has a controlling function.
– The importance of structural conditions with regard to the reasons why individuals drop out, fail to obtain an education or fail to play an active role in the labour market is rarely analysed, and posibilities for changing the structural conditions are not mentioned as recommendations.
– There seems to be a tendency in career guidance research to individualise social issues, and to refrain from challenging and exploring the options of individuals participating theoretically or empirically (Callesen & Thomsen, 2005a).

4

In many areas Danish career guidance research faces the same challenges as those outlined in the British reviews. There are very few longitudinal research projects, and short studies (in terms of both time spent and length of reports) do not support theoretical deliberations and discussions.

4.1.1 Commissioned career guidance research

These critical reflections connected with career guidance research should be seen in the light of the fact that a great deal of this research is commissioned. Commissioned research is expected to provide answers to questions that have been formulated from the client's perspective, and commissioned career guidance research therefore largely focuses on how society can benefit from effective career guidance practice (Callesen & Thomsen, 2005a). The clients involved in the field of career guidance are often the Ministry of Education or other organisations with an interest in career guidance. The association representing Danish folk high schools (FFD) has been extremely active in relation to producing knowledge about the career guidance provided by these schools; and the association representing Danish *Efterskoler* (residential schools for young people in 9th and 10th grade) is now doing the same by implementing studies of its own career guidance practice in collaboration with research institutions. There is a good deal of EU funding for career guidance studies, which means that the problems (and solutions) involved focus on the goals of the EU programme granting financial support (the Leonardo da Vinci programme or the EU's 7th framework programme, for instance).

International studies are carried out for organisations such as the OECD, the EU or the World Bank, which demonstrates a great deal of political and economic interest in career guidance. Studies of career guidance in Denmark and internationally are often carried out in connection with the creation of policy briefings. This means that reviews or data collection studies are created with a particular objective and from a particular perspective that can be characterised by the fact that the knowledge presented is intended to form the basis of political decisions – which often leads to a reduction of complexity, the absence of any criticism of ideology, and the absence of any problematisation.

4

In connection with the production of policy documents for international organisations, knowledge is collected with regard to the career guidance systems in various countries. This knowledge is then analysed by researchers in several different publications. A report entitled "Guidance policies in the knowledge society" by R.G. Sultana is one example of an analysis of trends, challenges and responses from career guidance experts in 29 countries. It was carried out for the European Centre for the Development of Vocational Training. This report draws on a questionnaire survey which the OECD (supported by the EU and the World Bank) carried out in 37 different countries (Sultana, 2004, p. 7).[8] Another policy document in which the same data has been analysed is entitled *Career Guidance and Public Policy – Bridging the Gap* (OECD, 2004). These policy documents focus largely on communicating knowledge about the career guidance systems of various countries; the desire to communicate knowledge about a large area in a short, clear fashion does not leave much space for problematising any issues that might arise, which is why many of these publications display a high level of normativity. In particular, the normative assumptions appear in the following notions:

- Career guidance is a benefit provided by the welfare state (and it is always good).
- There is a connection between the educational and vocational choices of individuals and the development of the welfare system.
- Career guidance can create inclusion and cohesion in society.
- By empowering the citizens of any country, career guidance can help to produce a democratic society with active citizens.

These are assumptions which are not connected to any empirical analyses which might make it possible to produce theoretically based analyses of career guidance practice or to examine dilemmas, complexity and contradictions.

4

4.1.2 Levels of analysis of career guidance

The picture of career guidance outlined above makes it possible to identify various levels of research analysis focusing on career guidance. One level of analysis is the societal level, in which career guidance is analysed via political documents and general descriptions of political objectives in connection with educational, vocational and welfare policies (see Sultana, 2004 and Watts, 2004, for instance). This level focuses on the way in which career guidance can play a role in the educational choices of young people and in the way adults change their jobs. These analyses are often based on a sociological approach in Denmark.

Another level of analysis is the institutional level, at which career guidance is analysed or evaluated as a practice with a particular focus on the fulfilment of political objectives. This focus can be found in the evaluation of career guidance for young people produced by the Danish Evaluation Institute (EVA, 2007). On the concrete level of practice, career guidance as a (psychological) form of intervention and the career guidance practitioner's theory and method are made the subject of analysis. The focus is placed on the dialogue situation as a form of interaction between career guidance practitioners and individuals. See, for instance, Gunnel Lindh's doctoral dissertation (*Samtalen*, Lindh, 2000), Gunnar Schedin's PhD dissertation (*Expectations and experiences of career counselling: an exploration of interpersonal behaviour*, Schedin, 2007), or Lund's investigation of biographical methods of career guidance (2003).

Another focus at the concrete practical level may provide insight into the actual structure and organisation of career guidance practice, and the way in which this practice is connected to other practices and forms part of the everyday lives of participants. This is the level at which most of my analytical focus lies. The focus can also be placed on the participants in career guidance as groups with different qualifications for participation, with one group being young people (Jensen, 2005), and another group being the elderly (see "Third Age Guidance", Clayton, Greco & Persson, 2007). And finally, the focus can also be placed on career guidance as a subject and career guidance

4

practice as a profession (Lovén, 1995). So research into career guidance can consider various areas of the field, and in many cases the study questions explored will require an understanding of a number of different levels.

It is also possible to examine career guidance from a variety of perspectives such as the perspective of career guidance practitioners (a professional perspective); the perspective of the participants/users (a user perspective); or the societal perspective (a political perspective on the social function of career guidance). The challenge for Danish and international career guidance research as described in the reviews is to produce more qualitative, comparative studies of career guidance that incorporate theoretical discussions. Studies of the connection between the organisation of career guidance, its concrete practice and the options for participation that this creates are rare. Such research projects call for methods such as observations of career guidance and repeated interviews with the participants over time – demanding a great deal of time and resources, particularly if an attempt is also made to include the context of career guidance and study what happens before, during and after career guidance. For instance, on emight considerthe impact of career guidance on the everyday lives of the participants.

This book contributes knowledge about:

- A contextual approach to career guidance research based on empirical and theoretically informed analysis.
- Experiences of practice research as a modus in career guidance research.
- A participant perspective on the meaning of career guidance.
- Research based on a dialectic perception of the individual/ society which supports a theoretical discussion of the connection between individual and society and challenges the problems of individualisation.

4

4.2 **Summary**

There are certain problems associated with research-based knowledge about career guidance. The field is characterised by the presence of a large proportion of research commissioned for use in drawing up political documents. This seems to preclude dilemmas, problematisation and critical approaches. The study questions explored are often based on political objectives with regard to career guidance, and the solutions proposed generally imply that career guidance can help the individuals to act differently. This research field is under development, and both in Denmark and abroad there is a wish for more longitudinal and comparative analyses of the field of career guidance which are more theoretically informed.

4

5 Career guidance as an individual practice

In the previous chapter reference was made to criticism of career guidance research because it may help to individualise societal issues. Viewed from a post-structuralist perspective, it has also been pointed out that the individualisation and processing of individuals in career guidance interventions means that career guidance can be regarded as a form of governing technology. Conceptualising career guidance as a form of governing technology is one way of perceiving the connection between individuals and society. Governing technology or self-technology refers to the fact that when individuals participate in various practices in which professionals ask them questions and they talk about themselves and their expectations, they inadvertently steer themselves in a socially desirable direction without such professionals exerting obvious authority or laying down concrete guidelines for their actions (Rose, 1998, p. 344). In this chapter a range of analyses will be described from this perspective.

5.1 Career guidance as a governing technology

In recent years there has been some criticism of career guidance as a governing technology, inspired by the work of Michel Foucault and Nikolas Rose.[9] This criticism takes its point of departure in career guidance as an individual and individualising practice in which exploration of the life histories of the individual by career guidance practitioners, and allowing such individuals to confide in such practitioners, is claimed to constitute a powerful governing technology.

In the article "Subjects, networks and positions: Thinking educational guidance differently", Usher and Edwards draw parallels between Foucault's study of confessional practices and career guidance. They underline that several career guidance methods have their roots in humanistic psychology, for instance Carl Rogers' client-centred approach, describing the consequences of the link between career guidance and a therapeutic discourse in which the goal of self-realisation seems to be a goal in itself: "Here therapeutic notions of the importance of feelings to the authentic all round expression of self are translated into educational discourses and practices where self-development and self-realisation become framed as a central normative goal" (Usher, 2005, p. 398). The parallel to Foucault's confessional practices and the concept of governing technology are illustrated by the following quotation: "Due to their basis in the process of confession and circulation of pastoral power, the very guidance processes through which people's difficulties are meant to be resolved actually result in further dislocation, as the sense of individual responsibility for one's condition, for the development of an autonomous and individualistic subjectivity and its accompanying stress displaces more social sensibilities. Thus, confession can be seen to play a central aspect in the individualisation characteristic of contemporary society" (Usher, 2005, p. 403). Usher and Edwards connect individualisation with a governing perspective, writing that "Guidance, it could be argued, has become a technology of governing. The humanistic discourses of guidance which individualise learners are already part of an edifice of pastoral power, of a new form of governmentality that itself needs to be problematised and addressed" (Usher, 2005, p. 404). In the light of Lovén's conclusions that as professionals career guidance practitioners seek to maintain the idea that in their work they can focus purely on the interests of the participants (Lovén, 1995), this is a relevant criticism. Lovén also points out that in some ways career guidance practitioners seem to have convinced themselves that they base their guidance practice solely on the interests of individual. In the sessions that he has studied, so much time is spent on exploring and charting the life histories, wishes and motivations of the participants that there is no time for explicit information about specific opportunities for education and employment (ibid.). So Usher

5

and Edwards' criticism is relevant, but their analysis can be criticised in two ways. Firstly in their analysis they do not consider career guidance practices which assume an open, unconcealed wish to influence individuals in particular directions. And secondly, it seems as if career guidance is regarded as the only influence to which individuals are exposed. As we saw in the two introductory quotations in this book from Tine and Poul, they definitely share their thoughts about "career guidance questions" with the communities of which they are part at the folk high school and company respectively. Usher and Edwards' analysis makes it look as if a linear connection can be drawn between the individual's participation in career guidance, the confession that occurs and the actions that individuals then perform. But the empirical analysis in this book supports the idea that there is no such linear connection. Career guidance practitioners are by no means the only people that individuals consult with regard to their thoughts about educational or vocational choices. Discussions with their friends, colleagues and family are also regarded as important for the way in which people perceive their own lives and opportunities.

In my article entitled "Reflection – an empty category", I discuss the fact that when reflection occurs in career guidance practice there is a danger that it may be aimed at politically created discourses about the things that young people are expected to do (for instance that young people should refrain from having gap years and from dropping out, Thomsen, 2007). In this article, career guidance is regarded as a practice through which individuals are expected to develop ways of managing themselves in relation to a perceived socio-economic perspective which defines certain expectations for young people – or in other words: career guidance is a practice in which young people develop what we call "self-technologies" (Thomsen, 2007). Whilst fulfilling the goals of career guidance, practitioners are turned into representatives/guarantors of the socio-economic goals of career guidance. And the young people also focus on the expectations they feel they have to live up to. When viewed against this background, career guidance can also be characterised as a way of teaching people to make highly focused, ambitious and correct choices in relation to the societal expectations represented by career guidance practitioners and the young people themselves. This analysis similarly does not provide any insight into the fact that the young people involved in career guidance also participate elsewhere and are influenced by other people as well. The points made in the analyses above indicate that individuals regulate themselves through their participation in career guidance. The criticism I raise now is that the theoretical lens through which these conclusions are drawn does not permit an analysis of all the many different contexts for action in which people are involved and by which they are influenced. The self-government of individuals in career guidance through their thoughts about education and vocation can hardly be reduced to a consequence of their encounter with a career guidance practitioner. A governing-technology angle on career guidance fails to perceive that career guidance practice is only one aspect of the everyday lives of individuals, and that it interacts with other practices. The ambition of this book is to contribute knowledge in both areas.

Danish educational and vocational guidance has been analysed as an element of a neo-liberal governing technology by Lene Otto. In an article entitled "Livshistorier og biografisk subjektivitet" ("Life histories and biographical subjectivity"), she deals with the educational records kept by Danish school pupils from the 6th grade onwards. She points out that the work done on these records can be regarded as a form of self-evaluation through which the self-perception of the children is shaped (Otto, 2001). She also discusses whether this self-regulation through self-perception helps to individualise educational issues, leaving individual children with the impression that their situation is their own responsibility. She points out that we seem to have abandoned the idea that our collective history has an overall governing principle or goal which has to be achieved, and that as a result the history of the individual has gained increasing focus (Otto, 2001, p. 4). The significance of this is that children become responsible subjects with their own free choices, and that the responsibility for failure in a school context is largely installed in each child. Lene Otto underlines that the explanation of this focus on the individual can also be found in pedagogical changes in Danish schools and in the role of career guidance practitioners. She says that the authority of career guidance practitioners or teachers has disappeared along with their power to force young people to do anything – or to free them from responsibility (ibid.). She also points out that "self-interest" should not be seen as something which is mentally or biologically determined, but something which is embedded in everyday practices involving material objects and the way we do things (Otto, 2001, p. 6). This means that the way in which career guidance is organised and practised has an impact on the way in which people perceive their situation and the kind of help they think they need.

Lene Otto argues that it may be important to decide whether career guidance should be organised as an individual or a collective practice. She points out that collective forms of organisation allow participants to understand their situation as a shared, common problem as well as allowing them to use each other to explore potential solutions and opportunities.

Jo Krøjer and Camilla Hutters have carried out experiments involving "Storytelling workshops" as a way of overcoming the individualisation problem in the educational and vocational guidance provided by folk high schools (Krøjer & Hutters, 2006). In the article "Kollektivet som korrektiv" ("Collective or corrective?"), they study both how the experience of pressure by young people is connected with the neo-liberal individual work invited by their choice of education, and whether neo-liberal discourses can be transgressed when educational choices are thematised in a collective context (Krøjer & Hutters, 2008, p. 72). Krøjer and Hutters are particularly interested in collective methods because such methods, they argue, can potentially transcend individualisation tendencies generated and amplified by neo-liberal governing technologies (Krøjer & Hutters, 2008, p. 73). They conclude that the stories told by the young people clearly show that power (and thus the neo-liberal governing of educational choices) works because it offers incentives for realisation, for producing self-understanding (ibid.). This argument makes it seem as if governing efforts produce self-understanding. The two authors discuss the way in which self-understanding is also linked to the communities in which individuals participate. They conclude that, from a Foucauldian point of view, the regulation that occurs in connection with educational choices can be perceived as the exercise of power which functions not only as an external pressure but also by creating productive promises about attractive selves (Krøjer & Hutters, 2008,

5

63

p. 86). Storytelling workshops cannot reverse neo-liberal subjectifi-cation, but the collective may seem like a corrective factor for unique, empowered and self-optimised individuals who are able to choose the right education freely (Krøjer & Hutters, 2008, p. 85). So viewed from Krøjer and Hutters' perspective, the organisation of career guid-ance does have an effect on whether (and how) career guidance indi-vidualises societal issues.

In Denmark career guidance is often organised in the form of in-dividual sessions, and in the following sections I explore the way in which career guidance methods, legislation and research all support this practice.

5.2 Methods that individualise

There are various reasons why career guidance is largely organised individually in Denmark. For one thing, the previous inspiration of humanistic psychology still means that many people associate career guidance with a form of therapeutic practice which is not only per-sonal but also private, which is why it should take place on a one-to-one basis. In addition, many career guidance theories and methods support an individual mode of delivery and organisation rather than a collective form. This can be observed in the Danish psychologist Tove Løve's thorough consideration of career guidance and career guidance methods in her book *Vejledning ansigt til ansigt – Teorier og Metoder i den individuelle vejledning* ("Career Guidance Face to Face – Theories and Methods in Individual Career Guidance"), a book which is required reading on many career guidance diploma courses in Den-mark.

Løve distinguishes between *individual career guidance, collective career guidance* and *group career guidance*. Collective career guidance is described as the transfer of information; Løve draws a distinction between the potential outcomes offered by collective and individual career guidance respectively. She says that whereas collective career guidance can inform people and give them a practical opportunity to learn more about their educational and vocational options, indi-vidual career guidance allows space for reflection on how these options are perceived in relation to the life situation of the individual concerned (Løve, 2005, p. 82). Løve does not use the term "collective" in the same sense as Krøjer and Hutters; she describes collective career guidance as a form of collective supply of information in which individuals relate to their *own* life situation – not to a *shared* life situation and *shared* conditions. Krøjer and Hutters, on the other hand, use the term "collective" to focus on connections between participants in the collective (Krøjer & Hutters, 2008).

Løve points out that educational and vocational guidance is connected more to individual and collective career guidance than to group career guidance (Løve, 2005, p. 376). She then stresses that this may be precisely the reason why it is important to focus on group career guidance – to find out whether it provides opportunities for developing new methods which are suitable for small groups of students with special needs (ibid.). With reference to Borgen et al.'s book on Employment Groups (Borgen, 1989), Løve concludes that the research shows that well planned and well managed group guidance can help more people achieve a common goal faster than working with the same number of people individually (Løve, 2005, p. 378). In Løve's description of group career guidance there seems to be no appreciation of the potential of group career guidance for drawing the attention of the participants in a community to their shared situation and the issues facing them as a group. For instance, she says that in comparison with collective and individual career guidance, it is mutual support and honest feedback in concrete situations that is the strength of group career guidance, constituting the basis that enables participants:

– To increase their awareness of their own situation
   by listening to the reflections of others about it.
– To perceive their problems as acceptable because they discover
   that other people have similar problems (Løve, 2005, p. 378).

There seems to be no awareness that group career guidance might have the potential to give the participants the opportunity to perceive their problems as common problems which can be changed. In Tove Løve's presentation of group guidance, the participants remain in their own individual perspectives. They listen to each other, but only with a view to increasing their awareness of their own situation and their perception of their problems as being acceptable. By contrast, Krøjer and Hutters say that the collective experience of recognition helps to make it clear that the difficulties facing the individual are not only individual but actually reflect shared conditions (Krøjer & Hutters, 2008, p. 74). Krøjer and Hutters conclude that collective experiences make it possible for young people to transcend educational problems such as pressure and loneliness (ibid.).

In this book I follow Krøjer and Hutters' understanding of the term "collective", but generally use the concept of "community" to focus on contexts for action, with people also being part of the conditions for each other. Providing career guidance for several participants at the same time is neither a new nor an unusual practice in this field, which employs concepts such as collegial supervision, Socratic dialogue groups and group career guidance; it would be fascinating to find out whether these methods provide individuals with an awareness of the conditions that they share. However, such a study falls outside the scope of this publication.

5.3 Legislation that individualises

Expectations regarding the task and the organisation of career guidance are also reflected in the legislation governing this field, which constitutes another basic point of departure both for our understanding of practice and for the organisation of practice. The example of legislation illustrates another individualisation tendency, since various legislative documents and guidelines emphasise individual career guidance more often than group career guidance and collective forms of career guidance.

The Danish executive order relating to educational and vocational guidance (2008) states that career guidance for pupils in 6th-8th grades is individual, and that individual career guidance should be arranged in collaboration with the school. It also states that as far as possible, career guidance for other young people should also be individual at the educational institution in question.

The Act on educational and vocational guidance establishes seven Study Choice Centres to provide advice about courses of further education, and to offer young people a place to discuss their situation. The fact that guidance regarding choices of further education should be individual is not underlined so strongly here, and a number of these Study Choice Centres are currently testing other ways of organising and providing career guidance.[10]

In 2008 guidelines for the completion of courses at educational institutions were added to the Act, and collective career guidance is now mentioned in section 12a:

> 12a. Institutions of education under the auspices of the Ministry of Education which provide training courses for young people or courses of further education, and which offer the students individual and collective guidance regarding the completion of these courses, shall lay down guidelines for the guidance that they provide. (Author's translation)

This is followed by subsection 2, which again underlines and supports the idea that guidance should be organised in the form of individual interviews:

> Subsection 2. If an institution of education feels that there is a risk that a student will break off a course of education, this institution shall offer the student concerned an individual career guidance session. (Ibid.; author's translation)

The Danish legislation apparently supports the idea that career guidance should primarily be organised in the form of individual sessions between the student and a career guidance practitioner.

5.4 Summary

Career guidance can be criticised for individualising societal problems in several ways. The blame falls first on a normative assumption that there is a connection between the choices of individuals and social development. If career guidance is installed to contribute to the solution of societal problems, there could be a danger that such a practice will help to individualise the responsibility for social development rather than anchoring this responsibility in collective decision-making processes. Popular career guidance methods originate in humanistic psychology, which may lead career guidance practitioners to focus methodologically on identifying life histories and living spaces. Danish legislation encourages practitioners to organise career guidance in the form of individual sessions rather than in more collective forms. In addition, in chapter 4 we saw that studies and research projects in the field of career guidance also fail to challenge the individualising tendency in many cases, since they too focus on the way in which changes in individual actions can help to solve societal problems such as high drop-out rates or gender-specific choices.

This leads me to focus on the research choices made in this book. One way of meeting problems of individualisation involves studying career guidance practice in settings which are not based on individual sessions. Krøjer and Hutters say that the aim of choosing study settings on the basis of the way in which they organise their career guidance is to study collective organisations, because as a form of organisation the collective creates oppositional opportunities for thinking (Krøjer & Hutters, 2008). If the organisation of career guidance in predominantly individual sessions helps to individualise societal problems, empirical descriptions of alternative forms of organisation will be a point of departure for expressing criticism. Or as Lave points out, detailed descriptions of people normally regarded as "the low" (individuals participating in career guidance in this case) will challenge theoretical characteristics. This calls for studies of career guidance practices at places settings where they are *not* organised individually – out in the field, where they are more often organised in interaction with existing communities.

6 **Theoretical point of departure**

Chapter 6 describes the theoretical point of departure of this book, focusing on the way in which critical psychological categories can contribute to a dialectical understanding of the connection between the individual and society. The analytical categories that conceptualise this connection, which are important for the analysis in this book, are as follows: participation and participant trajectories, personal conduct of everyday life, self-understanding and "conditions, meaning and analysis of reasons". These are considered in this chapter. Critical psychology was chosen as an analysis partner owing to the wish to study career guidance from a participant perspective which also focused on the concrete organisation of practice. Critical psychology seeks to address the dialectics of inner and outer factors with regard to human development. Social-constructionist theory adopts a different approach, with discursive factors (outer elements) being attributed the greatest importance with regard to human development; cognitive approaches provide another contrast with critical psychology, since they explain development with inner factors (Christensen, 2003, p. 194).

As shown in the previous chapters, it is a common assumption that career guidance practice is located in a field of tension between the individual and society. In criticising dualistic issues, Lave points out that one way of studying such issues would be to study practice concretely and refrain from trying to separate the two poles. If career guidance is understood as a practice which seeks to solve both individual and social educational and vocational problems by talking to individuals and by changing their actions, analyses of career guidance call for theoretical understandings which can handle the perspectives both the individual/subject and society. It must therefore be assumed that a theoretically informed analysis[11] which uses analytical concepts that can help to avoid a distinction between individual and society will contribute to new understandings of the basic dilemma of career guidance. This book is based on a research approach offering analytical categories which can help to reveal the complex connections between the individual and society in the analysis of the empirical data it contains.

The book contains practice research based on a critical psychological approach (see for instance Dreier, 2008; Nissen, 2001; Mørck, & Huniche, 2006; Kousholt & Thomsen, 2012).[12] which is connected to social practice theory (see Lave, 1993). The German psychologist Holzkamp is a central figure in developing the perspective of critical psychology (Holzkamp, 1983, 1993). Other researchers categorise critical psychology as phenomenological and rationalistic in its basic philosophy (Christensen, 2003), a form of categorisation to which I shall return in this chapter. Holzkamp himself places this perspective within dialectic materialism (Holzkamp, 1991). In Denmark it has been developed in the direction of social practice theory, where it is often combined with socio-cultural learning theory (Morin, 2007; Mørck, 2003) and learning as changing personal participation (Dreier, 1999a). According to Jartoft, the central issue is that even though people are determined by their conditions, they also seek to create and change these conditions (Jartoft, 1996, p. 183).

Within a critical psychological framework, the connection between the individual's conduct in everyday life and participation in society is maintained through various analytical categories. I will now discuss the foundations on which these categories are based.

6.1 The subject and sociality of career guidance

Klaus Holzkamp focuses in particular on the relationship between the overall societal process and the individual life process. In connection with the ambition to gain understanding of the particular dual function of career guidance it is important to explore this relationship theoretically. The overall societal process or structure describes the way in which we arrange ourselves as a society in relation to each other so that we do not all need to be self-sufficient or to perform all the functions required of our life together.

In the book Critical Psychology, Holzkamp's chapter entitled "Societal and Individual Life Processes", describes the way in which the nature of Man is socially embedded – it is a societal nature. We are able to develop our society on an ongoing basis as we develop ourselves. Holzkamp says that it must be the case that as our socio-economic way of life developed historically, the "nature" of all living creatures must also have developed, enabling them to participate in – and have a share in – the new "economic" process, the societal production of the necessities of life ("Lebensmittel") and life conditions (Holzkamp, 1991). But it is not just a question of *being able* to participate with others: participation with others is regarded as a basic condition of human life. Holzkamp points out that individual existence is always a partial aspect of social life. So the individual life conditions of human beings are always individually relevant societal life conditions in some form and to some extent (Holzkamp, 1991, p. 58). The way in which we have divided the work done in our modern society means that we depend on each other's work and efforts for our own existence; collective interests are linked to participation by other people in the maintenance of our collective societal life conditions. This means that the issues dealt with by career guidance practice, for instance choices of education, *cannot* be understood and analysed as an individual practice in which the individual has a problem in relation to the conduct of their own life. What is perceived and described as the individual's problem must be understood as an element of the shared, societal maintenance of life.

6.2 Career guidance as a tool in a critical psychological understanding

When career guidance is described as a socio-economic tool (Plant, 1996; Watts, 1998), this is based on an understanding of the fact that career guidance can achieve political objectives such as economic development. From a governing technology perspective this quickly turns into the idea that *somebody is trying to achieve something with other people*, and career guidance is understood as a practice in which outer government turns into self-government via concepts such as

71

self-technologies. However, if this is perceived in the light of Holz-kamp's concepts of presentation of societal life conditions (Holz-kamp, 1991), something else becomes apparent as well. Using critical psychological concepts, career guidance can be understood as a fea-ture of the collective life maintenance process, as a way in which we as a society have arranged things based on the need to cater for shared interests (which may also be contradictory). Institutional arrange-ments for career guidance make it possible to coordinate social inter-ests in the direction in which society should develop.

Ole Dreier criticises Holzkamp's concept of an overall mediating social structure as an insufficient guide for studying persons as par-ticipants in and across particular contexts (Dreier, 2009), and points out that in using this concept the researcher risks working with an abstract concept of structure (Dreier, 2006). Dreier repeats Holz-kamp's point that social structure is regarded on an overall social level and as an overlapping context of action and the synthesis of meaning structures (Dreier, 2006, p. 4). And Dreier criticises this perception, calling it inadequate and too abstract in relation to the concrete lives of individuals in social contexts (ibid.), because, as he points out, when structure is regarded as an overall mediation structure it seems to be localised far from the concrete lives of individuals (ibid.). This resembles the same abstraction as that which occurs in the field of ca-reer guidance when a policy argument is made for the (abstract) con-nection between career guidance and economic development, but the abstraction does not explore and describe the connection in concrete terms in relation to people's life situations. Instead, Dreier argues that structure should be perceived as something that is practical: the ar-rangement of multiple practices in social practice structures (ibid.). In order to avoid this abstraction, structure is *not* analysed on an over-all social level in this book. The meaning of structures is analysed by considering the concrete and practical ways in which people conduct their lives and their encounters with career guidance in concrete in-stitutional arrangements.

The political expectation that career guidance should be con-nected to overall structures and can help to promote societal changes is in itself an abstraction of practice. In my empirical work it was important for me to avoid making the same abstraction, which risks explaining changes in human actions as being caused directly by career guidance efforts. Changed actions are analysed locally, concretely and in interaction with other considerations. Career guidance is understood as part of social practice occurring in various local contexts. Dreier defines context as a delimited location for the performance of a social practice such as a home, a school or a workplace (Dreier, 2008). As mentioned above, career guidance can take place in various local contexts such as a career guidance centre, a workplace or a folk high school. When career guidance is regarded from a societal point of view as a means of helping individuals in the transition between education and work, the movement of labour between education and work can be regarded as an overall structural issue. But it is also a structural issue which seems different for each individual depending on the context from which it is considered. For instance, my own participation in my education as a researcher and my own transition to the labour market seem different depending on whether I consider it from an educational context, my family context or in the light of gender distribution in academia. As Dreier points out, this means that individuals participate in different ways in different contexts, making structural issues appear different by turns (Dreier, 2009)

One of the employees at the company in my study pointed out that he might choose not to apply for a job at all, preferring to take unemployment benefit for a while instead. He defended this choice by pointing out that he had paid a premium for unemployment insurance for many years, so he felt comfortable about getting something back from the social system. In this way he was connecting his problem of redundancy with other arrangements for insurance and solidarity between the members of his trade union. But he also reported that he was soon to be a grandfather again, and that his daughter would be glad to have him available to help look after the baby when she herself returned to work. His reasons were by no means unambiguous or narrow, and they were connected to the way he conducted his family life across different contexts.

6

6.2.1 Meanings

When people participate in career guidance practice they do so based on the meaning they attribute to this practice. This meaning is not necessarily the same for both the career guidance practitioner and the person participating in career guidance (indeed, it will probably not be the same). Sometimes participation is based on the fact that people feel they are obliged to participate. A number of the employees at the company claimed that they did not participate in career guidance practice even though they subsequently referred to their meetings and discussions with Ulla, the career guidance practitioner. They clearly did not define what they were involved in as "participation in career guidance practice". Charlotte Højholt also points out that practice and people's understanding of what practice is are by no means always the same thing: "In a social practice human beings *act together* and in relation to particular historical objects and means, or you might say particular 'agendas' – there are particular things at stake and it is important for the understanding presented here that these things are 'at stake' since the participants are exactly *acting* with these and ascribing them different personal meanings" (Højholt, 2006, p. 87).

In social practice (or in this study career guidance practice) people act together and in relation to a particular history and particular meanings and "agendas". Højholt underlines the importance of maintaining that these objects are "at stake", which means that each individual acts subject to his/her understanding of the situation and ascribes it personal meanings. By analysing both the individual actions (my participatory observation) and the explanations given by individuals regarding their actions (my interviews), I can gain knowledge of the particular history to which career guidance belongs and the social, shared and personal meanings which career guidance has. Højholt goes on to explain how we create knowledge about the general by focusing on acting: "In our acting we adapt common – and structural – dilemmas, and regarded in this way specific (and personal) experiences and perspectives may tell us about the general in all its variations" (Højholt, 2006, p. 88). Dreier writes that we need to study concrete structures broadly as systems of concrete practices, the aim being to capture the meanings of these systems with regard to ongoing practices and to the participants in their different contextual arrangements (Dreier, 2006, p. 6). As shown above, in the field of career guidance there are various systems of practice (conceptual, legislative, historical and methodological). These systems, it is argued here, seem to be largely based on a binary division into societal and individual interests, leading to individualisation of the responsibility for changes of societal issues in career guidance practice which in turn lead to particular possibilities for participation, understood as participation in individual interviews. But other possibilities for participation can be glimpsed when the organisation of career guidance is different. Seen against this background, my study of career guidance in two different practices can provide knowledge about variations on precisely the theme of career guidance. These are not random variations. They are specific because they are variations on the theme of career guidance which are connected to other variations and representations of the same theme in other practices. As a result, shared and structural dilemmas connected to career guidance will be accessible through my study.

Furthermore, meaning is influenced by the community in which it occurs. In communities it is possible to talk about the meanings which the individual and others attribute to their conditions, and it is possible to understand these conditions in a new light and perhaps perform other actions as a result. Changes do not happen until action is taken, but other actions may seem impossible owing to the meaning that individuals or others attribute to their conditions. The social structures become visible in the form of conditions in various ways and at various times, so additional meanings are never either clear or final. Nor are they individual; but they are personal in the sense that the meanings that individuals allocate to their conditions are always connected to the conditions of other people. The ascription of meaning takes place on a continual basis and every day in the conduct of a life.

6.2.2 Participation and participant trajectories

The concept of participation is often connected with learning through participation, and described as the theory of communities of practice (Lave & Wenger, 1991; Wenger, 1998). In Denmark a special research group called *Praksisforskning i Udvikling*[13] (Developing practice research) has developed the concept of participation further. Learning is connected to possibilities for participation. "When we relate learning to participation in social practice, it becomes obvious that the individual possibilities for learning are related to possibilities for participation" (Højholt, 2006, p. 103). From the point of view of the organisation of career guidance practice, it would be interesting to consider what it is that the participants are being given the opportunity to take part in. The possibilities for participation that career guidance practitioners arrange do not necessarily match the possibilities for participation that individuals subjectively see and use. In this book the focus is placed on the way the participants, both students and company employees, perceived various possibilities for participation. This perspective is supplemented by insight into the efforts of career guidance practitioners, folk high school teachers and the company to organise possibilities for participation in the form of career guidance corners and career guidance space. The concept of participation leads to questions such as: what are the possibilities for participation generated by the way in which career guidance is organised, and how do possibilities for participation change as practice develops in interaction with the participants?

Dreier describes the theoretical consequences of regarding people as participants in practice. "First, to adopt 'participation' as a key concept in a theory of the person means to conceptualize subjects as always already involved in social practice" (Dreier, 1999b, p. 5). This means that in my study of career guidance practice I must acknowledge that the participants in career guidance practice and research practice are already participants elsewhere as well. This acknowledgement helps the researcher to avoid making career guidance practice omnipotent, the sole influence on the educational and vocational thoughts and choices of the participants. Regarding individuals as always already involved in a variety of contexts ivites questions such as: What are they participating in? And how are they participating in it? It makes it possible to study career guidance as one context among many others, which in turn makes it possible to carry out detailed descriptions of and obtain analytical perspectives on the interaction between the contexts of action of which career guidance is part.

Ole Dreier distinguishes between personal life-trajectories of participation and institutionally arranged trajectories (Dreier, 1999a and, 1999b). He defines personal life-trajectories as follows: "Across the life-span the person participates in a changing configuration of particular social contexts, and the person composes these changing contextual participations into a personal life-trajectory" (Dreier, 1999b, p. 19). He explains what institutionally arranged trajectories are by using an example of an educational trajectory: "… school is a particular institutional context with a particular significance in the students' composition of a conduct of everyday life across their various contexts which encompasses particular person-al relationships and meanings. At the same time school is arranged for a particular population which is obliged to participate in it for a period in their life-trajectory" (Dreier, 1999b, p. 19). In other words, personal life trajectories and institutionally arranged trajectories (exemplified here by the education system) may coincide for a while – especially if participation is obligatory for particular sectors of the population (as in the case of a number of institutional arrangements for career guidance). Seen as such, the concept of lifelong learning and the various practices established in extension of this concept can be regarded as (new) institutionally arranged trajectories for participation. In this light the government's establishment of the option of competence assessments can be regarded as a point of departure for a (new) education trajectory, with a particular group of individuals (people with a little or no further education behind them) being given special possibilities for participating in education via an assessment of their competences rather than taking a more traditional route which often continues a previous participation in the edu-cation trajectory. If lifelong learning is regarded as an institutionally arranged trajectory, it becomes possible to identify and analyse external interests associated with lifelong learning and thereby refrain from regarding participation in lifelong learning as being in the interests of the individual alone (and being their sole responsibility as well).

6

In relation to the education trajectory, incentive structures are established on an ongoing basis with a view to matching the individual's personal life-trajectory with the education trajectory. Within the field of further education in Denmark, these structures include the option of increasing your average examination grade at upper-secondary school by applying for further education within two years of completion of upper-secondary school. The aim of this kind of incentive structure is to match the personal life-trajectory with the institutionally arranged trajectories for education at an earlier stage.

Personal trajectories of participation are not static – they can be influenced and are changeable. Career guidance is often carried out in the transition between specific institutionally arranged trajectories. This reflects a political interest in ensuring that transitions are made based on the best possible information, as smoothly as possible, and in the "right" directions. "In institutional arrangements for trajectories transitions in life-trajectories with their necessary processes of personal reorientation may also be arranged for. These transitions must be accomplished in relation to existing social structures of practice and they may also be guided or misguided by observations of others and advice from others" (Dreier, 1999b, p. 20). In other words, education trajectories are not the only ones to be institutionalised. If we consider career guidance as an institutional arrangement, this leads to questions such as: Who is the arrangement arranged for? How do participants use career guidance in their ongoing reorientation in life-trajectories? When and how does an institutionally arranged trajectory gain importance for the personal life-trajectories of individuals?

Participation is not limited to a single trajectory and context, but takes place in and across several trajectories and contexts at the same time (Dreier, 1999). As a result, transitions between trajectories do not only occur at specific times and places – they take place continuously. Dreier points out above that transitions are accomplished in relation to existing social structures of practice. I should like to add that new transitions are occurring all the time, and that transitions between trajectories also occur outside institutionally arranged trajectories. Plenty of people change jobs without receiving career guidance, and plenty of young people apply for (or change) their courses of education independently of career guidance.

"A theory of structures of social practice with institutional arrangements and trajectories may guide our analysis of how the social world lends order, direction, and significance to ongoing personal activities" (Dreier, 2008, p. 40).

6.2.3 Personal conduct of everyday life

When individuals participate in several contexts of action and conduct their lives across these contexts, they have to undertake particular actions to ensure the coherence of their lives. People have to conduct their lives actively. This is primarily a practical challenge that is vital in ensuring that the individual's life does not fall apart. Holzkamp calls the task of designing and conducting a coherent everyday life "the personal conduct of everyday life" (Holzkamp, 1998).

He says that the conduct of everyday life is the superior entity under which all areas of the reality of life are structured based on a subjective perspective (Holzkamp, 1998, p. 17). The conduct of life is a relatively new concept in critical psychology, which Holzkamp calls the communicative category between subject and social structure (Holzkamp, 1998, p. 24). He includes a definition provided by the Munich Group:[14] "The conduct of everyday life is an activity 'every single day' with a view to organising, integrating and constructing daily life in such a way that the various contradictory demands with which the individual is confronted can be united and 'sorted out'" (Holzkamp, 1998, p. 27; author's translation). He reinterprets these definitions from a subject-scientific point of view, in which he adds what he calls an *elementary cyclicity* to the conduct of everyday life. This cyclicity means that I do not have to reconsider the world every single day, but can make a routine of some of my reasons for action in order to make life easier for myself. It is emphasised that routines do not mean that the life cycle will run automatically. The subject must still decide to undertake actions. So in a concrete study of a given social practice, the participation of individuals should be analysed from a first-person perspective because people handle their situations and conduct their lives subjectively and personally – as my own personal configuration of our shared conditions. The concept of conduct of everyday life is a holistic one because it

6

collates and integrates the actions of individuals and the various contexts for action into a single whole. *Home, school, the workplace, compulsory employment of the unemployed, career guidance* and *the sports club* are all examples of such contexts for action. So using the concept of the conduct of everyday life, no contexts for action can be understood in isolation. They can only be understood in relation to other contexts for action in human lives.

Holzkamp explains that in today's society nobody tells you what to do. We know we should be busy without being able to appreciate or see the connection with the overall mediating social structure within which we are expected to be busy; meaning is not (always) created for us – we have to create meaning ourselves (ibid.). At this point I should like to emphasise that creating meaning "yourself" also implies creating meaning *together* because our personal meanings must be seen as the personal configurations of social and joint expectations regarding what it means to have a personal meaning. If anything is to be meaningful for me, it must be meaningful for other people too.

The fact that individuals are never left completely alone with their meanings is made clear when Holzkamp points out that we also maintain each other's life conditions. In other words, he says, in principle my life is also maintained when I do not participate in this reproduction of the system and individually the social necessity for action is only a possibility of action for me (Holzkamp, 1991, p. 59). At this point Holzkamp is describing something that may be central to the understanding of why career guidance sometimes fails to work. One example of this is what looks like an attempt made by the Danish government and the Confederation of Danish Industry to persuade young people to start courses of further education earlier by reducing the number of gap years the reason given was demographic: within ten years of 2007 Denmark was going to be short of manpower.[15] This course of action for young people was (is) presented by the government and the Confederation of Danish Industry as necessary in order to ensure the supply of labour and consequently the future of the Danish welfare state. But at the same time 54% of the population (including young people themselves) supported the idea of taking a gap year before starting a course of further education, their reasons being that gaining experience and becoming more certain of their choice of education, would make it less likely that students would drop out or change their course of study. A course of action which was presented as necessary from one perspective (policy and industry) was seen as only one possibility among others from another perspective (youth and general).

This also means that the perception of the individual from a critical psychological perspective which Christensen characterises as rational must be explained in greater detail (Christensen, 2003). Critical psychology does *not* refer to a logical, objective rationality, but to actions which appear meaningful to the individual acting on the basis of their situation and their participation in various contexts. In her PhD dissertation, Hutters (2004) demonstrates that the Danish government tried to stop young people having a gap year in order to ensure that they completed their education faster. But upper-secondary school leavers said that they taking a gap year to ensure that they made the right choices instead of starting on one course and then changing horses mid-stream (this too would delay the completion of their education). For them the choice of a gap year seemed rational and well founded.

The concept of "conduct of everyday life" makes it possible to analyse human actions as being constantly connected to social structures. The conduct of everyday life is a personal configuration of the individual's participation in different, contradictory contexts of action. This points my study in the direction of a particular study perspective: the first-person perspective, which I will account for below.

6.3 The participant perspective

How can a study anchored in the dialectics between the individual and society use the perspectives of the participants in career guidance to help us to understand the meaning of career guidance? It can do so by exploring the way in which career guidance influences the lives of participants, and the possibilities for participation provided by two institutional arrangements for career guidance seen from the perspective of participants.

The key reason aspect of studying a practice from a first-person perspective is that this perspective should connect a subject who is socially anchored and a participant in social life with an intentionality deriving from the subject's participation. According to Højholt, this perspective generates particular analytical opportunities. She says that "the new conceptual opportunities for exploring psychological phenomena in social practice are based on a method of analysis that takes its point of departure in the way in which social conditions have personal meaning and can therefore be analysed as reasons for action" (Højholt, 2001, p. 83; author's translation). According to Højholt, the intention of the trilogy of concepts known as condition, meaning and reason is to pinpoint potential connections between practical conditions and moods of participation (ibid.) .

Conditions contain possibilities and limitations, but should not be seen as determining the subject even though they may *seem* to do so for individual subjects owing to the conditions on which such subjects *justify* their possibilities for action (Holzkamp, 1998, p. 24). It is the *meanings* that the subject ascribes to the conditions that determine the subject's possibilities for action. In this way the analysis of conditions, meanings and reasons is used as a conceptualisation of the connection between the subjective and the social (Jartoft, 1996; Højholt, 2001).

Focusing on this connection makes it clear that conditions are perceived differently by different participants. For instance, one of the folk high school students (Peter) did not seem particularly interested in career guidance or the need to get feedback or concrete help. This was because he had already qualified for admission to his chosen course of further education. His thoughts and frustrations seemed to focus more on his future social relations on the course of his choice. Would he enjoy life as a student? The other students seemed to have considered this already (or to have put it off until a later date), because all their energy was focused on gaining admission to the courses of their choice. Peter and the other students did not only have an inner intentionality; the intentionality was linked to their concrete possibilities for participation, which is socially determined but personally understood and handled. The potentials of the condition, reason and meaning analysis are explained in section 8.5 ("New possibilities for participating in education").

6.3.1 Self-understanding

The concept of *self-understanding* is an extension of the perspective of career guidance participants. Holzkamp points out that "self-understanding primarily means understanding yourself with regard to a certain issue (in this case the conduct of your life). I try to make something that I already know in one way or another reflexively comprehensible to myself by making the implicit explicit and the unclear clear ... Something that has not yet been said clearly, or something which could not be said before, must be expressed in words, so the other is potentially also included in the process of self-understanding" (Holzkamp, 1998, p. 21; author's translation).

Holzkamp's definition of self-understanding assumes that two or more people are present, because coming to an understanding with yourself involves a process of explication which forms the basis of renewed reflexivity. In her PhD dissertation, Line Lerche Mørck develops his use of self-understanding theoretically by proposing that Holzkamp's conceptualisation of *coming to an understanding with yourself* should be extended by adding a "we" (Mørck, 2003, p. 216; author's translation). The aim of this is to underline collective subjectivity as a central aspect of a person's self-understanding (ibid.). This explanation of self-understanding may explain why the individual always acts in relation to others. These others are present as soon as individuals try to understand themselves.

6.4 **Summary**

The figure below systematises the links between the categories mentioned above and shows how the analytical strengths of these categories are related to the basic dilemma of career guidance (individual – society). The categories help to perpetuate the individual/society unit because the reasons of each individual are based on social conditions as they are given meaning by individuals through participation and the conduct of their lives in communities and contexts of action. The dialectics take place between the individual and society, which are physically different but mutually balanced and determined by each other and which are therefore regarded as different parts of the same unit.

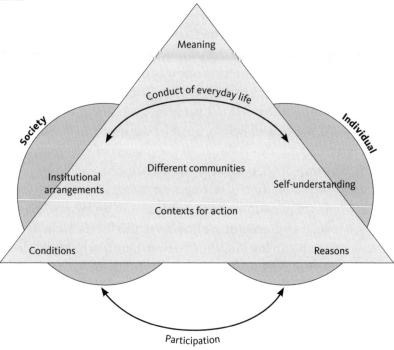

Figure 2. Connections between analytical categories.

The circles illustrate society and the individual, which are physically distinct units. Changes in either the individual or society are shown as being connected in the same unit (the triangle); to maintain the dialectics of the analysis, analytical categories are used, each of which constitutes a sub-division of the individual and society (the categories of meaning and self-understanding). The figure is based on the *a priori* assumptions that participation is a fundamental condition of human life, that life consists of participating in various communities

84

and contexts for action, and that this participation is coordinated via the personal conduct of everyday life. Participation and the conduct of every-day life describe the activity of the individual.

The categories form a basis for avoiding a division into individual and societal interests with a view to creating new understandings of what the field of career guidance presents as a binary problem and describes as a basic condition. The analytical categories do not permit one-sidedness in the analysis and separation into poles because each category contains connections to others. The strength of each of the categories lies in constantly forcing the attention of the researcher towards *both* the individual and society and towards connections between reasons and conditions, institutional arrangements and self-understanding. The research question explored in this book, which seeks to discover how to understand the meaning of career guidance seen from a participant perspective based on the study of two different institutional arrangements for career guidance, calls for the use of analytical categories which allow for the participant perspective on career guidance. Moreover, the presentation of the objectives of career guidance in the form of a normative division into individual and societal interests calls for a dialectical understanding of the connection between individual participation, institutional arrangements for career guidance and the self-understanding that is produced through participation in various communities and contexts.

In the introduction the term "practice research" was used to describe the method used for the research project on which this book is based. The next chapter contains further thoughts on methodology in relation to the field of study, the research question and the theoretical assumptions described above – as well as discusses the methodological consequences involving the interaction between these aspects.

6

7 Practice research – co-researchers

Chapter 7 contains methodological considerations in relation to the efforts of practice research to study something with someone else. Who are we studying with? What are WE studying? How did we agree to cooperate? The strategy of co-research is explained, and using examples from my empirical evidence the potential and limitations of co-research in my research practice are discussed. This leads to an account of the analytical work carried out in the research on which this book is based. How was the material arranged for analysis, transcription, coding in ATLAS.ti, analytical longitudinal movements in the individual interviews and across the whole material?

7.1 Design of study and selection of settings

The PhD research on which this book is based was a practice research project with the emphasis on the participant perspective regarding career guidance. In order to gain insight into the significance of career guidance in various ways, I have emphasised differences in the cases (different ages, different genders, different interests, different regions of Denmark, different career guidance practices etc.). Choosing a folk high school that prepares students for further education and a production company that was being closed down as my partners meant that I could comply with the requirement for differences. Career guidance is often provided in transitional phases in people's lives, and in my material there were two different transitions: the transition from a folk high school to further education; and the transition from having been in the same factory job for many years to finding a new job.

86

Many of the young people at the folk high school had just completed upper-secondary education and had applied to folk high school to give themselves time to make a decision about further education – or to improve their qualifications and make admission to the course of their dreams more likely. At the company the employees had not chosen to close down production, and it was the company that had decided to purchase career guidance services for them. They had not decided to look for career guidance themselves. The idea of choosing different study settings was that different participant perspectives on different institutional arrangements for career guidance would illustrate and illuminate each other.

The choice of a folk high school and a company gave me the opportunity of studying the way in which career guidance was organised in different conditions: (1) as part of everyday life at the folk high school, with a career guidance practitioner who was part of everyday practice and available outside the planned career guidance activities as well; and (2) at the company, where the time spent with the practitioner was more limited and the practitioner was not part of everyday practice, and would probably not be available outside the planned career guidance activities.

In order to find a suitable folk high school I contacted The Association of Folk High Schools in Denmark, which set up a meeting for me with the person responsible for career guidance at folk high schools and a consultant from the association. At this meeting I explained my interests, after which they suggested a folk high school that might be a good study setting. They also contacted this school and presented the project. The principal of the school was interested in participating, so I contacted the school and arranged to present the project to the entire staff. It was then decided which teachers I should observe and I was allowed to approach the students myself. For an explanation of the concrete research activities, please see section 7.1.3 ("Schematic presentation of empirical data").

To find a suitable company I contacted VUS Kontakt – an adult education service which was originally set up by Copenhagen County, Copenhagen Municipality and Frederiksberg Municipality as well as various parties from the Danish labour market. VUS Kontakt was established in 1992. I met the manager of VUS Kontakt and the prac-

7

titioner I was later to observe, and presented the project, the issue to be studied and my wishes with regard to collaboration with VUS Kontakt. We chose an international company (one of their clients) which was closing down its production department in Denmark. VUS Kontakt approached this company and asked them whether they would like to take part. They were interested, and after a meeting with the company's HR consultant, foreman and the VUS Kontakt practitioner I was allowed to visit the company whenever I liked. Before this meeting the HR consultant, foreman and VUS Kontakt practitioner had chosen five employees who I could ask to take part in the research project. They all agreed.

7.1.1 The process of empirical data collection

The collaboration at each study setting started with a meeting with the management and a contact/practitioner/shop steward to discuss the research project. I tried to identify and define their expectations regarding my participation in practice. Both these meetings ended with a guided tour. In both cases I was asked to introduce the research project to the employees/students myself, which I did at a meeting of employees and at morning assembly respectively. I briefly explained my interest in career guidance, but I explained my method in greater detail: I wanted to observe the participants in their everyday lives as students/employees. I would arrive when they arrived at work or went to have breakfast, and I would observe them for two days and round off the second day with an interview. I also explained the principles of anonymity and sovereignty, as well as their right to terminate their participation at any time during the period of observation.

I chose to observe five informants at the folk high school, and five at the company. At the folk high school I tried to choose students from different courses of study. My informants were selected based on a very short questionnaire, the purpose of which was to allow the students to state whether they wanted to participate in the research project or not. At the company it was not my job to choose my informants – they were chosen by the HR consultant in collaboration with the foreman and career guidance practitioner. My most important criterion was that the people chosen should be interested in participating in the research project, and that they should represent a certain amount of variation in terms of working area and age. These variations would give me the chance to observe several different sides of practice. I could have chosen a larger number of participants, but this would have forced me to cut down on the number of observation hours. I felt that in order to discover the impact of career guidance on the participants, and the possibilities for participation that these two particular institutional arrangements gave the participants, more hours of observation would be preferable.

One week of participatory observation of general practice
5 × 2 days observing the production employees, ending in qualitative individual interviews
Then: 2 days observing the career guidance practitioner, ending in a qualitative interview and an interview with the HR consultant

Figure 3. Design of observation process at the company.

7.1.2 Schematic presentation of empirical data

	Observation and interview	Interview	Observation
Company	5 employees 1 practitioner	1 dept. manager	– Lunch room – Production dept. – Job application course – Individual career – Career guidance interviews – Foreman's office
Folk high school	5 students 2 teachers	1 teacher responsible for career guidance	– Valuable Competencies course including teachers' meetings – Discussions of competences – A career guidance interview – Preparatory discussion, journalist – Staff room – General teaching, first-aid course, recreational area, cycle trips, art, etc.

Figure 4. Schematic presentation of empirical data.

89

A total of 15 interviews with employees, students, teachers, career guidance practitioners and the HR manager were conducted. This data is documented in the form of a field diary, minutes of meetings, notes from meetings, observation notes and transcripts of interviews.

7.2 Research intention

The aim of the dissertation on which this book is based had several aspects for which the methodological design had to allow. First I had the intention of describing how career guidance practice interacts with the everyday lives of the participants, and how career guidance was organised at the two study settings. This aim was pursued through observations. Then I also had a theory-driven intention that I sought to include and apply critical psychological categories in a study organised according to a practice research methodological approach to the field of career guidance. The theory-related intention was pursued in the analysis process, with critical psychology categories being used to highlight themes from the empirical data for the researcher and reader alike. The theory-driven intention moves onto a theory-generating level in relation to critical psychology, which to the best of my knowledge has not been used as the basis of a research study of career guidance practice before. When critical psychological categories are examined in a new field, the aim of the analysis is to contribute to the development of those categories. I also had a theory-generating ambition in relation to what is described as the basic dilemma of career guidance, similar to the approach of Jean Lave, who points out (when describing the goal of empirical research with Steiner Kvale) that if empirical research is to have any purpose, it should change your theory just as much as your theory influences your empirical work (Kvale & Lave, 2003, p. 191).

7.2.1 What is co-research?

Critical psychology has ambitions for research *with* people and *for* practice, which are linked to research based on a first-person perspective as described by Højholt, who says that subjects must not be con-

7

fused with objects when we wish to study them. Objects can be observed, influenced in various controlling manners, and then registered in terms of their reactions. Subjects, on the other hand, are characterised by their active intentionality directed at the world around them (Højholt, 1993, p. 20). The relevance of this active intentionality is that as soon as I am present as a researcher with a wish to research people and practice, the people that I meet and who meet me via their intentionality will be drawn into the research process. Consequently, in this understanding research as it takes place in practice in everyday life at the company or folk high school cannot take place in isolation from the influence and intentions of the participants – whether these intentions involve actively seeking out the researcher with questions and contributions, or quietly sneaking past them on the corridor. My research became part of their everyday practice for a while. And in this way the participants in the practice in which research takes place will always influence (and be co-researchers in) the research process.

With this understanding of people's intentionality and the ambition to understand career guidance from a first-person perspective, it is important in a research process to use methods that provide the opportunity to reveal the interests and standpoints of the parties involved from *their* point of view, position and perspective (Mørck, 1995). The first-person perspective has been used in a variety of ways in research anchored in critical psychology. One of these ways is via an understanding of research as practice research and with a shift in perspective involving a movement from thinking of *the objects being studied* as objects of the research process to recognizing *the co-researchers* as subjective participants in the process (Forchhammer, 2001, p. 27). In Hysse Forchhammer's understanding, this kind of perspective makes it possible to ensure that the subjective experiences, reasons, actions and interests of the objects being studied do not become sources of erroneous information – but are important, positioned perspectives and reasons for subjective actions. The joint interest lies in understanding and developing the shared field of study (Forchhammer, 2001, p. 31). This makes it possible to understand both the researcher and the participants as subjects participating in the research process with a shared interest in developing the field of study constituting concrete practice. At the same time it is also important to point out that the concept of co-research does not mean that the interests involved are *shared*, because the wishes of the participants when it comes to developing practice may easily differ.

7.2.2 Having an eye for contexts

When Dreier writes that we need to stop studying individuals in a single context (Dreier, 1999a, p. 83), he is making particular demands on the way the research process is organised – requiring the researcher to accompany individuals in various contexts because they participate in various contexts during their everyday lives. I will argue that this can be done in various ways. You can adopt a cross-contextual approach in concrete terms, as in Dorthe Kousholt's study (Kousholt, 2006) called "Familieliv fra et børneperspektiv" ("Family life from a child's perspective"), in which she accompanies children when they go home to their families after spending the day in childcare. She sees the children in various places and contexts of action. In her dissertation Anne Morin shows that a cross-contextual approach may also look like a single-context approach to outsiders: for example, the context of school (Morin, 2007). Morin observes the participation of children in both standard classes and special-needs classes, which from the perspective of the children constitute two different contexts – both within the context of school. But the question is whether the researcher should physically move between different contexts. How can we refrain from studying people in a single context? My point is that the participation of a researcher in a single context gives access to knowledge of several contexts at the same time: contexts of which the individual's participation is part.

The folk high school students referred to their participation in other contexts when talking to me and with each other. For instance, they told me about their time in upper-secondary school or their family lives at home. In a sense they showed me that contexts of action were all connected, and that participation at one place involved not only that individual context but a number of contexts at the same time. As a result, I argue that when participating in one context of action it is

92

possible for researchers to remain open to the connections to other contexts about which individuals give us information. Participatory observation in which there is enough time and space to talk allows connections to other contexts to appear and assume importance.

The fact that I was not physically present in other contexts (work and family life, for instance) did not mean that other contexts did not exist for me. This is a question of the researcher being aware of the interaction between contexts and interests and asking about such links. Knowledge of many contexts is available thanks to the co-researcher's description of their participation in other contexts seen from their point of view. So when Dreier writes that we need to stop studying individuals in a single context, I believe that there is more than one way of doing this. We can be physically present in various contexts; but we can also be sensitive to the issue of context in the research process. Context sensitivity in this sense means that the researcher is aware of and asks questions about how participation in one context affects participation in other contexts.

7.2.3 Participatory observation

Working with context sensitivity requires time and trust, which can be developed by participatory observation (as argued by Line Lerche Mørck). She claims that participant observation is typically a good way to develop a trusting relationship because it gives the participants plenty of time and opportunities to get used to the researcher (Mørck, 2003, p. 174). This was confirmed by the participants in my study. One of them said:

RIE: OK. What's it like to be interviewed? Although I haven't finished following you around yet.

TINE: It's been really nice actually because I haven't felt like I had to sit up straight or say anything I was supposed to say. I think it's been great – it's like having a chat with you, and we've had plenty of conversations while you've been here. If you just turned up out of the blue one day I might have felt a bit … but it hasn't been like that at all.

In writing about participant observation, Spradley (1980) says that the difference between the researcher and the ordinary participant in practice is that the ordinary participant only has one goal (taking part), whereas the researcher has two goals (taking part and researching). However, in the light of my theoretical standpoint the distinction between research and participation does not make any sense. Research is also participation – I participate through my research, or I participate with my research. I felt that my participation in practice at the folk high school and company made a new activity possible for the participants at those places: helping me with my research task. They explained that they made themselves available so I could do my job. In this sense my presence gave them another option for participation. They participated in their everyday lives, and they participated in helping me with my research project.

Line Lerche Mørck also points out (Mørck, 2003, p. 174) that participant observation is characterised by the fact that the researcher can gain an impression of certain conditions in practice which the people being interviewed regard as relatively obvious, implicit parts of their practice. Naturally such observations are controlled; but it is not possible to control the impressions provided by practice. In the subsequent analysis process the observations often constitute an important supplement as the focus of analysis changes and becomes more precise during the research process. When I lacked knowledge on themes about which I had not asked in the interviews, I was often able to use my observation notes to gain insight into and knowledge about new themes which I had not thought of asking about in my interviews. So it was important for the analysis process that the empirical material was both focused and broad at the same time.

Participatory observation also means taking part – not only being present when things take place, but also being willing to share your knowledge with the other participants in practice. So I always tried to give answers when people asked what I was writing in my field diary. These answers often resulted in new, shared reflections. If I had not answered such questions, my participatory observation would have failed to comply with the goal of creating trust. I was trying to understand from a participant perspective, but co-research means that the participants study my perspective as well. This requires me as a researcher to make my knowledge available. I wanted to democratise the accessibility of knowledge during the research process, and this meant considering the accessibility of my own knowledge. These considerations are explained in greater depth in section 12.2.2 ("Research as knowledge sharing – also throughout the process").

The wish to carry out co-research is therefore closely connected to the researcher's understanding of knowledge and knowledge production. In her PhD dissertation, Tove Borg writes that theory development or knowledge aquisistion with a view to changing practice cannot occur in the form of theoretical work in isolation from practice. The concrete practice, experiences, development interests and perspectives of individuals must be allowed some space in the process. On the other hand, the development of practice requires theoretical reflections based on broad theoretical and often cross-disciplinary contexts (social practice). In order to produce development – both theory development and practice development – an interaction between theory and practice is necessary. And to achieve this, actors who are relevant to the conditions being studied must be involved (Borg, 2002, p. 67).

Borg's presentation of the task of practice research indicates that inclusion is necessary to ensure the interaction between theory and practice. The people included must be actors who are relevant to practice. Borg does not specify any special qualifications in the people included, apart from their importance with regard to practice. Their importance with regard to practice must be determined by the researcher when dealing with the material, but their inclusion also depends on something else: anyone regarding themselves as important with regard to what is taking place in a research project can become involved, force their way in and express their views. This is exactly what happened to me when an interview in the lunch room developed into a group interview as more and more people wanted to tell me what was on their minds. See section 8.3 ("Career guidance in the company").

7

95

7.2.4   Ethical considerations

Neither of the study settings asked for anonymity. On the contrary – they both announced my presence and the purpose of the research project in press releases or by taking part in interviews in trade magazines. This placed me in a dilemma with regard to the anonymity of the participants. In the introduction to the observations and interviews I told the participants that they would be anonymous. They all replied that this was not necessary. It was difficult to say whether this was a carefully considered answer or simply an attempt to be obliging. Even so, I decided to make the study settings and participants anonymous – although I am also aware that total anonymity is not possible, and that my decision could just as easily be regarded as unethical because I failed to respect the wishes of the participants, who did not want to be anonymous. The decision was taken because the participants were slightly less explicit with regard to the absence of anonymity. It will always be possible to identify the study settings, so I decided not to spend time producing detailed biographical portraits of my informants. The age, gender and ethnic group of each participant have not been described because this information would have made it possible to identify the participants.

7.3   Collaborating in interviews

I started my observations in each setting by visiting for a week. During this week I tried to ensure that my observations were not focused, and I did not restrict my observations to activities which had already been defined as career guidance. I simply observed everyday life at the folk high school and company. During this week I also made arrangements with the people I was to follow subsequently. These weeks of participatory observation formed the background knowledge that enabled me to draw up an interview guide for the semi-structured interviews with which I concluded my observations. I drew up four different but similar guides (see appendices 1-4). They vary in terms of their wording, which has been adapted to suit the context in question (the school or company). Each guide is divided into themes containing suggestions for questions. These questions were not asked in the same way every time, and the order of the themes also varied somewhat. The differences were due to the fact that I wanted my observations of practice and shared experiences with my informants to form the basis of the dialogue in the interviews. Before each interview I prepared by reading through my observation notes and underlining events, activities or other points that I wanted to ask about in the interviews. I regard these themes as an objectification of the issues in question and an attempt to make the research concrete in the form of a common third (Højholt, 2005).

My intention was that each interview should constitute a shared process of study. To ensure that this happened, I also tried to install another common third to avoid falling into the trap for which I have criticised other career guidance practitioners: objectifying by studying the other party involved (Thomsen, 2007). The common third was a sheet of A3 paper on the table between us, which we could use to take notes. This strategy did not seem to work: I did not feel any need to take notes, and nor did my co-researchers. This was perhaps because the common third was actually the issue at stake itself and our shared experiences – not a piece of paper. After a couple of interviews the paper was removed, although I did retain the (ritual) introduction to the interviews, which went as follows (in a number of variations):

RIE: I thought that I would ask a few questions, but that what we should actually do is share the task of exploring what it's like to be at a folk high school.
MADS: That's fine by me.

RIE: I thought that we could use these interviews to explore a bit. Because I've been with you a while now, and I'd like to include some of the things I've observed or seen while I've been here, and then we could look at them a bit more closely.
OLE: Yes.

7

97

7.3.1 Interview criticism

When I retrospectively analyse my intentions of exploring various issues in partnership with the participants, I can see that the students at the folk high school, their teachers and to some extent the career guidance practitioners at the company were all given the same introduction to the interviews, expressing the wish for a joint effort. But the employees at the company were not given the same explicit introduction to my intention concerning co-research and the use of the paper as a common third in the interviews. I was not aware of this at the time, so subsequently the following question came to mind: do I think that in this situation the employees at the company were aware of the fact that they were to be involved in studying various issues in the interview, in which I asked a series of questions? The two interview guides also differ with regard to this point. The introduction was not included in the interview guide for the employees and career guidance practitioner at the company. Apparently my feeling about the study settings and the people I met there led me to introduce the interviews in different ways. It was interesting to reconsider the interviews at a later date, to see whether there was a difference in the degree of co-research going on. It was clear that the only difference was that my intention was expressed explicitly in the folk high school context, whereas it was implicit in the interviews at the company. On the other hand, the questions with which I concluded all the interviews seemed to invite co-research to a far greater extent. This question was "Is there anything I haven't asked about that you thought we were going to talk about?"

7.3.2 Visibility of co-research in the interviews

I have treated the co-research perspective analytically in my empirical material to see whether it was possible to find any points at which a shared analytical sense of curiosity was apparent. Passages were marked as co-research in the interviews when the interviewee asked questions, expressed surprise or took the initiative to examine a new theme in other ways. It was clear in all the interviews that this only started to happen when we were about half-way through. One obvious trigger seemed to be my final question: "We're almost finished with the things I wanted to talk about. Is there anything else that *you* thought we were going to talk about?" This question often led to a counter-question or the ideas of the interviewees, contributing additional knowledge or experiences from a new angle which they themselves introduced. The interesting thing is that I tried to conclude the interviews at a point when I felt my questions had been answered and when I felt that we were starting to repeat ourselves, and yet ending the interview with an open, curious question often led to entirely new ideas. In other words, the co-researchers were able to ask themselves and us a question which led to new reflections – reflections to which I would not have had access if I had concluded the interviews with a closed statement.

7.3.3 The limits of co-research

But what are the limits to co-research? Are the people involved at first hand the only ones who can be co-researchers (in this case the chosen folk high school students, employees, teachers and career guidance practitioners)? Or are there any other co-researchers involved during the process?

7

Conceptualising career guidance as an institutional arrangement means acknowledging the fact that practice gains its direction from many different places: from the participants in concrete practice, from the participation of the participants elsewhere and therefore also from the input gained by practitioners via their participation in other career guidance arrangements. Along the way I have presented thoughts and preliminary results for career guidance practitioners, who have reflected on the research themes in relation to their own practice, experiences and knowledge of the field. This has resulted in a number of good dialogues, supplying the research project with broader knowledge from the field and occasionally problematising the current points. For instance, see section 10.3 ("Ethics and confidentiality"). Consequently, I argue that co-research is not limited to the people involved at first hand, but that it can be broadened out to include other practitioners in professional communities.

7.3.4 The limits of privacy

In designing the project I wanted to consider the impact of career guidance on the lives of the participants and in interaction with other contexts of action. As a result, I did not wish to limit my observations or perception of career guidance to activities taking place with a career guidance practitioner. This was why I observed the students at the folk high school and the employees at the company over a lengthy period of time: from morning to evening, and for more than one day. Even so, I did not see many folk high school rooms. It was as if the students drew a line in the sand at the doors to their rooms – even though they were extremely cooperative and helpful. One girl invited me into her room, but all the others met me in the dining room or at morning assembly. Some said "I'm just going down to my room – can we meet in the dining hall in a few minutes?" Even though as a researcher you try to observe your co-researchers in all contexts, your participants also have an influence on the research process. And the students did not imagine that I would be interested in seeing their rooms. It also seemed out of the question to ask the employees at the company whether I could observe them in their everyday lives outside the company, at home, or when they went to recreational activities. But many of the company co-researchers were very willing to tell me about their private lives, hobbies, childhood and youth, school experiences – indeed anything that seemed like a natural extension of our shared exploration of the interaction between career guidance and their everyday lives at the company. As such, the other contexts in which the participants took part did have an influence on the research project when the participants told me about them.

One of the issues discussed in research is whether it is an advantage to know something about the field you wish to study as a researcher. The quotations below reflect contrasting attitudes regarding the previous experiences of researchers in the field which they are studying. Spradley writes that "The *less* familiar you are with a social situation, the *more* you are able to see the tacit cultural rules at work" (Spradley, 1980, p. 62, emphasis in the original). On the other hand, Dreier points out that including people who have knowledge of (or who are affected by) any practice which is being studied shows that personal interest in a research project does not necessarily have a negative effect on your perception (Dreier, 1996).

I knew both a great deal and very little about the study settings in my project. I have a variety of experience of career guidance. For instance, I have participated in career guidance in various contexts as a school pupil and university student. I have also participated in the training course for career guidance practitioners, and worked as a career guidance practitioner for the 6th grade at a Danish school. I have also lectured and taught on the subject of my current research. But career guidance was only one context of action for the participants in my study settings, and I know very little about what it is like to be a 50-year-old man who produces paint – or what it is like to be a student at a folk high school, because I have never been to one.

7.3.5 Interviews and career guidance are closely connected

It may be particularly difficult to interview people about career guidance because career guidance itself often involves an interview/dialogue. I was a researcher in this context, and needed to avoid assuming the role of a career guidance practitioner. Despite my awareness of this fact, I did end up assuming this role on a couple of occasions. This happened once at the end of an interview, when I must have felt like giving a student a little more self-confidence. I started to praise him and said that I was sure he would be a good doctor, researcher or anything he decided to be:

RIE: So I hope you'll get into university. I think you'd be a good student and become a good doctor, medical man or anything you decide to be.
MADS: Thanks a lot! I hope so too.

On another occasion I was aware that this was happening during an interview. A student had asked several times to be challenged on his choice of further education, and after the end of the interview I asked:

RIE: But why do you want to study medicine?
PETER: Well ...
RIE: Come on – what's your answer?

Peter then answered my question at length, after which I acted as a good career guidance practitioner should and asked some follow-up questions to expand on his reflection and decision-making process. Perhaps some form of exchange was going on here. He helped me in the interview and allowed me to observe him for a few days, then it was my turn to give him something back. The schism can also be related to my point that democratising the research process also involves me making my knowledge available. When the research process is conceptualised as cooperation, I regard it as counterproductive if one of the participants withdraws from instead of contributing to the joint process of cooperation. Researchers who wish to work with participants in practice with regard to studying practice cannot expect to participate at a distance from a privileged position solely as observers and collectors of knowledge. For further discussion of this point, please see section 12.2.2 ("Research as knowledge sharing – also throughout the process").

7.4 **Transcription**

7

The interviews were all transcribed *in extenso* by the same student assistant.

> TRANSCRIPTION GUIDELINES:
> – Transcribe word-for-word including supporting sounds such as "mmm", "yes" and "no".
> – Start a new line for each new person.
> – Breaks of less than three seconds should be marked by three dots.
> – Breaks of more than three seconds should be marked by [break].
> – Any lack of clarity should be marked by writing "unclear" plus the time, and then (in brackets) an interpretation of what had been said.
> – If the interviewee stresses any particular words, this should be marked in bold type.
> – Emotional outbursts (laughter, for instance) should be marked in brackets (laughter).

7.4.1 From transcripts to quotations in the analysis process to quotations in the book

Owing to the length of the dissertation on which this book was based, it was not possible to include passages of the length I considered in the analysis process. The quotations in the dissertation were edited accordingly in relation to the following parameters. Supporting sounds were omitted because they increased the length of the quotations significantly – they were marked by a new line and a new person every time someone said "mmm" or "yes". I carefully transformed the quotations from spoken language to written language to reduce the number of breaks and repetitions. People often change topic rapidly in spoken language, which seems very confusing when it is written down, and so I edited the quotations to ensure that the topics dealt with were dealt with together. The aim of the transformation was to make reading the quotations easier, which meant changing the word order of the transcribed text into a more natural word order for written language. This meant that the attention of the reader could be fixed on the point I was trying to make, rather than being confused by the kind of sudden switch in topic which is so common in spoken language. Occasionally it was necessary to explain what (or to whom) something referred. This was indicated in brackets.

7

7.5 The process of analysis

There are various different attitudes to the possibility of explicating analysis processes in research work, as illustrated below.

Henning Olsen (Olsen, 2002, p. 9) says that the process of analysis can be made clear by drawing up a motivated and implemented analysis strategy from among the available strategies or as a particular strategic mix: Should a perspective from below be given priority? What position should conceptualisation and conceptualised procedures be given? How does interpretation play an analytical role?

Henning Olsen pleads for total transparency, and says that when this is not possible the task of the researcher is to persuade the readers that the limit to additional transparency has been reached (Olsen,

2002). At the other end of what could be called the transparency continuum of analysis we find a perception of analysis and interpretation
strategies that is almost esoteric.

In his method book *Den skinbarlige virkelighed* (The incarnation
of reality), Ib Andersen says that interpretation is a form of creative
procedure that cannot be described and controlled in the same way
as traditional methods of analysis. In other words, the methods contain an important artistic element, which may be the reason for the
lack of method books in this field. It is impossible to tell people how
to dance ballet like Margot Fonteyne or how to paint like Rembrandt
– and it is also impossible to describe how we should actually carry
out a qualitative process of interpretation from A to Z (Andersen,
1999, p. 247).

At this end of the continuum the limit has apparently already been
reached before explication has begun. I attempt to place myself somewhere in the middle of the two poles.

Within the field of critical psychology there is a good deal of focus on the part of the research process that takes place in practice and
alongside co-researchers. There are plenty of descriptions of organising the research process in cooperation and drawing up issues jointly (Højholt, 2005), based on practice (Rasmussen, 2003), and of understanding problems from a participant perspective (Borg, 2002).
There are also descriptions of how to arrange the empirical material
for analysis. Proposals for concrete analytical measures, however, are
rather thin on the ground. The most recent of these proposals are provided in PhD dissertations by Anne Morin (Morin, 2007), Dorthe
Kousholt (Kousholt, 2006) and Ida Schwartz (Schwartz, 2007), with
the analytical categories being used to look for connections and link
the social with the personal.

7.5.1 From coding to analysis theme

This section contains an example of my analytical efforts and of the
transition from thematic coding to analysis theme. In coding the
material from the company I tried initially to code on the terms of
the material itself – in other words, using concepts that were used
in the interviews. One of these was education. On several occasions

I came across stories and references to the participation of the employees in supplementary training and other courses. Initially I coded these references under the heading of "education". Later on in the task of analysis, based on my theoretical set of concepts and the focus the categories gave on connections and links (see the figure in section 6.4 "Summary"), it became apparent that the situation facing the employees (they were being fired) was related to their perspectives on participating in education. New perspectives on education now applied, and therefore new possibilities for participation. So the first code ("education") was placed in the analysis chapter entitled "New possibilities for participating in education" (8.5).

Some analysis themes make sense in both study contexts, while others do not. Differences in study settings, situations, participants and career guidance can help to indicate issues and terms connected to issues extending beyond the practices studied here, a point to which I return in section 7.5.2 ("Example of creation of categories").

As a practical support in handling my material I chose to import and code the interview transcripts in the program ATLAS.ti. ATLAS.ti is based on grounded theory, offering the option of connecting codes and making families of categories – functions that I did not use in my analysis work. For me, the primary aim of using this computer program was to organise my material. As the analysis themes developed I read and re-read my observation notes and interviews. The codes formed the point of departure for themes that were supplemented with material from my observation notes. The initial codes were not the same as the analytical themes and discussions that were presented in the dissertation on which this book is based. When first coding the material in ATLAS.ti I coded relatively long sequences of interviews, because I wanted to use the function in ATLAS.ti enabling the user to retrieve a transcript of all quotations under the same coding in all the interviews. In this transcript I wanted to present the "whole story" in the interviews. For instance, in sections dealing with "education" I went back to the point in the interview at which this topic started, then went through the interview marking all the text until the topic was abandoned once again. So at the start of the analysis work I worked with relatively long interview sequences. The codes I started with were:

7

– CV	– Past, present and future	– Previous career
– Culture	– Understanding competences	guidance-education
– The individual and	– Concrete help	– Choice of folk high school
the community	– Co-research	– Career guidance
– Professionalism	– Relationship between	– Self-confidence
– Credit	teacher and student	– Organisation

Figure 5. The first codes.

I started by coding the material from the folk high school. I did not intend that the codes should necessarily be repeated in coding the material from the company. I remained open to the idea that other new codes might arise in the course of my work. Some codes were of a general nature ("education", "concrete help", "career guidance" and "self-confidence", for instance). Others were more specific in relation to the issues I was exploring and my theoretical understanding ("co-research", for instance). But codes also arose gradually as they formed patterns of meaning during my re-reading of the interviews ("The individual and the community" and "Past, present and future"). Not all of my codes were used in the analysis. As I formed patterns between codes, theoretical concepts and my research questions, the codes turned into analytical themes.

My explanation of what occurs in the analysis process places me somewhere between complete transparency and the completely esoteric, since I seek to account for an interaction between patterns of connections in the empirical material which are compared to and inspired by the theoretical categories, which in turn demonstrate sensitivity to the empirical contributions. This means that the process of analysis moves constantly between empirical material and theory, finally being frozen in an instant of time to constitute a unit of theory and practice (this book).

7.5.2 Example of creation of categories

I mentioned above that ATLAS.ti is based on grounded theory, and this section represents an example of the way in which the process of interpretation in practice research can be distinguished from the process of interpretation within grounded theory.

7

This idea about generating theory from the flow of incoming data in research has prompted the name of the procedure: grounded theory methodology (Corbin & Strauss, 1994, in Axel, 2002, p.618).

Axel goes on to describe the way in which data processing with grounded theory continues as a reduction in complexity by identifying common denominators. Comparison reveals common denominators, and these are described as categories (Axel, ibid.).

By contrast with this approach, in my analysis I was interested in finding contradictions and differences. One example of this is a sense of wonder that things needing processing in the individual are conceptualised differently in different career guidance contexts, for instance in the form of the concepts of realism or motivation. Young people seem to have a need to make a realistic educational choice. People with little or no further education have to be motivated to take part in education. Both concepts start as themes in the analysis, with the theme dealing with career guidance and spotting what needs to be tackled in career guidance. The differences between the concepts made me aware that they are connected to the social embeddedness of career guidance. Connecting the two different concepts from two different practices to the function of these concepts in relation to the societal objectives of career guidance makes it possible to see how their differences are an expression of the same mechanism: an adaptation of individual interests to what is regarded as societal interests. The fact that young people are encouraged to be realistic in their choices should be seen in relation to both the education system as a sorting mechanism, and the fact that the young people's educational wishes need to be directed into areas in which a shortage of labour is expected. The two concepts, which initially seemed so different, become an expression of the category called "adaptation" in the analysis.

Critical psychology provides very few instructions for concrete analysis, which can be explained by the fact that the basic assumption about the unity between theory and practice requires the analytical concepts to be grounded in the local context. Consequently, it is in the confrontation between the explored field of practice and the basic set of concepts in critical psychology that a concrete set of concepts

7

can be constructed for use in analysis (Dreier, 1996). Another explanation could be that anchoring concepts in a local context makes them
appear to be everyday concepts. All we need to do is consider concepts in other theoretical areas – for instance intersectionality (an approach used to analyse power imbalances), or the concept of self-technology (as explained in a previous chapter), compared with concepts
such as conditions, participation and perspective. In critical psychology the latter are both practical and analytical categories, and as analytical categories they have an effect on our everyday assumptions
when we use them to gain insight into connections, contradictions
and differences.

7.6 **Relevance and validity**

The fact that I maintain the unity between theory and practice calls
for consideration of whether the knowledge contributed in this book
may have an impact on the study settings and other practices. Dreier believes that the connection to existing problems and revelation of
possibilities for action for the participants provide criteria for the relevance and validity of practice research (Dreier, 1996). He twists the
concept of generalisability and emphasises that we can talk meaning-
fully about generalisability because the problems and possibilities of
the world are not unique but typical in typical contexts. Generalisation does not determine actions. It merely indicates theoretically a
(new) practical possibility: generalisation makes it possible for us to
imagine previously overlooked possibilities for action (Dreier, 1996).
From this perspective, generalisations are possibilities for thought
and not statements claiming that something applies in all practices
at all times.

Researchers working on a critical psychology basis seek to achieve
a form of research that both (from the inside) establishes a subject
perspective by subjectifying in a community and (from the outside)
transcends and generalises the same subject perspective by changing
(constructing) objective meanings (Mørck & Nissen, 2001, p. 57). The
aim of generalisation is that people should join forces to transcend
and extend their potential by generalising the meanings attributed to

the objective structures. In this way, generalisation can create a path leading to changes in concrete practice structures. The potential for self-transcending actions is therefore connected very strongly to the potential for conquering more general conditions and forming wider communities (Nissen, 2002, p. 71). The fact that you can achieve more in communities, transcending your understanding of your own life situation by inclusion in a community and thereby gaining an overall extension of the potential of communities, may indicate the importance of community for career guidance and the importance of examining this area in research.

7.7 Summary

Chapter 7 is entitled "Praxctice research – co-researchers", and this idea becomes important in the light of the ambition to understand the way in which career guidance influences how individuals conduct their everyday lives and vice versa. By participating in practice via participatory observation, I sought to study career guidance and the way in which people conducted their lives in cooperation with the individuals concerned. I tried to develop common points of reference between myself and the students or employees involved which might give us common knowledge of practice to which we could both refer in the interviews. So I was not studying individuals – I was studying their participation in cooperation with them based on what we had experienced together. Naturally, this was supplemented by my knowledge gained through practice in other contexts (research practice, studies of the literature etc.), which also helped to influence my curiosity and interest in the research process. Similarly, the students and employees involved also contributed various aspects in participating in this context or connected their participation in this context to their participation elsewhere.

Henning Olsen has studied Danish qualitative interview research by assessing 15 studies in comparison with quality criteria derived from Danish and international method literature. He points out that the general criteria for assessing qualitative interview studies are *transparent and motivated methodological procedures* and *thematic/*

7

methodological/analytical/scientific consistency (Olsen, 2001). The aim of this chapter of the book is to link the previous chapters together and summarise the connections and consistencies between them. Not all the choices made and rejected are dealt with here, but the most important connections are outlined.

The field of career guidance faces a basic dilemma relating to a binary problem involving the connection between the actions of the individual and the development of society – a basic problem that is often presented normatively. From a neo-governmental perspective, there is criticism of the fact that societal problems are individualised through career guidance practice, leaving the individual with responsibility for societal development and change without connecting this responsibility to structural possibilities and common issues. Among other things, the critical psychology perspective is derived from a challenge from the philosophy of science against the idea that knowledge is created by establishing a research distance from the objects being studied (Højholt, 2005). By contrast, critical psychology seeks to argue that knowledge is created and exists as a commitment to practice and is developed and found in shared actions and cooperation regarding dilemmas and problems in practice. From this point of departure the basic dilemma of career guidance is challenged by conceptualising the relationship between subject and society as a dialectic and exploring the importance of career guidance via a participant perspective. Most studies in the field of career guidance in Denmark can be characterised as commissioned research, so they do not tackle the basic dilemma and they rarely contain detailed descriptions of practice which could form the basis of theoretically informed analyses of practice. Consequently, my point of departure is descriptive in relation to communicating knowledge about the more collective forms of organisation that I experienced. In order to deal with the critique of individualisation, I study career guidance at places in which it is not organised individually. Before starting this research I did not know whether individualisation was connected to the organisation of practice, or whether the tendency would be the same in the more collective forms of organisation which I had chosen.

7

8 Career guidance in the company

8.1 Vignette – welcome to the company

Work starts at six in the morning. The building complex is big and old, a jumble of yellow plaster facades, red brick, plastic sheeting, tiles, asbestos cement and tall brick chimneys. Erik walks through the gate to the factory area, passing large pallets of blue plastic tanks containing the raw materials used in production and sacks containing various substances which are always hot even when there are sub-zero temperatures outside like today. He registers his arrival by waving to the foreman, who is sitting behind his window. He does not need to be told what to do today because he was pouring paint into cans yesterday and he simply has to continue doing that now. He smiles as he passes the office and pushes his way through the plastic strips that reduce the draught in the factory a little – though you can still drive through them with a fork-lift truck. He turns left through the door to the lunch room and is met by a mixed smell of coffee, sandwiches, hot chocolate and cigarette smoke. He recognises the smell – it hasn't changed for the past 28 years. Behind the lunch room there is a changing room, where he changes into red work trousers and a red jacket. It's cold today, and even though heat lamps are dotted around the factory and many of the products are hot when they are stirred (more than 50° C), there is still a draught from outside through all the many gaps in the old walls of the building. The state of the building and its location are part of the reason why the employees are now in their current situation. The management has announced that it is not possible to increase production here because

8

the factory is in the middle of a housing area. Erik walks into the factory and over to what is known as the pouring line, where he works next to Jim. The factory is a confused jungle of pipes, huge mixing machines, taps and conveyor belts. It seems to have been built using iron Lego bricks on various levels and platforms. Erik and Jim are standing underneath a platform on which Michael is working. The mixed smells of the raw materials merge to form a slightly sweet aroma which tries to live up to the sweet looks of the girls adorning the walls. The factory smells of paint, glue and varnish. Erik explains that the smell has improved a great deal over the years. When he started almost 30 years ago they also had to work with solvents, which smelt terrible. Your stomach felt awful for about a month until your body had grown used to it, he explains. Erik and Jim are pouring paint into 20-litre metal cans. First Erik has to open the tap, then he pushes the heavy can out onto a manual conveyor belt and through to Jim, who seals it with a lid and lifts it onto a pallet standing nearby. The pallet is picked up by a fork-lift truck and the process starts all over again. The factory is very noisy: fork-lift trucks driving around, metal cans landing on hard plastic conveyor rollers, machines applying lids and other machines mixing or pouring paint into cans. Michael is mixing paint on the platform above. He pours various products into huge pallet tanks, empties the tanks into large mixing vats, adds the right dyes and starts the mixing process. The mixing process generates a good deal of heat, causing many of the products to emit the characteristically sweet smells of glue and varnish. The foreman walks past occasionally shouting, "Is 43:40 ready yet? When you've done that, we're going to need 32:10". Some mixing processes take several hours, and while this happens Michael starts mixing other products in other tanks. He is always busy picking up and mixing various products. Once a product is ready, it has to be approved by quality control. Michael draws off a number of samples in small plastic flasks and takes them to the laboratory. After about half an hour he is told to mix more or add more, or that the product is ready for pouring into the finished cans. The others say that Michael is good at getting the products approved, but sometimes this is a slow process and he has to test the products as he goes along – adding a little at a time, mixing and taking samples. Sometimes the laboratory tells him what to add, and

8

sometimes he uses his own experience of the products and chooses the mixture that he thinks will give the right result. Very occasionally they simply cannot get the mixture right whatever they do. The paint forms lumps that prevent it from being filtered, or they can't get the right colour or consistency. Sometimes a whole batch of 10,000 litres has to be discarded. Michael is very anxious to avoid any wastage, and tries to use reject products in other production processes. Once a product has been approved, he tells Erik and Jim to pour it into cans. They take turns having their breaks so the production process is not interrupted. They each get more breaks if they can manage this, they say. During their breaks they sit in the lunch room drinking coffee or hot chocolate, smoking, chatting, and "teasing each other". They eat their sandwiches and read the newspaper. Erik has been working here for 28 years. "We're part of the furniture," he says.

8.2 Losing your job

In this section I try to characterise the situation in which the employees found themselves. What were their perspectives with regard to losing their jobs? While I was there their contracts were extended. What did this mean for the way in which they tackled their situation? What did they think about the future? The situation and the way the employees viewed it were part of the context in which career guidance functioned at the company. I wanted to carry out a decentred analysis of career guidance, so my analysis starts broadly by characterising the situation facing the employees.

In August 2004 the employees were informed that the company's production of paint and varnish in Denmark was to be discontinued as of 31 December 2005. A new factory in Sweden was taking over the production activities in Denmark. But the factory in Sweden burned down, so 12 of the Danish employees had their contracts extended until the autumn of 2006. The employees said that they had a good severance package – so good that they did not want to leave the factory until the final day of their employment. The foreman said that this severance package of course helped to ensure that the company could continue its production, but he was less certain about whether it was a good deal for the employees: "They've got a really good deal here so why should they bother to try and find another job?" Frans explained why there was no point in looking for new jobs if they were committed to remaining at the company until the final day: "We won't be looking for management positions, after all. We're shop-floor workers and we have to be ready to start a new job immediately – not in four months' time." In the interviews I asked them to explain their thoughts when they were told that the factory was closing down and they realised that they would be losing their jobs.

JAN: We were told we were shutting down, and even though we'd seen it coming it was obviously a pretty emotional day. We had to say goodbye to 27 years of our lives. We were all pretty shocked actually. But luckily we were able to keep our spirits up somehow. People started talking about training courses and severance packages and negotiations – just what you'd expect.

For Jan the announcement of the closure produced an emotional reaction. Even though many of the employees had expected the factory to be closed, it was still a shock when the announcement was finally made. Jan was not only losing a job – he was saying goodbye to 27 years of his life. But new routines were quickly established. He emphasised that they were able to keep their spirits up, and a number of employees told me that these good spirits were an important part of their workplace. Their new everyday situation involved planning training courses for everyone, severance packages and all the negotiations required when people lose their jobs.

The thought of potential unemployment made Jan think about any special skills that he might have. In the next quotation he explains how he started wondering about whether he would be able to sell himself. He had never had to write an application before.

JAN: I was never much good at selling myself. I can't deny it.
And I've never had to write an application before in my life.

So losing his job meant that Jan now faced a situation in which he needed to learn new things – for instance how to write an application or a CV. Poul had similar thoughts:

114

RIE: What kind of things do you think you'll need help with?
POUL: Writing a CV for instance – 90% of us or even 100% of us.
    We didn't have a clue. When Ulla handed out a CV it turned
    out to be pretty simple, but I'd never tried it before.

Jim had applied for jobs before. He is a skilled labourer and seemed
to approach the situation with a certain amount of confidence. He
knew what to do. He was unlike the other employees because he knew
how to apply for jobs and was not afraid of the writing task involved.
Like most of the others he started by saying that being fired did not
matter much.

JIM: I haven't thought much about the factory closing down.
    I'm not bothered. I'll find something else. I haven't got any big
    financial commitments. No small kids, and our house isn't a
    huge financial burden. Our finances are reasonable and pretty
    stable, know what I mean? I don't think we'd be in a crisis
    if I was unemployed. I was unemployed for a year and a half
    many years ago. It was OK – of course we felt it a bit, but it
    wasn't anything major.

The situation is connected to several aspects of each individual's
personal life conduct, and this quotation reveals that being fired also
generates thoughts about their future financial situation. As far as Jim
was concerned these thoughts did not cause any alarm and despond-
ency. He did not feel dependent on having a new job as soon as he lost
this one. Do Jim's thoughts conflict with the goal of career guidance in
terms of meeting society's needs for a labour force in the future? His
thoughts certainly constitute a challenge to the consensus idea that the
needs of the individual and society are always in accordance with each
other.

8

    Jim went on to explain that the situation had led him to reconsid-
er his working life. He had actually always wanted to do some further
training (as an architect, for instance). He wanted to do something
different. He also told me that he did not really regard this as realistic because he was 55 years old. He was also toying with the idea of
starting his own company to produce furniture and deal in second-
hand furniture. The shared situation resulted in a variety of options

for action for each individual – options which were connected both to their shared situation (losing their jobs) and to the ways in which each individual conducted his life and the wishes generated by this (some of them similar, and others different). For instance, Poul wanted to change his working life too.

POUL: I thought I wanted to stop doing such hard physical work, but it's hard to find anything different. When we were told that we were going to be fired I thought "What are you going to do?" Of course I've been looking in the newspapers and trade journals and there have been plenty of jobs. And Ulla has been a fantastic help and support. I didn't know what I was going to do until I got a chance at a removal company called 3x34.

For Poul the situation generated thoughts about the kind of job he would like in the future ("I wanted to stop doing such hard physical work"). Losing his job made him think about the future course of his life, and new opportunities became apparent. These new opportunities should also be seen in the light of the wish for everyday life to follow new routines in the future. For others the prospect of new routines led to anxiety about their new everyday lives in very concrete terms (some of them were worried about how they would actually arrange daily transport to a new workplace, for instance).

FRANS: How am I going to get a new job where I won't have to write stuff on a computer and have a driving licence? Some people don't have a driving licence you know, and I'm not going to bloody well get one. I live in the city and use public transport. Where the hell am I going to find a job close to home? With a reasonable salary and without loads of stupid demands?

Factories employing unskilled labour are gradually moving away from the centres of our cities and out into the peripheries of our conurbations. This makes new demands in terms of the time spent on getting to work and having a driving licence, for instance. For Frans the closure of the factory meant that his everyday life would change – he would have to spend longer getting to a new place of work. The situation created uncertainty about the future and the physical location of a new job. What kind of transport would he need? Would a new job demand qualifications which he and a number of the others did not have (knowing how to use a computer, for instance)? But the situation also extended beyond the concrete into a more general issue: how can you best protect your own interests when you lose your job?

FRANS: I think that most of us are pretty relaxed about looking for a new job. You don't have to find one overnight. It's all been so gradual, so people have had a reasonable chance to find something new … if that's what they want, know what I mean? Some of us have agreed to an extension of our contracts. It wasn't our fault that one of their factories burned down in Sweden. So we'll help them here for nine months, won't we?

As described by the foreman, the company had offered to extend the severance package. This package meant that they were paid an extremely good wage during their final months – more than they would be able to earn in a new job. This meant that it was a good idea for them to stay on for these final months – but it also meant that many of them did not apply for new jobs during this period because they were not immediately available to take any new employment. As described by Frans above, unskilled workers are expected to start new jobs more or less immediately. So this was a two-sided situation. It was in the company's interest to know which employees they still had for which months, so they offered terms that were so favourable that the employees would find it financially attractive to stay on. But the system also prevented the employees from pursuing other courses of action: applying for jobs during the period in question. The career guidance practitioner had to operate in this dual situation, in which conflicting interests were at stake. The practitioner had made an agreement with the company, so she had to act in accordance with the company's wish to keep its employees for a while. But her professional ethics required her to focus on the interests of the individual, and the goal of her employer was that she should seek to provide supplementary training for people with little or no further education behind them. The idea of offering and recommending supplementary training courses seems like a compromise catering for the inter-

8

ests of most people during the severance period. I shall return to this point below.

Most of the employees thought that the company had treated them well. The company had paid for training courses, arranged career guidance with Ulla, and provided a generous severance package. Everyone had apparently had their interests catered for. But this did not apply to everyone, and Erik was by no means satisfied with the idea of losing his job. He distinguished between the local management at the factory and the international management that had taken the decision to close down production in Denmark. He was angry about this decision – an anger which he expressed in no uncertain terms:

ERIK: First of all I think that the local management have been weak when it comes to comparing the factories with each other. They haven't done anything at all to tell the international management that we didn't deserve to be closed down. They should have explained that compared with how many people work here we produce a lot at a reasonable price. Looking back on it all now it's clear that the worst factory in the whole world is the factory over there in Sweden. It might be big, but what's the use of being big when you sit around twiddling your thumbs all day long?

Erik did not believe that the decision to close down production in Denmark was rational. He did not feel that the local management had protected the interests of the employees. I asked whether the closure of the Danish factory was due to the fact that it was difficult to expand because of the proximity of an area of housing.

ERIK: Bloody hell that's a load of crap. They could try asking themselves "What are we trying to achieve at this company?" That's the main thing. They said they could produce acid-hardening varnish in Sweden, but that factory burned down anyway even though they were supposed to able to cope with the fumes. So instead of having water-based standing around over there they could produce acid-hardening over there ... and what they did was keep the production of something we could do much better than they could in Sweden.

118

If you ask me they've been a bunch of spineless lazybones …
all of them.

In Erik's experience the Danish factory was good at producing paint – better quality, quicker and cheaper. This experience made it difficult for him to accept that the decision to close down the Danish factory had been made on a rational basis. He talked about the responsibility of the management; felt that if they had explained how good their employees were, other people (the international management) would have had the opportunity of acting differently. Erik could not accept the idea that he was bad at doing his job. He did not think that people had been fired on an individual basis, and he did not accept the structural reasons for closing down the factory with which he had been presented. Erik's thoughts can be seen as an example of the fact that structural reasons are also given personal meanings; from Erik's perspective the meanings with which he had been presented could be given meanings in different ways resulting in different priorities. From his perspective, decisions that were presented as "objective" and rational (the impossibility of expanding the factory owing to its location) could just as easily have resulted in priorities regarding which products should be produced where. The situation was ambiguous and full of conflict.

8

8.2.1 Analytical perspectives – losing your job

Initially, losing your job is a shock. Everyday life is suspended for a short while on the day when you are fired, after which normality returns relatively quickly. The situation at the company was characterised by a wide variety of differences. Losing your job was given different meanings in relation to the structural conditions which were provided as the reason for closing down the factory. Most of the employees accepted that this was inevitable. But Erik challenged this acceptance, which shows that what might appear to be "objective" condition structures must also be linked to different perspectives and interests. In this intersection of interests the employees faced a transition which the career guidance practitioner was required to address. All the employees were in a transitional situation, but their perspectives differed widely. For some of them this was a chance to think concretely about how to organise transport so they could get to a future workplace. For others their financial future determined whether they needed to find a job quickly or whether they could relax and consider their options (finding a new type of job or retraining, for instance).

In her PhD dissertation on apoplexy patients, Tove Borg compares a variety of situations in human life such as illness, accidents, divorce, job losses etc. – all of which are characterised by the fact that they occur suddenly and unexpectedly with consequences that may have a profound effect on everyday life and require its considerable reorganisation (Borg, 2002). The loss of your current working life leads to thoughts about how to establish a new everyday life and new routines. Most people prefer a working life that creates a certain amount of stability. Some people are anxious about recovering their everyday lives, while others focus on the opportunity to try something new. As pointed out by Holzkamp, breaks in cyclicity generate new resigned questions: why do I have to get up every single morning – and for what – when life is now no more than "a burden" to me (Holzkamp, 1998, p. 30)? Breaks in cyclicity create transitions to a new cyclicity which has to be arranged by the individual concerned based on interaction between various areas of life. People live their lives differently, which is why the thoughts arising in such situations vary so much. Some of the employees at the company were worried about transport time, others about their wages, and others about how to tread new paths in their working lives. However, what they all shared was that a break in cyclicity had created a transition, and this transition was associated with thoughts and ideas that could also occur in career guidance contexts (among others). Transitions create special conditions for career guidance because rearrangement is required in transitions and the demand for rearrangement is connected to other aspects of the personal conduct of everyday life.

8.3 **Career guidance in the company**

This section contains a number of examples taken from my interviews revealing the ways in which the employees perceived career guidance in the company. I asked them about their needs as far as career guidance was concerned and about the career guidance they had received. My aim was still to explorehow career guidance interacted with the way the employees conducted their everyday lives at the company.

When I asked the employees whether they had received career guidance from Ulla, most of them said "no". However, during the interviews it became apparent that the vast majority had spoken to her. So why did they answer "no"? In most cases my question was "Have you had any sessions with Ulla?" or "have you received career guidance from Ulla?". The way my question was phrased may have signalled an understanding of career guidance as being a particular form of intervention – a discussion between Ulla and the employees; but my observations made it clear that career guidance at the company was not organised in the form of individual sessions. This may be why most of the interviewees said they had not received any career guidance or had any discussions with Ulla, when they had talked to her, asked her questions and been given help in applying for jobs and drawing up a CV.

RIE: Well … have you ever received any career guidance …
about your choice of training or job?
JIM: No, never. I haven't … Well only with my Mum. She was
absolutely certain that I ought to become a dentist.

When asked about his experience of career guidance, Jim refers to conversations with his mother. This indicates that the concept of career guidance is interpreted very broadly, and that Jim regards his conversations with his mother as career guidance. As far as Jim is concerned, career guidance does not seem to be limited to the activities taking place with a career guidance practitioner. Instead, it seems to consist of the kind of issues that people talk about in all possible relations throughout their lives. Later in the same interview Jim explained his perception of career guidance in greater detail:

8

JIM: I feel that Ulla has been very active and has given us good, professional career guidance. I haven't seen much of her myself, so it's a bit hard for me to say much. But I know she's been very active with lots of the others – they've been doing CVs together and all that kind of thing.

RIE: Yes. Why haven't you talked much to her?

JIM: Well, I *have* spoken to Ulla a bit – I just haven't had any great need. Because all that about producing a CV. I've done it loads of times before and I've got plenty of them at home which I've used in the past. I've still got copies of them. So that wasn't a problem for me.

RIE: You said that you had spoken to her. So what did you talk about?

JIM: Actually I can hardly remember. We talked about this and that. About my views on things and my skills.

Jim started by denying that he had ever received any form of career guidance, and he did not think he had received career guidance from Ulla. And yet he reports that they had talked about his "views on things" and his skills. He explained that he had not taken part in any discussions because he did not need to do so, having already produced a good number of CVs. His perception of career guidance was linked to the difficulty of producing a CV. The CV was a central document in understanding the nature of career guidance at the company. One of the company's demands on Ulla was that her career guidance should result in all the employees producing a CV. As part of this Ulla used a tool for the production of CVs which is available on Jobnet.[16] Producing a CV can be regarded as a demand that underlines the institutional links of career guidance. Other people have decided what is required when applying for jobs, and the aim of career guidance practice is to help people to produce a CV to meet these requirements. Jim's rejection of any help in producing a CV can be seen as a rejection of the idea that he needed any help at all: "I just haven't had any great need," as he put it.

Ulla, on the other hand, regards the role of the CV as multi-faceted. For one thing, the need to produce a CV opens a pathway leading to guidance interventions and discussions with the employees. These

8

interventions lead to the joint identification of the skills of the employees, and together they can then try to link the skills of the employees to a future job situation. For Jim the connection between career guidance and the need for help in drawing up a CV indicates that he does not believe that career guidance can have any other points of focus than this. I shall return to this point later. The CV appears to create a link between current skills and future job opportunities, so it seems as if an adaptation perspective is at play here. It is more about finding a match between the current skills of people with little further education behind them and possible jobs than the development of skills to cope with a different type of working life. Jim's perception that career guidance involved interviews about CVs, or my presentation of career guidance as a particular form of intervention, meant that he did not regard his talk with Ulla as career guidance. On the other hand, Jim was extremely precise in his statements about what he wanted career guidance to be and to contain. With regard to his ideas about what good career guidance is he had the following to say:

JIM: The only person who could give me guidance is the sort of person that could listen to my wishes and say, "Look – there are some opportunities here!" I think I've checked out all my options, but a career guidance practitioner might be able to recommend a training course – a supplement to the training I've already been through, for instance. Not a long course, but it would give you a job. That would be a useful thing to do in my view.

Jim points out that in his view, good career guidance is all about opportunities. He describes himself and explains his wishes for a future working life. He thinks the job of a career guidance practitioner is to indicate any opportunities that he might have. He underlines that training courses need to be short, and that they should enable him to apply for a new type of job to suit his wishes. His expectations are that career guidance should help to identify new possibilities by finding connections between his wishes and the possibilities that society provides in the education system. This is actually a classic definition of career guidance (see Løve, 2005; and Plant, 1996, for instance). Ulla does actually offer this form of career guidance, but Jim

8

does not seem to realise this because he connects her career guidance with producing a CV. But Jim's rejection of career guidance can also be interpreted in the light of the fact that career guidance based on producing a CV reflects a perspective of adaptation in which Jim's skills can be matched with possible jobs. Jim sees things differently. He is more focused on developing his skills through supplementary training.

Ulla also attributes another meaning to the production of CVs: she explains that this is one of the first things people have to produce when applying for unemployment benefit. She believes that it is a good idea to work on the production of a CV before you lose your job, because then you can say that you already have a CV when you sign on to receive benefit. This may seem slightly contradictory, because the Danish unemployment schemes and job centres are also obliged to provide career guidance. If the people they deal with have already produced a CV, they will not be able to use the CV as a point of departure for their interventions with the individuals concerned. Ulla's motives can be connected to the basic dilemma of career guidance because she does not only protect the interests of society by making sure that people produce a CV – she also protects the interests of the individual because if they already have a CV they will have more influence on the kind of career guidance activities they are expected to participate in when they lose their jobs.

The CV is important in a variety of ways with regard to the possibilities for participating in career guidance. Some employees look for and appreciate concrete help in describing their skills and entering them in a CV, while others do not feel that they need any help to produce a CV. Some of the people from the latter group even feel that the work involved in producing a CV actually has a detrimental effect on their chance of getting a new job.

ERIK: I think it's just about as rotten as you can get. It shouldn't be necessary for people to produce a whole data-bank just to get a job. I've been on the labour market for so many years that if I lose my job some kind of attempt should be made to find me another job in the same line of business.

8

Not all that "Now let's sit down and make your CV and we'll put it out on a homepage and hope that someone can be bothered to have a look at it". Nobody's going to really consider taking on a 62-year-old man.

Erik demonstrates great reluctance to use the tool that Ulla uses in her career guidance: producing a CV. His reluctance seems to be linked to the fact that when he describes himself on paper his age will immediately become obvious to any readers – and he views this as a disadvantage when applying for jobs. When I looked at him and watched him working, I thought he looked like a 45-year-old and worked like a 25-year-old. Erik knew that he would have to meet potential employers and show them what he could do to persuade them to take him on. So from his perspective producing a written CV was a disadvantage. He would not be the one contacting potential employers – instead, they would be looking at his CV anonymously, and then deciding whether to contact him or not. I found that the theme of contact (or no contact) with employers via a CV was a matter of considerable importance for the group of employees who had already put their CVs out on the net and made them available to future employers.

ERIK: Let's take Hans for instance. He's 40, right? I don't think anyone's been in to have a look at his CV. So he might start thinking, "What's wrong with me? Is my CV too long? Or … what have I done wrong?" I think it's all wrong.

Erik believes that if his colleagues are not approached on the basis of their CVs, they might start wondering what was wrong with them. Were their CVs too long, or what had they done wrong? The question is whether the organisation of career guidance focusing on producing a CV pulls career guidance in an individualising direction, as was pointed out in the discussion of career guidance as a governing technology. Instead of joining forces in a shared situation of losing their jobs and explaining this by referring to a lack of possibilities in relation to structural conditions, it seems as if the work involved in producing a CV individualises the issue by focusing on the indi-

8

vidual and their competences or lack of competences. Erik's discontent can be understood as an expression of his frustration regarding the way in which the collective dismissal, which was not explained with reference to the lack of competences in individual employees, was now causing frustration for individuals even so. Erik thought that this was wrong, and his view of what was going on can best be characterised as a shift of responsibility from the company to the individual. Here are his views on a different way of allocating the responsibility for finding new jobs for the employees:

ERIK: The company ought to wake up and contact other companies. Not just some wishy-washy idea of doing some kind of training course. The company should stand up and say "We'll find a bloody job for you. We'll contact the people we know (banging on the table). We'll simply call them up. That's what they should do. Because there's loads of companies who still produce paint and we've got people with 15, 20 or even 30 years' experience here and someone must be able to use them. That's what they ought to do straightaway. That's the right thing to do – also for the sake of the company. Showing a bit of initiative. They give you DKK 100,000 but it's not worth damn all in the end because you can easily spend that in a few years.

ERIK: I don't think applications should be necessary. The company ought to concentrate on saying "OK, we've got someone here called Ole and we'll find a job for him by calling the companies we know who've got loads of fork-lift truck drivers. They just pick up the phone and call them, and as soon as they say, "Right. We need someone in January or February," the company should say they'll send Ole out to them for a chat. And off he goes and they can move on to the next man. That's what the company ought to do.

Erik mentions a different, more concrete way of helping the employees who have not yet found a new job. He believes that the company should contact other companies to find jobs for the employees it has fired. In this way Erik challenges the individualisation of responsibility in relation to unemployment. He places this responsibility on the company. The company made these people redundant, so the company should take the action required to remedy the situation. The responsibility Erik feels that the company should accept does not involve organising career guidance for each individual or helping people to produce an electronic CV. He thinks the company should actually help the employees to find new jobs which they can start the day after they lose their current jobs. Other employees at the company had similar views, and concrete proposals were made that the company should insert an advertisement in the local paper with photos of the employees and a brief description of each individual. This is an idea that clearly reverses the situation: the employees should not be responsible for applying for new jobs – this is a responsibility that the company should assume. If the company took this kind of action, the employees would be approached by companies interested in employing them instead of having to look for employment themselves.

The idea of inserting such an advertisement is both similar to and different from the situation that arises when employees publish their CVs on the Jobnet database. The similarities are (1) each individual is described, with potential employers considering each individual; and (2) the potential employers are anonymous, and they are the ones responsible for contacting the applicants. The differences are (1) the company is responsible for sending the message and looking for new employment for its redundant employees; and (2) the fact that the company inserts the advertisement shows that the individuals involved are not responsible for putting themselves in this situation – this is a shared situation caused by an event over which they had no influence. Seen in this light, a more shared situation arises if the company is made responsible for finding new jobs.

One of the characteristic features of career guidance at the company is that the term "career guidance" is not used – although the career guidance practitioner Ulla is often mentioned. She is mentioned in connection with what I would characterise as typical career guidance activities. My point is that when we consider career guidance from a participant perspective, it varies a good deal depending on the way in which each individual participates. Thoughts and discussions about the future are part of everyday life and involve many different people in different places and at different times. In this light, Ulla's presence and provision of career guidance must be regarded as being in interaction with all kinds of other relations which the employees deem to be of importance with regard to their future. The employees do not refer to their relation with Ulla as "career guidance". Instead, they say that "she's just here", and that she is available to answer their questions.

RIE: What do you mean when you say that Ulla is "just here"?
  I mean the fact that she turns up even though nobody actually has an appointment with her?
POUL: It's good because people rush to meet her every time.
  And that's good to see.
RIE: But why don't people make appointments with her?
  As far as I can see there's lots going on when she's standing in there putting up job adverts and people come in and …
POUL: That's because the factory is closing down very soon and people have hundreds of questions to ask her. She might make an appointment with Jørgen for a specific time, but if she hasn't got the time he'll go in and start looking things up for himself; and if Flemming and Alan have just written their CVs or applied for a job they might have some questions too. So I think it's good that she comes. Lots of people find out what to do themselves of course and have already applied
  for jobs.

Studying career guidance from a decentred perspective makes it possible to see that the employees consider their situation at various times – and not only when career guidance has been planned or appointments for sessions have been made. Thoughts about the future are not limited to the career guidance situation. But the fact that Ulla is available even though nobody has specifically asked for a session gives the employees the opportunity to ask her questions about their situation on an ongoing basis. When I consider career guidance from a decentred perspective, it becomes apparent that availability and flexibility are important. As the quotations below reveal, Poul is a representative example of this fact:

8

POUL: I don't know whether it's laziness, but if Ulla had
an office somewhere else I don't think we'd bother to go in
and see her. I'm absolutely certain that hardly anyone would.
I think people would start looking for and applying for jobs
themselves, and if they hadn't found anything by the time
they stopped here well … I'd better speak for myself. I
wouldn't have applied for anything. So it's brilliant that
she comes to see us here. It's fantastic, and if there are any
other companies closing down they really ought to get hold
of someone like Ulla to give a bit of support in lots of ways.
I think it's been brilliant.

RIE: What kind of questions do you ask?

POUL: If you bring in a job advert – I've seen the other eejits
doing this! What are we supposed to do, what should we
write? She looks at your CV and sends it with your application
and … kind of makes sure that you actually get everything
sent off in the right way. Know what I mean? And plenty
of the lads have never even touched a computer before now.
Ulla can make a phone call and find out what a job involves
and pull a few strings. Know what I mean? Because she can
use her experience to tell you what they're really looking
for and what they're not really interested in, and she can
tell you if your application is set up all wrong.

Poul refers to a variety of aspects of Ulla's job. She puts up advertisements for situations vacant, helps people with their CVs and job
applications, answers their questions etc. Poul underlines the importance of her practical assistance in writing things on a computer,
printing them out, getting them sent off and making phone calls to
companies. When calls are made to potential employers, the employees want to know more about what these employers are looking
for because this is important with regard to what they should write
in their applications. Sometimes Ulla knows what they are looking
for – but if she does not know, she is often the one who calls them to
find out. A contrasting form of career guidance would involve starting with the idea of self-help. This would probably involve the career
guidance practitioner sending applicants home and telling them to

call some companies before their next session. Ulla acknowledges the practical problems at stake and solves them with concrete, practical help. Her strategy involves helping the employees to help themselves by offering to discuss their options or teaching them how to write a CV so they can apply for jobs themselves. Many of the company employees had never had to apply for jobs before in their lives. If such individuals are only taught how to read job advertisements and apply for jobs, it is not certain that they will ever actually apply for any. They would of course have learned a number of things that might prove useful next time, and perhaps helping people too much deprives them of the opportunity to learn anything themselves. These thoughts lead to the question of what issues career guidance is actually supposed to address. Should it focus on the personality of the individual, or on personal learning and competences? Or on the problems and conditions with which individuals are faced here and now? I shall return to these questions in section 10.5 below.

Ulla participates part in many different contexts at the company every day. She organises courses on how to apply for jobs and appointments with employees (individually or in groups), and she provides concrete, practical assistance by making telephone calls, searching the net etc. Her acknowledgement of the concrete, practical problems involved and her practical help to solve them shows that she does not only help employees to help themselves – she also joins forces with them to solve their practical problems. Her concrete participation means that responsibility for the situation is shared. Ulla does not take responsibility for their redundancy, but she does take concrete and practical responsibility for helping them as much as she can, as well as telling them what they should be doing. But she does not necessarily expect the employees to transfer this information into concrete, practical action by themselves.

However, career guidance is not regarded as a positive thing by everyone at the company, and not everyone wants to avail themselves of the opportunity to get involved. Erik does not want to participate, and does not even think the employees should have been offered career guidance. He believes that it was the company's responsibility to find them jobs; He refuses to assume responsibility for himself. He opposes the idea that responsibility for finding a new job should rest with the individual, with career guidance providing the help you need to find a new job. Attitudes such as those expressed by Erik and Frans below may result in the rejection of career guidance. From their perspective, Erik and Frans had good reason to refrain from participation – reasons that can be interpreted as being linked to the social function and various interests of career guidance, and to the rejection of individualisation. In the quotation below Frans expresses frustration about his experiences at the job centre. This came at the end of an interview in the lunch room, where a number of men were having lunch. The interview developed into a group interview because the others joined in and added their views, asking what my job was all about. I answered:

RIE: So I'm here to follow what Ulla does and to talk to you about what you think should happen when a company closes down.

FRANS: That's easy to answer instead of all that career guidance. Just give us a job! We don't need career guidance, we need a job. (Raises his voice to drown out others.) You can give us all the career guidance you like ... but that's the best guidance I can give (interrupted by another man).

CARL: The problem has got much worse because other people are going to decide how we ought to look for new jobs. (Voices in the background).

The people deciding how they should look for new jobs worked at the job centre, I was told. I asked whether they could just avoid the job centre altogether. They pointed at the job advertisements on the wall: in some of these advertisements no company names or telephone numbers were mentioned. Their names and numbers were only available from the job centre. Some of them had tried calling the job centre, but had been told that there were already 30 men for that job, so they had asked for information about the employer in question so that they could send an application for jobs that had not necessarily been advertised. But they were not given this information. They pointed out that the job centre was like a middleman they had to get past in order to apply for jobs. The fact that other people had an influence on the way in which Frans and the others applied for jobs

8

runs counter to their self-understanding and life practice. They were used to taking matters into their own hands and approaching companies which might be interested in employing them. But now there was a middleman to assess their qualifications and competences before they could contact a company in person. They felt deprived of any control with their own situation. They were asked to surrender their autonomy when applying for jobs. They could only contact potential employers by publishing their CVs on the internet and waiting for these employers to contact them.

On the current labour market the job centres are not the only bodies thst function as middlemen. Agencies organising temporary employment do not publish information about their clients either. Anyone applying for work at such agencies has to convince a middleman of their competences before convincing a potential employer as well. An electronic application for completion on the company's homepage may also function as a middleman. Individuals do not always have direct access to the workplace in question or potential employers: the path to employment leads through an electronic application on company homepages. In the past there was a different form of contact between employers and their employees. One employee explained this as follows: "You had an uncle who took you along to the factory and said you were his nephew and asked if the company had a job for you". In this light, career guidance at the job centre can be seen as depriving you of all control over your own decisions about job applications. The way in which you apply for jobs, and your applications, are subject to the approval of other people before you are allowed personal access to potential employers.

8.3.1 Analytical perspectives – career guidance in the company

If career guidance is perceived solely in the form of a session with a practitioner and an employee, it would be true to say that many people do not feel that they have participated in career guidance. This perception seems to restrict people's potential for participation because the employees say that they do not need career guidance, or that they find it hard to plan when questions might arise. The employees can be said to do participate in Ulla's activities in the company if these activities are viewed in a broad perspective (finding job advertisements, putting them up, answering questions about how to apply, helping people to write and print their CVs and applications). This way of organising Ulla's work in interaction with everyday life in the company makes it possible for the employees to ask her questions in the lunch room when they are there for other reasons. There is also an opportunity for participation that resembles a listening position – the option of listening to the questions that other employees are asking and to the answers that they are given. This provides possibilities for participation that are not present when career guidance is organised in the form of individual sessions. The borderline between career guidance and everyday practice, between professionalised interventions and ordinary conversations between individuals, seems vague; and from a participant perspective the delimitation of career guidance does not seem important. But there are also perceptions of career guidance at play that seem to preclude the opportunity for participation. These are related to the idea that it is the company's responsibility to find new jobs for the employees it is making redundant, and to the fact that career guidance is perceived as the removal of the power to exercise control over your own affairs by approaching potential employers directly. The fact that the employees appreciated the concrete, practical help they were given may make it possible for career guidance to resist any individualising effect because it becomes possible to regard the responsibility as being divided between all the participants in career guidance (both the practitioner and the participant). Concrete, practical participation can also be seen as the abandonment of any idea that career guidance should help people to help themselves, because the concrete needs of the participants are met and made general via common actions.

The possibilities for participation are linked how individual employees perceive their situation, the responsibility for this situation and their options for taking action in relation to it, as well as being linked to the concrete way in which career guidance is organised and the way in which other people participate. For instance, a listening position is only possible if other participants ask the questions.

A decentred perspective on career guidance reveals particular problems and dilemmas in relation to career guidance in interaction with everyday life practice, with career guidance not being regarded as purely positive. At the same time we also gain insight into how career guidance can indicate new possibilities for the employees, the way in which (particularly by providing concrete, practical help to handle problems) it seems to deal with the conditions experienced by the employees.

In the next section we shall take a closer look at the concrete interaction between career guidance and everyday life at the company by studying the way in which everyday practice at the company changes career guidance practice. These changes lead to particular options for participation.

8.4 Career guidance corners

In this section I describe a concrete change of practice: from a career guidance corner in one building to a "career guidance wall" in another building. Jean Lave criticises research into everyday life by pointing out that the relationship between individuals taking action and the socially material world in which they act is often overlooked: "Theories of situated everyday practice insist that persons acting and the social world of activity cannot be separated. This creates a dilemma: Research on everyday practice typically focuses on the activities of persons acting, although there is agreement that such phenomena cannot be analyzed in isolation from the socially material world of that activity" (Lave, 1993, p. 5).

A good deal has happened in this field since 1993. For instance, in their book *Doing Things with Things* Dreier and Costall (alongside the other contributors) seek to shed light on the relationship between the material and the social. In order to show changes in and of practice, I pursue this analytical path in my empirical material. Lave discusses two different perceptions of context in the fields of activity theory and phenomenology: "The major difficulties of phenomenological and activity theory in the eye of the other will be plain: Those who start with the view that social activity is its own context dispute claims that objective social structures exist other than in their social-interactional construction in situ. Activity theorists argue, on the other hand, that concrete correctedness and meaning of activity cannot be accounted for by analysis of the immediate situation" (Lave, 1993, p. 20). Engeström adds further detail to the problem of the phenomenological understanding of context: "This makes context look like something that can be created at will by two or more persons in the interaction, as if independently of the deep-seated material practices and socioeconomic structures of the given culture (Engeström, 1993, p. 66). Bearing in mind on Engeström's point, context must be analysed correctly. This can be done by describing the concrete, physical location in question and considering its significance.

Dreier has problematised the concept of context in relation to psychotherapeutic practice, indicating that psychoanalytical practice must be understood as being contextualised and tied to the daily conduct of everyday life and inter-contextual participation of the participants concerned. He says that the subjects can therefore only be studied in an adequate manner in relation to the particular context of action in which they are placed and in which their actions take place (Dreier, 1993, p. 25). He follows this point up with criticism by saying that despite this, *psychotherapy* is often practised and presented as if it took place in a vacuum or in a strange, *privileged idealised space* with no connection to an objective social world. It is perceived as if it could occur anywhere and nowhere. The dominant perceptions of therapy are *decontextualised*. They are based on the implicit assumption that the concrete context is not important, that it has no influence on what takes place there (Dreier, 1993, p. 25, emphasis in the original). This shows that context can be perceived as something that is created by people in social interaction, which leads to the assumption that career guidance can take place in the same way anywhere and at any time. Places, however, are more physical. They have a concrete geographical location, concrete buildings, furniture and a specific use.

In the previous section Poul was quoted saying that he did not think he would participate in career guidance if it took place in an office somewhere else (at a job centre, for instance). This is a familiar phenomenon to which a variety of solutions have been proposed over the years: establishing career guidance corners in companies, for instance. Career guidance corners are now a familiar concept in Denmark, as shown in the description below taken from the homepage of a Danish adult education college called Herning VUC. The text

8

advertises the career guidance corners that the college can set up in companies:

> Our career guidance corners are a special offer to companies and their employees, providing educational and vocational guidance. Career guidance corners consist of an information stand with folders and posters providing information about opportunities for supplementary training, salary subsidies for companies etc. These folders can be supplemented by a computer with career guidance tools and the presence of a career guidance practitioner for an agreed period (in the lunch break a couple of times a week, for instance).[17] (author's translation)

This description of career guidance corners can be found in similar versions on the homepages of various trade unions, adult career guidance centres and institutions of supplementary education in Denmark. The actual concept of "career guidance corners" was introduced by the Danish women's trade union (KAD) in the 1990s to provide a special form of career guidance in the workplace. These corners were introduced because the union's members did not use the guidance services provided by the union, and they represented a new way of organising career guidance (Plant, 2002).

There are very few variations in the available descriptions of the way career guidance corners are designed and what they should contain. Their design and concept are relatively fixed. But as Costall and Dreier et al. point out in *Doing Things with Things*, there are many reasons why things should not be regarded as final and independent of human practice: "... the kind of understanding of things presented in this book – things not as fixed and independent of human beings, but as themselves transformed, even coming into being, within ongoing human practices, and which, in turn, transform those practices. We learn much more about both people *and* things by studying them as worldly, though not just as in the world, but as incorporated in *practices* in the world" (Holzkamp, 1996 in Costall & Dreier, 2006, p. 11). Career guidance corners contain special things, folders, posters, computers etc. These are part of the concept of a career guidance corner, and should be used in special ways. As Costall and Dreier point out, things come into being in practice in special places, and things help to transform practice, which in turn transforms things and places. In other words, what is involved here is a dialectical perception of the interaction between people and things. According to the geographer Edward Casey, this argument can be developed. He points out that concrete, physical places also transform practices: "... places gather things in their midst – where 'things' connote various animate and inanimate entities. Places also gather experiences and histories, even languages and thoughts" (Casey, 1996, p. 24).

The reason why the Danish women's trade union set up career guidance corners was that the wage agreements to which its members were subject (involving piecework) made it unlikely that they would spend time going to a career guidance office outside the company where they worked. It was a wish for supplementary training for its members that led the union to experiment with the way career guidance was organised (Plant, 2002).

In 2002 various alternative career guidance initiatives in Denmark were evaluated.[18] Career guidance corners were presented as an alternative form of organisation because the traditional form of career guidance involved face-to-face interviews with a career guidance practitioner in their office at an agreed time (Plant, 2007b). In this evaluation, Peter Plant pointed out that successful career guidance in the workplace required that it:

8

- Be close at hand: actually in the workplace instead of somewhere else, no matter how centrally located this "somewhere else" might be.
- Make career guidance personal: tailor-made training, individual adaptation, personal career guidance.
- Allow plenty of time: career guidance with enough time to think things through. (Plant, 2002).

Plant underlines the importance of an alternative form of organising career guidance: actually at the workplace in the sense of being *among the employees*. The evaluation did not focus on potential problems that might arise in relation to the organisation of career guidance among the receivers concerned. This gives the impression that moving career guidance from one place to another would not affect career guidance practice. However, this is not the case in this research: I will show that practice does not simply move from one context to another. Instead, practice changes when it is organised differently and is influenced by the ordinary everyday practice of the workplace in question and the normal use of various locations in the workplace. I will also show that although career guidance can change its location, this does not happen without career guidance and the problems it seeks to solve being influenced by the location to which it is transferred. Here is a collection of my observations of Ulla's work at the company, an interview with her and observations from the company in general.

"THEN WE OCCUPIED THE WALL"

Ulla arrived at the company and was shown a room in which the career guidance corner was to be set up. She was given a bookcase, a table, two chairs, a notice board and a computer. The bookcase was stocked with brochures about various supplementary training courses, and various job advertisements ("situations vacant") were posted on the notice board. The computer was on the table and there were two chairs: one for the career guidance practitioner, and one for the employee receiving career guidance. The career guidance corner was located on the ground floor in a building which was separate from the production hall and administration offices. The production manager and the staff responsible for salaries, logistics etc. had their offices in the same building. Production took place in the production hall about ten metres away from this building. The production hall also contained the foreman's office and lunch room, as well as showers and changing facilities for the production staff. The HR manager, advertising department, reception and company refectory were located in another building at a different address in the next block.

We join the interview at a point when Ulla is explaining that the trade union (3F) has visited the company to discuss supplementary training courses for the employees. VUS Kontakt, Ulla's employer have also been involved, and she explains expectations regarding the task that VUS Kontakt is going to perform. The interview is conducted in the office where the career guidance corner was initially set up. Ulla explains that the corner will be moved; in this quotation she mentions Tonny, the company foreman.

ULLA: The career guidance corner was placed in the corner
of this office and we were given a desk and chair. The staff
sat over there. I'd already been round and introduced myself. We had a meeting and a couple of employees came over
when Tonny sent them over. This was not the best idea,
so I started to find job adverts and hang them up on the wall
in here. People started coming in to have a look at them. So
Tonny and I agreed – or else it was Tonny who said , "You'd
be better off coming over here, wouldn't you?" So I moved
over there and started using the wall in the lunch room, and
started basing myself over there and got a desk and chair.
They stared at me at first … I was a stranger, after all. And
then … it suddenly became obvious that this was a situation
they weren't very keen on … They could see me on the premises, so they started thinking they were going to be fired any
minute now or the place was going to be closed down and
they knew that redundancies had already been mentioned.
So it was a sensitive situation.

RIE: I see. How did you cope with that situation?

ULLA: Well, at first I sort of tried to … I wouldn't say I tried
to be invisible, but I tried to sort of approach them without
forcing myself on them. We'd sort of occupied the wall in
the lunch room, so I could put up some job adverts so
we had something to talk about at least.

Ulla explains how she handled the challenges implicit in the way the
career guidance corner was organised: at first nobody came to see her
apart from the people that Tonny had sent over. She points out that
the career guidance corner plan did not turn out as expected. So instead of using the familiar concept of a career guidance corner, she
started using a career guidance wall. Why did this happen? And how
can it be analysed? At first my attention focused on the location of
the career guidance corner and on the fact that it was too far away
from the everyday lives of the production staff. But this does not fully explain the meaning of *location*. Why was it necessary to move?
How was the move accomplished? And what happens to career guidance practice when it is transferred to a new location?

Costall and Dreier repeat Estrid Sørensen's point about the design of practice as follows: "Thus, it is necessary in general, Sørensen argues, to study the continual interplay between design and practices, and how this interplay leads to orderings in and of practice ... Sørensen proposes that we should regard design as politics, in which a design is proposed, picked up, continued, and either changed or left unchanged" (Costall & Dreier, 2006).

In this understanding, the design of career guidance corners can never be more than a proposal for the ordering in and of practice: a proposal which is picked up in practice and negotiated there, and which then continues in an unchanged (or changed) state. The definition of career guidance corners and Plant's evaluation of them both indicate that they should be located as close to the employees as possible, so it is surprising that the career guidance corner at the company was not set up in the production premises or the adjacent lunch room from the outset. But the example demonstrates that things are not always possible at before such things can happen. Design and practice need to be negotiated and changed first. Initially Ulla was placed a long way away from the production premises and in the same building as the production manager and logistics office – a building which the employees never set foot in "unless there was some kind of trouble", as they put it. Gruenewald points out that self-understanding is also linked to location when he writes that "... selfhood and placehood are completely intertwined" (Gruenewald, 2003, p. 626). Seen in this light, the physical location of the career guidance corner had an impact on the way the employees perceived Ulla. She became "one of them". Later on, when Ulla moved into the lunch room and set up her career guidance wall, this position changed and Ulla became "one of us".

In Denmark career guidance is often organised in the form of private, personal dialogues between two people. This form of organisation is backed up by both legislation and methods, as shown in chapter 5, and may help to explain why career guidance in the company was initially organised in a room some distance from the production premises. This room made it possible to offer both individual and private career guidance – a private sphere which was impossible to establish in the lunch room because this room was also used by the employees to take their breaks at various times. The lunch room was the beating heart of the production premises, and not least a room in which the employees enjoyed having a laugh and teasing each other. So it was not regarded as suitable for use as a career guidance corner in which privacy and a quiet atmosphere were apparently required. However, Ulla discovered that she could not do her job because nobody came along to her career guidance corner when it was located in another building. This fact can be understood in relation to my previous point that the rejection of participation in career guidance can also be perceived as the rejection of individualisation. Ulla walked into the production premises with her file under her arm, and this change in the way career guidance was organised led to other changes: changes which also had an influence on the understanding of problems on which individualised career guidance is based.

In the quotation above in which Ulla describes the change, she uses the image "visible/invisible". She uses "invisible" to describe the way in which she functioned in the production premises. But the terms "visible/invisible" also reveal something about the interaction between career guidance and everyday practice at the company. When career guidance practice was located at some distance from the production premises, any employee deciding to look for career guidance became visible to all his workmates when he went to talk to Ulla, and his problemtherefore became visible as well. But when Ulla moved over into the production premises, she had to make herself invisible in order to talk to the employees. The physical movement required also signalled that each individual had to deal with their problem themselves in collaboration with a career guidance practitioner. But when Ulla moved into the production premises, she was the one who became visible because she was the one who could help them with the problem they were all facing: how to find a new job.

Moving practice from one location to another means exposing practice to new things and new (everyday) practices; moving from one location to another always means a change of practice. "A place … has its own 'operative intentionality' that elicits and responds to the corporeal intentionality of the perceiving subject. Thus place integrates with body as much as body with place" (Casey, 1996, p. 22).

When Ulla moved the career guidance corner from one location to another, she was also exposing the design of the corner to interaction with the new location and changing its original design. In the article "Politics of Things", Estrid Sørensen asks the following question: "Does a fixed end and standardised design result in a rigid practice, and does an open design bring along flexible practices?" (Sørensen, 2006).

Design is used by Estrid Sørensen to refer to the interaction between inscriptions and practice in the sense of intentions and practice. The intention of the career guidance corner seems clear, but its design in practice prevents this intention from being fulfilled. Ulla decided to change the design in order to get closer to the intention, with the design being a career guidance corner and the intention being the provision of career guidance for the employees who had been made redundant by the company. The physical movement influenced the career guidance practice: instead of consisting of individual, private dialogues it became a more shared and collective practice largely centred on a career guidance wall featuring job advertisements in the lunch room. The function of the lunch room as a place for taking collective breaks influenced the career guidance, which could no longer insist on the establishment of a private sphere in the new place.

The result was that career guidance became more collective, with several people listening in and asking questions at the same time. This meant that career guidance could be provided without interfering with the normal function of the lunch room, but not without changing the appearance of the new location, because the lunch room now had physical reminders in the form of job advertisements that the employees' employment at the company was temporary. There is a dialectic element at play here between the influence of the location on practice and the influence of practice on the location – influences that also have an impact on the way the employees perceived the contribution made by Ulla. It is possible to move practice and thereby also to change people's perception of the situation. As a consequence of the fact that career guidance practice in the company was influenced by the location in which it was embedded, career guidance took place in a different way. Ulla described what happened when she put up job advertisements in the lunch room:

RIE: I've noticed that something happens when you put
   up job adverts. What is it that happens?

ULLA: They all come running (laughs).

RIE: Yes (laughs). But not actually to look at the adverts?

ULLA: No … no. But the reason is the same. It's not a threatening situation.

RIE: And what can happen in an unthreatening situation?

ULLA: Well, for one thing they can have an informal chat with
   me even though it's about something formal. Because they're
   going to be out of work soon. It's an informal situation so
   they feel comfortable and unthreatened. If I go too far and
   say, "Have you sent off that application?" and push them a
   bit, they can pretend that I'm talking to someone else. This
   (situation) is not threatening. And then they've got each
   other – I think that's important too. I think they need to hear
   what the others have to say. And then sometimes I wonder
   whether they're actually in competition with each other for
   the same jobs. Although at the same time they say things like
   "What about that? Don't you fancy applying for that one?"

In this excerpt Ulla uses a different form of dualism to describe the
movement in practice: the movement between formal and informal
career guidance. Instead of accepting that some types of career guidance are described as formal and other types as informal, in the light
of Lave's idea that binary problems generate a particular type of issue
it is interesting to consider what it is that the career guidance practitioner uses the terms formal/informal to explain. Ulla describes the
informal situation as unthreatening, thereby identifying the employees as people who might be afraid. For Ulla the terms formal/infor-
mal provide an explanation of when the employees are willing to participate and when they are not. But this is also an explanation that
fails to allow for interaction between the design of career guidance
and the structural embeddedness of career guidance. Instead, this is
Ulla's way of maintaining that what she is providing is indeed career
guidance – what else should she call an everyday talk with the employees in the lunch room? No particular methodological instructions are being observed here. There is no particular set-up and the

8

dialogues do not take place in a particular isolated, confidential, concrete location. The use of the term "informal" can remedy this by including the interaction in question in career guidance. Formal career guidance is characterised by special instructions and takes place in particular locations on the initiative of one of the participants. Informal career guidance lacks these factors and occurs in interaction with everyday practice in a far more random manner. Ulla uses the dualism threatening/unthreatening to refer to what happens when an employee rejects her demands. She is expected to help the employees in particular ways: by suggesting supplementary training courses or helping with the production of a CV. But some employees do not wish to participate in this and do not want to be helped in this way. Career guidance practice as an institutional arrangement has clear ambitions on behalf of the participants; in order to handle these ambitions vis-à-vis other adults they can be positioned as individuals who are in need of help. But the movement of practice may also reflect the way in which the employees wish to participate. Career guidance on an individual basis did not seem to work because the employees showed no interest in attending. But career guidance to deal with a common problem in collaboration with a number of other employees seemed attractive. This is dealt with in sections 10.5 and 10.6 of the discussion.

8.4.1 Analytical perspectives – career guidance corners

The analysis has demonstrated that the physical location of career guidance has an influence on each individual's possibilities for participation. These include the opportunity to participate in individual sessions, to ask questions of general interest, or to listen to questions asked by other people and the answers they are given. It seems to be the case that organising career guidance in a new location means that it is associated less with private and personal dialogues and more with collective, common and shared issues, and that the employees can also help each other. The analysis has also shown that focusing on the context may not be sufficiently concrete when it comes to realising the importance of the physical location with regard to the design of career guidance practice. Analytical awareness of the importance of location with regard to practice seems to help to concretise and contextualise the analysis with a view to gaining insight into the links between career guidance design and the problems which career guidance as an institutional arrangement seeks to solve. Placing the career guidance corner in an office block far away from the production premises meant any employees attending career guidance became visible to the others, as well as individualising the common problem facing all the employees. But moving the corner to the lunch room enabled several employees to ask questions at the same time, and they might all benefit from hearing the answers to other people's questions. The problem seems to become more collective in such a place.

8.5 New possibilities for participating in education

The participation of employees in supplementary training courses was a theme that occupied the shop steward and the foreman, as well as occupying me during the course of my study. They told me that before the employees were fired there had been very little interest in such supplementary training courses, but that this had changed significantly when they received their notices of redundancy. The theme of supplementary training is closely connected to career guidance, and VUS Kontakt's aim in offering career guidance at companies is to develop the competences of the employees and provide them with supplementary training. In other words, VUS Kontakt subscribe to the view that career guidance is one way of motivating employees to participate in supplementary training courses. The aim of analysing the way in which the employees' interest at the company in supplementary training changed is to demonstrate that the reasons for taking part in training courses vary, and that the conditions applying to training both influence and are influenced by the community, in which significance is attached to these conditions in various ways.

In my analysis strategy I pointed out that the analysis of conditions, meanings and reasons makes it possible to focus on possibilities for participation. As pointed out by Morin (2007, p. 24), focusing on participation as an analytical concept opens up for a double focus on the participant and on the conditions of their participation.

8

145

Focusing on the way in which the employees' perception of participation in education changed in a new situation and when facing new conditions makes it possible to show how the meaning attributed by the employees to participation in training is founded both in the new possibilities offered by the situation and in the the employees' understanding of these possibilities.

The separation of conditions, meanings and reasons is an analytical approach designed to distinguish between the three for a brief moment. In concrete terms they are interconnected, which means that changes in one of the three cause changes elsewhere as well.

FOCUS ON CONDITIONS

The employees of the company are facing a situation in which their concrete terms of employment are being changed. These are the concrete conditions that are in focus at this level.

FOCUS ON MEANINGS

At the level of meanings, the focus is on how the changed conditions have personal meanings and on how these are expressed as reasons for new possibilities for participation in training.

FOCUS ON REASONS

At the level of reasons, the focus is on the reasons given by the employees for their choices with regard to participating (or not participating) in various training courses, and on how these reasons are connected to the personal conduct of their everyday lives, to their perception of the situation and to their participation in the working community at the company.

This section demonstrates that new possibilities for participation are not only linked to the actual availability of training courses, which were also available before the employees were fired. They are also determined by how the employees view the possibility of participation and the meaning they allocate to this opportunity. It is only when the meaning they allocate changes in various ways and for various reasons

8

146

that they avail themselves of the opportunity of attending supplementary training. When they are actually made redundant they are given a new reason for explaining their participation in training courses.

8.5.1 Concrete conditions for participating in education

The HR consultant, former shop steward and current shop steward reported that the employees had always been able to participate in training courses but that nobody had shown much interest in doing so. This changed when the employees were made redundant, with more people expressing a wish to take part. The HR consultant and shop steward both viewed training courses as a perk for the employees, and were surprised that there had been so little interest in them.

Most of the employees at the company wanted to stay there for the rest of their working lives, so they saw no reason to take any additional training courses. They had never imagined changing jobs before. The problem of the failure to participate in supplementary training is linked to the perspective from which the lack of participation is regarded. The HR consultant's perspective focused on securing a qualified workforce, while the shop steward saw training courses as a perk that also equipped individual employees to meet the challenges of the labour market of the future. So the problem of participation (or non-participation) in training courses is complex, involving far more than merely considering rational reasons for gaining qualifications in a process of lifelong learning. It has been argued that the option of competence assessment would motivate people with little further education behind them to take part in supplementary training (Holsbo, 2005). If the opportunity for participation was sufficient in itself to make people act, one could argue that there would be no need for career guidance. The need for career guidance can be seen in the light of how it is explained in relation to concrete individuals. In relation to people with little further education behind them, the need for career guidance is often related to the problem of a lack of motivation. In such cases the task addressed by career guidance is a motivational one.

Before being made redundant, the employees at the company were not very interested in taking part in supplementary training courses. In other words, the opportunity for supplementary training and the

8

public discourse regarding lifelong learning were not sufficient to inspire them to participate. This can be explained by the fact that people's personal conduct of their everyday lives must be understood as "relatively autonomous": not directed by social factors but simply based on them as options for action (Holzkamp, 1998, p. 24; author's translation). Holzkamp expands on the relation between options for action and reasons by pointing out that the meanings given as alternative actions in such a possible relation that the subject actually converts into actions depends according to our conception on the reasons related to the subject's interests in terms of attitude to the world and life quality (ibid.).

8.5.2 Interest in supplementary training prior to losing your job

During one of my observations while we were sitting in the foreman's office, Flemming (a former shop steward at the company) told me that he used to encourage the employees to give supplementary training courses a chance – but that this had been hopeless. They were simply not interested. However, now they knew the company was going to close down a good number had taken such courses. He was unable to explain this, but thought that the employees might be keen to make the most of the final few benefits from the company before it closed down. He actually used the expression "they've got a knife at their throats now". Flemming thought that the extra training had been a good experience for the employees, and the trade union (called 3F) had visited the factory to draw up training plans for the employees. He did not know why the employees were so willing to attend courses now – but something had changed, and he was surprised at the level of interest. The fact that my research process was designed in the form of practice research with the intention of including any sense of surprise that was registered in the field led me to ask the employees why they were interested in supplementary training courses now, and why they had not been interested previously. The current shop steward offered another explanation: the courses offered previously had been of a different nature.

JAN: We talked about training courses about six months
   before we were made redundant, but we have since found out
   that the company already knew we were going to be closed
   down – so that's why they agreed. Before that they used to say
   that the company *already had* a training committee, and that
   was true enough. But it was only for the office staff and not
   for the shop floor – we were never offered any training courses or anything like it. But that's when it started. The HR manager and I discussed it, then the management
   got involved, and we started to define what kind of courses
   we wanted. And then we were told we were closing down
   – and *then* there was no alternative.

During my observations Jan told me that it was difficult for him to motivate his colleagues to sign up for these courses. "Why should we?",
they used to ask him. But "When we found out we were closing down
they wanted to do courses in Danish, maths and loads of other subjects. Perhaps they thought these courses would give them the chance
to take time out and relax a bit". If the employees had imagined that
they would be spending the rest of their working lives at the company,
they would of course not be particularly motivated to take part in any
supplementary training courses – unless they were required to do so
to keep their jobs. This situation changed when they were fired.

Frans explained that he had done a course in farming. He had not
done so previously because he saw no point in learning about farming if he was going to work at a paint company for the rest of his life.
But when the company closed down, a new situation arose in which
supplementary training courses were connected to a different perspective on the future. The employees did not know what kind of job
they would be able to find, so relatively broad training courses seemed
attractive. At the same time the fact that the company was closing
down meant that training courses were perceived as a perk, so the
employees felt entitled to ask for courses designed to meet their own
wishes rather than being designed to meet the needs of the company. The reasons for participating in training courses changed in line
with the new and unexpected perspective on the future. The employees did not base their wishes for supplementary training on the ar-

8

149

guments that abound in the public debate relating to lifelong learning, individual employability and the flexibility of the workforce. This
dilemma is dealt with by Leif Hansen in his article "(Nogle) voksnes
lærings- og undervisningsbegreber" ("The learning and teaching concepts of (some) adults"). He refers to a Danish study of the motivation and barriers of some 40- to 60-year old men in relation to taking
part in adult education, in which Christensen et al. (1997) point out
that training becomes a partial, defensive and ad hoc measure designed to reinforce a house that is collapsing (the slow disappearance
of the industrial shop-floor worker) instead of building a new house
to meet the needs of the future (the post-industrial knowledge society and its unpredictable changing nature) (Christensen, 1997). The
fact that the employees of the company did not perceive supplementary training as a long-term solution is connected to their focus on
staying in their current jobs until they retired. Long-term reasons
seemed to be absent as long as they thought they would be staying
on at the company. However, the new situation required action in relation to a new potential future, and this new situation meant a complex change in their self-understanding and the personal conduct of
their lives. They used to say that they were not interested in training
courses because they did not know what to use them for – they were
not relevant in relation to the way they conducted their lives. But
in the new situation they justified their participation in supplementary training in a variety of ways.

These reasons did not only change for the individual. It is necessary to study these reasons in concrete terms and in relation to the
changed concrete conditions for participation in training. Jim pointed out that the courses attended by individuals were not necessarily
connected to the performance of their current jobs.

JIM: I've been offered courses and extra training and that kind
of thing, and I've done quite a bit of it. Lots of people have
got their driving licences that way as well as other things that
weren't really necessary for their jobs. It's always an advantage
to have a driving licence for lots of jobs, of course. But it's not
absolutely vital for most jobs, is it? I've done a course in entrepreneurship and a computer user course as well. I actually only

did the computer course so I could put it on my CV and say that I had some computer skills. But the course in entrepreneurship was purely for my own sake, know what I mean?

Jim's choice of a course in entrepreneurship was connected to his self-understanding. I have already pointed out that Jim wanted to move his life in a new direction, so his choice was probably based on this wish. But his reason for taking part in the computer course was to gain a certificate confirming that he had computer skills so he could add this to his CV. It was not enough for Jim to know that he had computer skills – he needed documentary evidence as well. In this way people's reasons for participating in training courses are also connected to the conditions occurring in institutional arrangements for career guidance – for instance the production of a written CV. The task involved in producing a CV gave reasons for participating in supplementary training courses with a view to gaining the official stamp of approval or documentary evidence of particular skills. As far as training courses were concerned, the employees felt that they had greater freedom of choice after they were fired. Such courses no longer had to be relevant for the company, which meant that the employees could consider their relevance with regard to the personal conduct of their own lives in general – not just their relevance with regard to their future working lives at the company. As a result, a wide variety of courses were chosen. I was told of basic adult education courses such as Danish and mathematics, courses at technical college, courses for industrial operators and cargo handlers, computer user courses, courses leading to driving licences for cars or HGVs, fork-lift truck courses, and farming and entrepreneurship courses.

8.5.3 Changing the concrete conditions

The foreman was not certain that the employees would have been offered training courses to the same extent if the company had not been about to close the factory; and in one interview the HR consultant Helene told me that the agreement on training courses had been the area that generated most disagreement between the employees and the HR department.

HELENE: It's never completely smooth and unproblematic
– they sometimes do and say irrational things because they
feel hurt and disappointed, and we understand them completely ... One of the issues was that we said we'd do what
we could to get them some training courses, but the agreement stipulated that these courses had to be relevant for
production. But they thought that they could go on courses
from day one and for the next year and a half. There was a
bit of disagreement about that. And some of them were very
slow starters. They couldn't understand that they weren't
allowed to disappear for a couple of months from one day
to the next just because they'd suddenly realised that
they wanted to go on a course.

There were limits to how much training each individual was permit-
ted because the company did not want the wheels of production to
stop turning. Helene's words reveal that the employees were not allowed to attend an unlimited number of courses. Concrete conditions
had an influence on these limitations, and failure to attend courses
(or limited attendance) cannot be explained solely by individual
or internal motivation factors. Participation in training courses had
to be relevant for production, which meant that individual possibilities for participation were embedded in the community. The greater
the number of colleagues taking part in training courses, the lower the
chance of other people taking part because production needed to continue. The same applied to any time taken off due to illness. These are
factors extending beyond individual motivation and into the conduct
of communal life. Even though the company explained its support
for employee training courses by saying that it had their best interests at heart, there were limits as to how far these interests went.

HELENE: There have been periods when (the company)
extended their contracts because there was a fire in Sweden
and the company needed extra labour the employees were
told that if they wanted to stay on they could. The employees
thought that if they stayed on they could continue to attend
training courses as well, but we had to say that this was

8

no longer possible. Of course we wouldn't necessarily say "no" if someone came along who had never been on any courses at all, but the general offer of training courses was taken off the table. Their contracts had only been extended in order to keep production going, and they got angry and said we had promised to do what we could. But those days were over and we were facing a new situation.

The employees were supposed to want to take part in training courses, but this was not supposed to get in the way of production. This meant that their "motivation" had to be coordinated in relation to the range of courses on offer and the participation of their colleagues in these courses. For instance, employees involved in the same production processes could not attend courses at the same time because this would result in a breakdown of production, so coordination was required in relation to the way individuals conducted their lives and participated in other communities. Helene explained that the training agreement only applied during the period between being made redundant and closing the factory. When the employees were offered an extension of their contracts, several of them found it hard to accept that their entitlement to training courses had not been extended as well. First they were encouraged to attend training courses, and then they were not. The conditions seem to be connected to far more than the motivation of each individual alone. Subsequently, Helene reported that the company was unable to grant very long courses (40-week courses, for instance). The company needed production to continue, so very few men could be spared at any one time; if the courses on offer were to be shared by as many employees as possible, they had to be short.

When this reasoning is connected to Ulla's career guidance, it becomes clear that in her practice she was also tied by various restrictive possibilities for action preventing her from working with the inner motivation of each individual alone. Instead, she had to work with the concrete possibilities for participation that existed, which had to be coordinated in the community constituting each individual's conditions for participating in training courses. She had to work with the coordination of the concrete courses available, the date on which they started and finished, and the wishes of employees in the light of the fact that production had to continue. Ulla had to coordinate in relation to the need to produce the products required by the company's order list; and each individual in turn had to coordinate the personal conduct of his life and participation in other communities (family, recreational interests, other work etc.) in relation to this need. These conditions meant that the career guidance had to be understood in the light of a highly concrete coordination of various interests.

8.5.4 Analytical perspectives – new possibilities for participating in education

Both the shop steward and the trade union had previously tried to motivate the employees to take part in supplementary training courses, but this had proved to be an uphill task. The redundancies led to new possibilities for participating in training in several ways. For one thing the variety and number of courses on offer increased, and in addition being fired led to employee's having new thoughts about their future working lives. New possibilities for participation appear thanks to interaction between a change in the conditions applying to participation and a change in the reasons for participation. This analysis makes it possible to discuss the extent to which the motivation of each individual should be explained as an inner motivation in the person concerned. This analysis suggests that motivation should be viewed in interaction with the conditions to which each individual allocates meaning and in which they justify their actions. New concrete conditions generate new opportunities for career guidance, and indicate that career guidance in the transitional period between jobs can help to create concrete possibilities for participation in training courses by coordinating the interests involved. Throughout this transition the employees found new reasons for participating in training, and their changed conditions lead to demand for knowledge about opportunities for courses and supplementary training.

This means that career guidance is important in connection with transitions in which concrete conditions, including the courses offered and future perspectives, are subject to changes. Career guidance may seem attractive, but it may also be perceived as invasive in its ambitions for encouraging participation in training courses (based on the discourse of lifelong learning), thereby failing to find its place in the structure of reasoning of each individual. Reasons are mutually determined by conditions and the meaning attributed to conditions, so changes in the structures of reasoning of individuals can only be understood in concrete interaction with changes in the conditions established by the company for employees wishing to participate in supplementary training courses. The courses offered used to be related more closely to production; but during their period of notice after being fired the employees had access to a wider range of course options. This availability meant that participation in training courses could also be regarded as a perk seen in the perspective of the way each individual conducted his personal life – it was no longer connected solely to new qualifications or competences that were of value to the company.

A decentred perspective on the interaction of career guidance with changed possibilities for participation in training leads to thoughts as to how career guidance can be included in a double change of the structures of reasoning: partly in the company, where a wider selection of supplementary training courses becomes possible because such courses are now regarded as a personal perk; and partly in the individual, who also regards such courses as a personal perk en route to a new working life. This means that the motivation for training cannot be analysed on a general, abstract level, but has to be analysed as situated in the context in question. This is a conclusion which Leif Hansen may also be close to when he summarises a number of studies of the motivation for attending training courses of people with little further education behind them. He says that there is a good deal of evidence that for adults with little further education behind them there are two things (possibly connected to each other) characterising their relationship with supplementary training: their motivation for training is closely connected with the world of work, so that keeping or (re)acquiring a job is the most important driving force in relation both to signing up for training courses and to which subjects are the most interesting (Hansen, 1999, p. 4). The realisation that the motivation for training is closely connected to the world of work may be the first step along the path leading to the conclusion that studies

8

must be concrete and situated. But even referring to the motivation for training (as opposed to concrete possibilities for participating in training) may be regarded as an individualisation of theissue. From this perspective we are unable to see how interaction between the concrete conditions and interests experienced by the individual as well as the meanings they attribute to these conditions and interests, can create new reasons for participating in training for the individual. This is a dilemma that is dealt with in section 10.5 of the discussion.

8

9 Career guidance at the folk high school

9.1 Vignette – welcome to the folk high school

Mads has just got out of bed. He didn't have time to take a shower before breakfast, but he doesn't care because this is not particularly important at the folk high school, where he has grown used to seeing people either bright as a button or unkempt and unshaven. He picks up some bread, tea and fruit and sits down at a table for six by the windows in the dining room. They seem tired today, and nobody says very much. He talks to some of the other students. It's cold outside, but the sun is shining and they are starting a project called "Valuable Competencies" today. He does not really know what to expect. This is his final month at the folk high school and he has already been here for five months. Up until Christmas everyday life here was divided into learning various subjects, and he has been specialising in medicine, which has been interesting. But in January the student's time has been split between a variety of projects. He looks around and smiles when he sees how different the old and new students look. All the new students have showered, dried their hair and packed their bags. They are absolutely ready for the day. Within about a week they will be much more relaxed – just like him.

A teacher takes the microphone and reads a list of names of the people who are on duty. This week Mads has to set the coffee table in the recreational area in the evenings. He leaves the table because he just has time to take a shower before morning assembly. He is late for the assembly, but sneaks in while they are singing *"Min Marie"*, which he thinks is Lars' favourite. They certainly sing it a lot. The ratio of young men and women is roughly the same in the new group of students as it was in the old group. Two-thirds of the students are women; but fortunately the men are not the quiet type. The assembly room has a red-brick floor and red-brick walls. The red colour is broken by a blue curtain in front of the stage and three long, narrow windows on each side of the room. Next to the stage there are two woven rugs featuring religious motifs in various shades of red and brown. Lars gives a short talk about competences and then announces the names of the students in the various groups. People have been allocated to groups on the basis of the role test they completed yesterday. Mads' group is given a room and agrees to meet there in fifteen minutes' time. Mads walks down the long corridor and out into the sunshine. He only manages a very quick smoke before it gets too cold to stand outside. Back in the group room with big windows, a brown carpet and black painted tables he joins Louise, who has just started on the journalist course. The group also includes a number of students from abroad, and this has an impact on their choice of theme. They decide to produce an introduction to the folk high school called "The Danish Maker". Mads feels rather sad because his time here is almost over. He looks at Louise and thinks that she still has five great months ahead of her. During lunch they talk about how to get into courses of further education when you don't have the required grades, and they discuss the entrance examination for the school of journalism. This reminds Mads that before the end of January he has to write an application stating his reasons for studying medicine in Odense and including a CV. He has heard several teachers say that they would be happy to help with this. He wants to avail himself of this opportunity, so he needs to pull himself together and make sure he gets their help before he leaves the folk high school.

9.2 **The situation of the students**

This section starts by describing the situation of the folk high school students. It includes several perspectives, each of which contributes to an understanding of their situation – a situation with which career guidance has to interact. The first part of the analysis focuses on the various reasons of the students for studying at the folk high school. These reasons are interesting because they are connected to the conditions experienced by the students with regard to their participation in society in general, and to the conditions related to participation in life at the folk high school.

The students at the folk high school when I started my observations in January were all involved in the course entitled "Valuable Competencies". For some of them (the autumn students) this was the final stage of their time at the school; for others (the spring students) it was the start of their stay. I met a mixture of old and new students. In February even more students started the courses run by the school, so in the space of a single month there were students leaving and two groups of students starting. The new students then spent 17 weeks studying various courses at the school.

9.2.1 Reasons for attending a folk high school

Students attend folk high school in Denmark voluntarily. They apply to the school of their choice and pay for the time they spend there, applying for any subsidies themselves. Their reasons for attending vary, but they are often connected to their thoughts about career choices and educational opportunities. Some of them say they study at folk high school because it gives them the chance to gain extra credits, thereby helping them to gain entrance to their chosen course of further education. Others say they want to find out what it is like to study particular subjects so they can decide whether these are the right subjects for them. Another reason given was that they wanted to challenge themselves in relation to the social competences which are required and can be learned at a folk high school. Their reasons vary, so the situation in which they find themselves varies too. Even so, there are also characteristics of their situations that they share – after all, they have all decided to study at the same folk high school. Some of these characteristics are expressed by the students below, serving to illustrate the situation in which they find themselves.

9

9.2.2 Extra credits and studying new subjects

One of the reasons given by the students on the nursing and medicine course is that spending time at a folk high school gave them extra credits and the chance to qualify for entrance to their chosen course of further education. But there were also other reasons, as shown in the interview with Mads:

MADS: Well, I didn't think about it (studying at folk high school) for very long. A guidance counsellor told me it would give me extra credits, so that's why I did it. It was difficult to find a job at the time, so a couple of days later I just went for it (laughs) ... I didn't think twice about it.

Mads was afraid of being unemployed. He could not find a job, so decided to try something else and applied for folk high school. Peter also had six months during which he needed something to do, and felt that studying at a folk high school would help him find out whether the subject of his choice was really the right one for him.

PETER: I always knew I wanted a gap year, and I knew I wanted to go travelling, but I didn't know what to do in the final six months of the year ... And I didn't just want to work for six months – I thought that would be boring. I wanted to be more certain about what to do the following year ... what kind of further education and that sort of thing. So I searched the internet and found this folk high school plus another one up in Skagen which also had medicine on the programme. And I thought I might as well try it to find out whether medicine was the right course for me. I also thought the social life at a folk high school would be good.

Peter's expectations are characterised by his desire to learn more about a new subject area, and in general students expect the courses they study at folk high school to resemble the courses of further education they are interested in doing the following year. Their expectations are also characterised by the idea that participating in new subjects will help them to choose the right course of study for the next year. For Peter there seemed to be a connection between the subject of medicine as studied at folk high school and the subject he expected to encounter in a course of further education. Subjects were apparently regarded as universal and identical entities at all institutions of education, despite the fact that folk high schools are not part of the formal education system in Denmark. Peter expected to gain insight in and experience of the subject area he was considering for further study. Finding out if medicine was the right course for him was high on his list of reasons – although he did add as an afterthought that the social life was important for him, too. This latter point is dealt with in greater detail in the next section.

9.2.3   Challenging yourself

Another characteristic expectation of the students si that the folk high school is a place where you challenge yourself to participate in a new kind of social life. They expect that living in such close proximity to so many people for such a long time will demand something special. I talked to Tine about her goals during her time at the school:

TINE: Goals and goals … well, I'd like to believe a bit more in myself. Believe that I can manage things.
RIE: How did you think the school would help you with this?
TINE: For one thing because there'd be so many of us living close together. I often used to feel that I needed to go into my room and shut the door behind me to be on my own for a bit … Away from it all. That's why I chose to share a room with someone else – I thought I'd learn most that way. And it's definitely worked, so that's what probably did the trick for me.

The situation demands something special of the students in relation to participating in the social life of the school, the invasiveness of which is not only a fundamental condition of life but also a learning opportunity which many of the students tried to make the most of, like Tine. Life at the school demanded special competences, said Peter. We talked about the influence of life at the school on life outside:

9

PETER: It might be a bit too soon to answer that one actually, because we might realise what the answer is later on. But I think I will be able to use the social skills I've learned here outside the school as well. I've learned not to be so shy or afraid, and you do tend to be shy and afraid when you meet new people and that kind of thing. I think it's gone really well and maybe I can use this later because I know that nothing terrible is going to happen. You just have to jump in at the deep end. I think I'll be able to use this later. Jump in at the deep end and have a go … I think this is one competence I'll be able to use later.

RIE: A "jump-in-at-the-deep-end" competence.

PETER: Yes – and how to land on your feet as well. (Laughs) Jumping isn't enough on its own.

The opportunity to develop social skills by participating in the community and social life of the folk high school was an issue on which many of the students focused a good deal. A number of them said that this was one of the reasons why they decided to study at such a school. In section 9.5 I discuss in greater detail the significance that the students attributed to their participation in the community.

9.2.4 Being in the same boat

The students at the folk high school often discussed their choices of further education. There were many common aspects of their situations. One of these was that they were all facing the decision of what to study when their time at the school came to an end. This was a different situation from that applying to their peers outside the school: some of their friends had already started further education; the young people who were unresolved about what to do, or who had been rejected, were excluded from the study community and placed in the position of observers while their friends made new friends and joined new communities. But at the folk high school a different situation applied because all the students were engaged in applying for further education – a position which allowed them to participate in the community and discuss their shared situation with other people at the school. Tine explained the significance of the fact that they were all in the same boat:

Tine: We're all thinking about what to do next and how to go about it. We're all in the same boat. And some people have tried already – applied last year and went to a few interviews, and some people have done a few courses at university. So we can all help each other somehow and get lots of different perspectives on our situation, and I think it's been great actually because otherwise people just tend to form cliques and talk about the same things with the same people all the time. But here at the school everyone talks with everyone, and I think it's been really great.

For Tine the situation is characterised by her focus on the fact that the students all have different experiences when it comes to choosing further education, applying for courses, going to interviews and taking courses. Tine feels that it is important that the others have thought about further education and have already gained some experience of it. She sees this as a resource from which she can gain insight by talking to the other students: an insight she uses in her own thoughts and actions in relation to choosing and applying for further education, *"So we can all help each other somehow and get lots of different perspectives on our situation"*. For Tine the uncertainty of the other students and their "failed" experiences of further education become a resource for the community. The teachers encourage the students to use the experiences they have gained in various ways, a point to which I shall return in section 9.5 ("The importance of community"). The fact that the experiences of the students are regarded as an important resource places the students in a situation in which the focus is on what the individual contributes to the community. This is a situation in which you are expected to participate and to share your experiences with other people. This is one of the conditions of participating in the folk high school community, and one of the things that the students feel helps them to make decisions about further education. The importance of community in helping students

9

to make their decisions is not one of the reasons for joining the folk high school community; but it is regarded as important when the students describe their thoughts about which specific subject to choose in their future educational careers.

9.2.5 A different teacher/student relationship ("adult to adult")

The students at the folk high school experience a new role for themselves when they meet adult teachers who seem to respect them as adults. They emphasise that their relationship with the teachers at the school is very different from the relationship they had with their teachers at upper-secondary education programmes (Youth Education see illustrations in appendix 7). This situation is characterised as a meeting between two adults, which is a new and positive experience for them. The statements by Peter and Louise while we were talking about the relationship between teachers and students illustrate this point:

PETER: I think it's great. You could say that at upper-secondary school there was a much bigger difference. The teachers were one thing and the students were another. You didn't talk to the teachers much. But we do here. Lots of the teachers join in some of the activities here. They treat you differently. You could say that we're one step further up the education system and closer to being adults ourselves. That's a pretty awesome thing to say, but we have grown up a lot I think.

LOUISE: At this school the students have a good time with the teachers at meal times. I really like the teachers here. I really do. I think they're really cool and I think that … even though some of them are a bit older … I think they're open and positive to us young people, and they seem to like young people. In general they seem to think we're interesting. After all, every six months or even more often than that there's a new group of students arriving here. But even so they can be bothered to find out about our lives and our dreams and wishes. I think that's fantastic. And they seem to be really proud of each

9

group of students. They seem to get involved in our every-day lives and they seem really keen to make sure that the new young generation growing up and starting life on the labour market are going to be good citizens who have learned something about life.

This situation is characterised by the fact that the students feel they are treated like adults and that they are allowed to be adults. The teachers take part in the same activities as the students, which helps to give a feeling of equality. Louise feels that the teachers are genuinely interested in young people. They find out about *"our lives and our dreams and wishes"*. She also feels that the teachers have ambitions on behalf of the students: *"they seem really keen to make sure that the new young generation growing up and starting life on the labour market are going to be good people who have learned something about life"*. The students are in a situation that is characterised by the fact that someone is interested in them as adults and future citizens in society. This interest demonstrated by the teachers implies a mutual sense of involvement and commitment. The students are expected to enter into the community by sharing their dreams and wishes with the teachers, who want to help them to become *"good citizens"*. This is apparently a situation that many of the young people have not experienced previously in the education system.

9.2.6 Participating in the activities that are organised

Studying at a folk high school is a situation that is characterised by the fact that the young people have to accept and subject themselves to various things in relation to their participation in the community. This observation is in contrast to other characteristic descriptions of young people as individualists who primarily do what they themselves regard as sensible (see Ziehe, 2005, for instance). The young people have to accept that they must participate in the school's activities and share their experiences with each other and with the teachers. They have to accept the fact that the teachers show an interest in their choices of further education. They have to accept that other people will keep asking them about their choices of further education, whether they have written their applications and sent them in. They have to accept the fact that they must participate in the everyday life of the school (teaching and planned leisure activities). But they also have to take part in activities designed to help them choose a future course of further education, as described by Maria:

RIE: You said that one of your goals was to gain a greater sense of clarity while studying at folk high school. Can you say what aspects of life at the school help you to achieve this?

MARIA: For instance some of the things we experience here – like when we visit various colleges and hear about the courses studied there. I think the people who want to study psychology learned a lot when we had a chat with a young woman who studies psychology at university. Because afterwards they said they didn't want to. We also visited a few colleges that train social educators, and the people who were interested in that course found out what they wanted to study and where they wanted to be because they thought these colleges were great! It was some of the *actual students themselves* who told us what it was like to be there. Suddenly you saw a few real live students and could picture what it would be like to study there yourself. On Thursday we're visiting an educational institution for the physically disabled. That might teach me a lot – if I could see what kind of people I would have to work with if I did that course and if I could find out more about the legal aspects of the job (Maria wanted to be a social worker). I think it might confirm that this is the right kind of thing for me.

The students have to choose their preferred course of study at the school, and each course arranges a variety of activities with a view to helping them decide about their future. The students are expected to participate in these activities: visits to particular colleges or institutions; dialogues of their own initiative regarding the time spent at the school; dialogues of their own initiative with regard to life after the school; and discussions about their own participation in the school's activities (project work, for instance).

9.2.7 Analytical perspectives – the situation of the students

The situation of the students at the folk high school is characterised by the fact that it contains a mixture of goals: personal goals (challenging themselves in relation to participating in social contexts); subject-specific learning goals (learning about the subjects they might decide to choose for further study, for instance); and qualification goals (gaining credits to boost their grades so they can study the courses they want). Even though the students have chosen this situation themselves (unlike the employees of the company, who had been fired), the situation still demands a variety of things from them. It demands active participation in the social life; it demands that they share their experiences with each other and with the teachers; and it demands that they think about and gain experience of their study choices and listen to the experiences and advice of others in relation to both the choice of further education and achieving what could be called *the good life*. The situation is also characterised by the fact that they are all uncertain about various things. Some of them are uncertain about which course of further education to apply for, while others are uncertain whether they will qualify for the course for which they intend to apply. By contrast with their previous discussions with friends, at the folk high school it is entirely acceptable to spend a lot of time talking about your uncertainty. And a lot of time is spent talking about "Plan B" – their strategies if they are rejected.

It is important that each student has certain experiences that they can share with the others. It is also clear that the students gain understanding of themselves and their own strategies by participating in the community. Holzkamp's concept of self-understanding as a joint project of understanding, in which the implicit is made explicit, makes it possible to see how people include each other in their own self-understanding projects. In this perspective, self-understanding is linked to the conduct of everyday life – my life and me in it – by contrast with a cognitive perception of self-understanding as inner structures which are made conscious. The folk high school students mix in various social contexts which require their participation: group work, sports activities, teaching and visits to various colleges, for instance.

9

Their self-understanding and decision-making seem to be linked both to their expressions of their experiences with each other and with the teachers, and to their concrete experiences of visits to colleges. In this way they gain insight into the "we" that Line Lerche Mørck adds to Holzkamp's concept of self-understanding. The folk high school students are expected to participate in their own projects of self-understanding with each other. In other words, there is a "we" (consisting of themselves, other students and teachers at the school) that helps to reveal possibilities for and expectations about their participation. This is important with regard to their opportunities for understanding themselves in general and their choices of education and wishes for a future life in particular. From this perspective, achieving self-understanding is regarded not as a reflective project for each individual, but as a shared project occurring in the community established around the situation in which the students find themselves, and which requires their participation in particular ways.

The fact that communities provide particular possibilities for decision-making is not something the students regarded as significant prior to attending the folk high school, and they do not mention it as one of their reasons for choosing to study at such a school. But in our joint analysis of their situation in the interviews (carried out by the students and myself), they did acknowledge that the community was important their decision-making process. For instance, this can be seen in the theme called "in the same boat", in which the importance Tine attaches to her knowledge that all the students are thinking about what to do next is relevant in terms of what the students feel it is legitimate to talk about. The importance of community is discussed in section 10.2 below ("Other people's experiences as a resource").

9.3 Career guidance at the folk high school

In this section I focus on career guidance at the folk high school by considering the way in which the students describe their encounter with career guidance. The concept of career guidance covers a broad range of activities. The EU's resolution on lifelong guidance refers to:

information and counselling, consultancy, competence assessment, mentor schemes, and advocacy and teaching in decision-making and career planning (Council of the European Union, 2004). In this book a participant perspective on career guidance is adopted, leading to an interest in finding out what it is that the students at folk high school describe as career guidance. The students explain their thoughts regarding both career guidance at the folk high school and career guidance in their previous school careers. I wanted to avoid defining what I meant by career guidance, so I asked open questions such as "What kind of career guidance activities have you taken part in?" Other questions were even more open than this, focusing on activities that they regarded as important in terms of their decisions about further education. In the statement below Maria describes the range of activities available:

RIE: Can you try to describe the career guidance activities you have been involved in since you started at the school?

MARIA: When we got here we started on the special course of study that we'd chosen. We had to define what we wanted to be and why. The teachers gave us career guidance as a group, and a bit later we were given a questionnaire and asked to answer various questions such as: why did you choose to study at a folk high school, and what kind of course of further education would you like to do, and how are you going to get in and that kind of thing. And we answered these questions and it sort of got us thinking. Afterwards we had a talk with the teacher about it, and the teacher asked us to give some more details and we had the chance to talk about our wishes with regard to further education and our goals. Then there was a whole day of student counselling when they visited us from Aarhus [*Regional Guidance Centre – ("Studievalg")*]. That was mostly for people who needed to boost their grades by gaining credits. But it was also the kind of meeting where people asked questions and tried to figure out what they wanted to study and so on. So, yeah, I think we've had a lot of different kinds of career guidance activities.

9

For Maria career guidance seems to be a broad concept that includes much more than individual dialogues between a career guidance parctioner and a young person. Instead, her definition of career guidance seems to depend on the content of the questions asked – they need to focus on education or the future. This can be connected to the way the folk high school organises career guidance: all the teachers provide career guidance, so it is not restricted to a particular individual practitioner or a particular design. Career guidance is included in, co-operates with and contributes to other processes of decision-making and learning at the school.

The students do not only include the career guidance they encounter at the folk high school in their descriptions. They also include their previous experience of institutional arrangements of career guidance. In the statement below, Maria describes a variety of institutional arrangements for career guidance, starting with the folk high school teachers and including career guidance at secondary school and encounters with student counselling at an institution of further education. She focuses on activities that have made a difference to her:

MARIA: There's our teacher, she often sits down with us and
talks about our thoughts, whether we've had any new ideas
or what's going on. It hasn't really been like that before. At
secondary school we had a few personal sessions of course,
but you didn't get much out of it because it wasn't really relevant for your education anyway. So I think it's better that they
get hold of you every now and then and ask whether you've
made any progress and what you've been thinking about
since the last time.

RIE: What is good career guidance in your view?

MARIA: If it's related to further education then it's often about
hearing the facts – just some clear answers about the facts –
but also about a guidance counsellor trying to relate to your
current situation. If the students say they want something
the guidance counsellor should try to start with that, and if the
guidance counsellor thinks it's impossible they should try and
suggest something else that's relevant instead. Because for instance when the guidance counsellor in there (at the social

worker training college) said she didn't think I was ready. Then I'd have liked her to suggest some alternatives about what she did think would be relevant for me. I think lots of the student counsellors I've known have been a bit negative and have actually thought that my questions were stupid. They told me to have a look on the net, and that's not a bad idea but when I call a guidance counsellor that's not the kind of thing I'm looking for, I don't want them to just say go and have a look on the net. I want to hear what they've got to say, because that's more of a help and it also gives me a better impression instead of looking on the net.

When asked what had made a difference to her, Maria did not mention specific activities but presented us with her thoughts regarding a particular relationship. She underlined the influence of a teacher who sat down and talked to her, asking her about her wishes for the future and new ideas. When asked what good career guidance was, she started talking about the way in which practitioners meet their students. She mentioned the importance of reliable, factual answers, but also said that practitioners should not simply refer students to facts that they can find on the net. She wanted to hear what the practitioner had to say, and she wanted to hear about other options – particularly if the practitioner was sceptical about her choice. The possibilities for participation connected with searching the net and phoning a career guidance practitioner must be characterised as different. Dialogues on the phone can develop in a way that searching the net cannot do. Telephone conversations made interaction possible by following up with further questions based on the information provided. Maria thought that factual information was an important ingredient of good career guidance, but she also thought that the way professional practitioners met students was important. Part of this professionalism involves knowing the facts and being able to provide guidance to help young people achieve their goals. In Maria's case a career guidance practitioner had apparently rejected her educational wishes owing to her lack of maturity, where Maria wanted her to give her some other alternatives instead.

9

Mads also said that career guidance practitioners should be able to present alternatives and possibilities. He believed that such practitioners should know a lot about *opportunities*.

RIE: What is career guidance in your view?

MADS: Basically I've always thought it was like the guidance counsellors we had at secondary school, who knew more about the options you could choose and who could tell you the best way of getting on and what you should be thinking about and that kind of thing. And in general: how to go about it.

Mads felt that career guidance practitioners helped to create a connection between the possibilities offered by society and the wishes of the individual in question. Career guidance practitioners were people *"who could tell you the best way of getting on"*, which meant helping students by matching information about the options with the experiences of the individual concerned in terms of their previous education and wishes for future education, and then telling them how to make progress as easily as possible. In a critical psychological perspective, the best way of categorising factual information is by using the concept of the conditions which the students felt had an impact on their possibilities for action. In this sense, knowledge about your conditions helps to create a greater range of possibilities. Mads wanted to know his conditions so he could take action accordingly.

9.3.1 The importance of conditions with regard to possibilities for participation

There is a general understanding of the fact that career guidance can be many different things, while people's wishes regarding good career guidance vary a good deal more and are connected to the concrete situation facing each individual. Maria wanted to meet a career guidance practitioner who supported her and accepted her choices, but Peter wanted a practitioner who challenged his ideas and study choices – as shown in the statement below, in which Peter refers to the introductory interviews that all the students had with the teacher attached to their particular corridor to introduce them to the school.

172

PETER: I don't think it helped. I think she could have been –
not a psychologist, exactly – but she could have asked why
you had decided on your particular course of study and so on.
Started talking a bit more personally to you. Those interviews
we've had. Someone probably said they'd be a good idea and
then they were put onto the programme. So I don't think it's
real career guidance and perhaps they could have changed
that and spoken a bit more directly to you.

Peter found it hard to define career guidance. Previously he had said
"They could have organised some lessons and called them career
guidance or something like that". He needed to give the activities a
title so he knew that career guidance was involved. He participated
in everything that was organised for him, including the personal
interviews with the teachers responsible for his corridor, with all the
students being asked to complete a questionnaire on which these
interviews were based. In his view these interviews did not count as
career guidance. He found them irrelevant. But he found it very easy
to say what he thought should have been done instead.

PETER: I'd like it to be a bit more concrete … For instance,
if we'd had a discussion about the study of medicine and if
they'd been a bit more direct with me – then I'd have been
forced to you know provide some reasons why … I wanted
to study medicine because I haven't really thought all that
much about it. And then perhaps they could have pointed
out some of the pros and cons of studying medicine, but
they haven't really done that either.

Later on he continued: "… I could have got more out of it if they'd
helped me to decide why I really wanted to study medicine."
Peter was interested in discussing his concrete thoughts about his
choice of further education. In connection with a visit by a student
of medicine, he explained what he meant by the term "concrete":

PETER: … he had actually just graduated as a doctor and explained what it involved. I thought that was really great. For
instance, he said he had a great number of really long duty

shifts. That's a bit negative isn't it? On the other hand it's also really great ... when you've learned something and you can actually use it in real life and that kind of thing. That's what I mean.

The concrete description of what it was like to work as a doctor gave Peter something to relate to in making his choice of further education. What kind of life would you lead if you were a doctor? Was that the kind of life he wanted? He wanted his choice to be challenged in relation to questions like these. A number of the other students were given this kind of challenge when asked to explain their reasons for choosing a particular course of further education, but these were the students whose grades were not sufficient to guarantee them a place. Peter's grades were good enough, so he was not forced to explain his reasons for choosing medicine. The different conditions facing the students meant that they had different views about what was important in career guidance activities; but it also meant that their possibilities for participation were different. Peter was not forced to explain his choice, but the students who did not have the necessary grades were forced to do so. The different conditions facing the students meant that they had different possibilities for participation, and therefore that their needs in terms of career guidance were different.

9.3.2 Career guidance does not determine your choice

In her description of good career guidance, Tine referred to the way in which other people helped to influence her opinion.

RIE: What is good career guidance in your view?

TINE: Perhaps ... that you are influenced a bit by other people's attitudes ... but only a bit so you still make your own decisions. I mean that you can sort of weigh up the pros and cons and say OK this sounds really good actually and perhaps it's the right path for me. That you get the chance to think it over and wonder whether it really is and that kind of thing ...

I don't mean you just get influenced by other people but that you don't just sit back and say OK what do you want to do then? And then say that sounds fine or something like that – that's no use to me. It's a good idea to be challenged a bit so you find out whether you're certain about your choice or whether there's any doubt and … if so where does this doubt take you.

On the one hand Tine wants to make her decisions herself – but she also wants to hear other people's opinions. She feels that being challenged is a good thing because these challenges help her to find out how certain she is, whether she might like to change her mind, and if so what this change of mind might involve. A new dimension appears here which is related to the exploration of why certain future opportunities might be relevant for me and why I might choose them. The individual's reasons for certain choices must be explored and challenged in the career guidance process. This was also what Peter wanted, and Tine returned to the point later in my interview with her when she said "a guidance counsellor ought to provide constructive criticism".

Criticism should be constructive – it should inspire her to think more carefully about what she really wants. Tine wants the reasons for her choice to be explored – not just the course she has chosen. The way in which career guidance practitioners challenge the reasons for making choices can be seen in the light of Holzkamp's concept of self-understanding, with the folk high school students wanting to use career guidance to help them make the implicit explicit and to make their educational choices comprehensible to themselves. What are good reasons in my own view? Reasons that I can see reflected in the way you and other people respond to them and the way you challenge them.

The students ask themselves questions about the opportunities that are available, and the opportunities that are available for them in particular. How do I gain access to the course of my choice? What do I need to do? Then other questions appear: What would it be like to study there? What will the social life be like? Maria expressed this

9

as follows: "What can I expect from that particular college, so I'm more or less prepared when I get in and it's not a shock". It is true that certain conditions have to be fulfilled; but each individual would also like their expectations regarding the study environment on the course they choose to support their choice. They ask themselves questions such as: is it really the right choice for me? Peter expressed this in the form of questions like "How many credits will it give me?," and questions designed to identify his own reasons for applying for admission.

PETER: There's lots of different ways of giving career guidance at this folk high school. There are concrete questions like how many credits will it give me? And what am I supposed to do with this application? And because I can't go and ask one of the teachers if they think I would think it would be fun to study medicine. That's a really vague question. They can't answer questions like that about what the actual course is going to be like. I think Karl is the only one who can do that. (Karl was a student of medicine who was involved in teaching the January course). The others are different – schoolteachers and that kind of thing. Of course they know something about their subject, but they don't know anything about the social life at various universities. They can't say anything about that. You have to visit colleges yourself to find out that kind of thing.

In this statement Peter underlines another aspect of his decision-making process. He wants someone to answer his question about what the social life of his chosen course of further education is going to be like, And he does not think the teachers or the career guidance practitioner know the answer. He needs somebody who has actually studied medicine. This new aspect of career guidance concerns knowledge about how practice communities function in relation to concrete choices about concrete courses of further education. This aspect can be added to the aspects regarding knowledge about opportunities, knowledge about individual competences and knowledge about the paths leading to these opportunities for the individual. Peter points out that the concrete experiences of a student of medicine gained

9

from participation in a concrete educational context enables him to ask questions that he would not expect a teacher to answer. This means that the individual's expectations of the participation of the other person involved in career guidance has consequences with regard to what kind of questions they ask. So career guidance practitioners cannot expect to be asked all the questions which the individuals regards as important. This argument supports the idea of providing career guidance in communities, where the fact that more participants are present with a variety of experiences may mean that more questions are asked.

9.3.3 Analytical perspectives – career guidance at the folk high school

For the students at the folk high school, career guidance is limited by their thoughts about the future in general rather than being limited by the nature of specially designed activities. This means that there are plenty of possibilities for participating in career guidance activities, and that many different activities can be categorised as career guidance, but it also means that the students themselves have to look for and determine the content of the career guidance. With reference to their experience of participation in career guidance at both the folk high school and other institutions of education, a distinction appears between three areas of content in career guidance.

The first area of content concerns the fact that career guidance practitioners have knowledge of various *opportunities*, and that they can guide people when it comes to matching these opportunities with individual competences and find the easiest/best way to achieve the individual's goal. Kofod also comments on this in her analysis of career guidance at folk high schools in Denmark. She concludes that folk high schools can potentially provide a social space which can support young people in their decision-making processes and ultimately empower them to make choices by focusing on their abilities and opportunities (Kofod, 2004, p. 47). Kofod calls this career guidance space. The analysis contained in this book indicates that an additional dimension should be added to this, because the social space

9

for career guidance is not same for everyone. Peter, whose grades are sufficient to guarantee him admission to his chosen course of study, is not faced with the same challenges and demands for reflection as the students who have to give reasons for their choices when applying for further education because their grades are not sufficient. The space for career guidance at the folk high school is not just a space in itself, but includes participation of the students elsewhere. Their required admission tasks can be interpreted as societal conditions that have a direct bearing on the career guidance space while at the same time creating a wide array of possibilities for student participation.

The second area of content concerns insight into what it is actually like to study a specific course of further education: what is the social life like? Peter doubts whether his teachers can tell him much about this, and says that only students with personal experience can answer this kind of question. This means that career guidance is limited by the personal experiences of the teachers; but it also means that various forms of experience are regarded as meaningful – indicating that career guidance in communities can benefit from the various forms of experience of the people involved. Naturally, a student counsellor with relevant experience will be regarded as a more legitimate representative of knowledge about the social life of a particular college than a folk high school teacher or career guidance practitioner with a completely different background.

The third area of content, which is not necessarily something that characterises the career guidance provided at the folk high school, but which is something that the students connect with good career guidance, involves somebody challenging their reasons for choosing a particular course of further education. A number of the students wanted career guidance practitioners to give them constructive criticism, thereby forcing them to argue more convincingly for their choices with a view to increasing their own insight into the reasons for these choices.

The experiences of career guidance gained by the students at the folk high school, and their wishes with regard to career guidance, indicate that career guidance practitioners need:

1. Knowledge about opportunities – knowledge about the education system – knowledge about the qualifications of the participants.
2. Sufficient knowledge about further education, enabling them to explore their reasons.
3. Experience of the social life that the students can expect.

These requirements generate various expectations with regard to the interaction between career guidance and the participation of the students elsewhere. For instance, career guidance practitioners cannot gain experience of what it is like to study at various colleges and institutions of education. Focusing on the interaction between career guidance and other practices makes it possible to deal with this dilemma, and various attempts are already made to do this (for instance by asking students already involved in further education to provide career guidance, or by arranging bridge-building activities or "Open House" events allowing potential students to visit the colleges or universities of their choice). In relation to point 3 above (experience of social life), it is important that career guidance and its practitioners acknowledge their limitations before considering how to fulfil the wishes of the students.

9.4 Career guidance space at the folk high school

Analysis of the concrete location of career guidance at the company showed that career guidance practice was influenced by the location in which it took place, and that the location was influenced by practice as well. The analysis section below explores the concrete context for action of the folk high school by analysing descriptions of the concrete location in which career guidance takes place and the opportunities for changes in the way in which it takes place.

Career guidance at Danish folk high schools are studied by Anne Kofod in *Kortlægning af vejledningsindsatsen på højskoler* ("Mapping of career guidance at Danish folk high schools"). Kofod writes that career guidance at such schools is an open concept, so decision-making involves more than the subject-specific competencies of the students alone. She names this career guidance space describing it as the overall

9

presence of an intensive process in which the community encourages reflection on the kind of person you are and what your future might hold (Kofod, 2004, p. 50). In this description of career guidance space, the concept of career guidance is extended in relation to its theme and not restricted to vocation-specific reflections. Kofod also writes that the community encourages reflection. In her study she focuses on the way in which the framework of the folk high school influences the decision-making processes of the students (Kofod, 2004, p. 16). She says that this framework provides particular opportunities for a sense of community. In her analysis of frameworks she does not include the significance of the physical location as a place containing special objects and opportunities (which is something I did in my study of career guidance corners at the company above). In this section I will look more closely at the folk high school as a physical location and explore the significance of this location in relation to the organisation of career guidance. In my interviews it was the teachers in particular who focused on the physical location and talked about *where* career guidance took place, so in this section I will adopt the perspective of the teachers.

The folk high school consists of a large complex of buildings. The central building, dating back to the 1970s, contains student accommodation, an assembly hall, classrooms, a dining room, and a lounge in the basement. It is a red-brick building with concrete frames around the windows and doors, and black woodwork. The dormitories and classrooms have large windows on one side, and there are long, narrow corridors with small, high windows on the other. The administration offices and staffroom are in a separate building, and this is where the room occupied by the teacher responsible for career guidance is also located. As was described by Kofod, the everyday life of the students is highly structured and planned (Kofod, 2004). Most of their time is spent in the company of other people, with teaching and other activities starting at 8 am and continuing until 9 pm. Consequently, the teachers are often engaged in teaching or other activities with the young people. They emphasise that they are either teaching or engaged in other duties most of the time. Teachers who do not live near the school sleep at the school when they are on duty. The teacher on evening duty often sits in the lounge in the evenings or takes part in the activities that the students plan for themselves.

9.4.1 The importance of architecture for the meeting

During my stay at the folk high school I observed that when the students and teachers moved from one activity to the next (between morning assembly and teaching or between teaching and lunch, for instance), the students often approached the teachers to ask them questions about their applications – or the teachers approached the students to follow up on some advice that they had given them earlier. The architecture of the school, with its long corridors, meant that the teachers were accessible on these corridors on the way to or from various activities. For instance, teachers might ask students, "Did you call that student counsellor as we arranged? What did you find out?" These questions often led to further dialogue and questions. The physical layout of the school, combined with the fact that all the teachers were responsible for career guidance, had an influence on the availability of career guidance for the students. The fact that all the teachers provided career guidance meant that they were all open to the idea of students approaching them to ask questions. This was important for the students because it meant that they did not have to wait for answers until they had made an appointment or until they met the teacher with special responsibility for career guidance. All the teachers were happy to discuss choices of further education, which meant that the students could ask questions whenever something occurred to them. Nor did the students have to wonder whether their questions were significant enough to warrant making a special appointment. This is a clear parallel to the way career guidance came to be organised at the company, which might also be a consequence of the fact that in both settings career guidance aimed to achieve immediate interaction with the everyday life of the company or folk high school.

The interaction between the architecture of the school and the way career guidance was organised may seem like a random affair, but in my interview with Lars, a teacher at the school, he explained his thoughts about how to organise everyday life with a view to ensuring more opportunities for talking to the students. In this interview Lars told me about the difference between the way everyday life during the January course called "Valuable Competencies" was organ-

9

ised and the way normal everyday life was organised. Towards the end of the interview I asked whether I had missed anything out that Lars regarded as important.

LARS: We could also talk about the framework of our informal discussions with the students, which involves plenty of career guidance – but I'm not sure if …
RIE: Certainly. I'd like to hear about that.
LARS: It's worth focusing on perhaps, because apart from January our everyday life is strictly divided into teaching and leisure time. And I sometimes think that what happens in January is that the borderline between the two tends to disappear. Our everyday life is with the students, and we do things together. It might be great to work a bit more with this so that our everyday life changed and we could do more things alongside the students and even assume the role of guidance counsellor so we could all experience some kind of learning process – although I'm not sure exactly how to do this. I just know that some things work in January which we could use in the other months of the year when things are divided more clearly into work and leisure.

Lars indicates that when everyday life is organised differently and the distinction between teaching and leisure time is drawn less sharply, there are better possibilities for assuming the role of guidance counsellor both in relation to a shared learning process and in relation to what he calls "informal discussions with the students", which involve plenty of career guidance. I asked him what his phrase "informal discussions" meant:

RIE: What do you mean when you say "informal discussions"?
LARS: I'm thinking about the things that just happen when we don't actually call it career guidance and spend an hour talking about it – when discussions arise of their own accord. Because I can see that this happens in certain places. It happens to Ole a lot because he does outdoor pursuits and spends a lot of leisure time with the students, and it would be very interesting

to work a bit more on that kind of thing and find out how
to create a framework so we could all have more of those ...
moments. Because I can see that it helps at the school. The
idea that we're co-actors, that we're all committed to the same
project. And I think we could definitely do some more work
on forms of learning which don't distinguish so sharply
between work and leisure time. And leisure could be when
we jointly explore some things together, things we think are
interesting. If it's music then we work with that and take
it as it comes, and then we can have discussions as and
when they arise.

Lars would like to pursue the opportunity of working on forms
of learning which do not distinguish so clearly between work and
leisure. His goal is to spend more time with the students, and he
points out that dialogues between teachers and students occur in particular places – for instance during Ole's outdoor pursuits activities,
when they all spend a great deal of time together. Lars connects the
organisation of everyday life with the locations in which opportunities for talking to each other arise. The organisation of everyday life
has an impact on where and how students and teachers can discuss
issues with each other.

In the more informal activities (which are still planned), the teachers have a reason for being involved. Sometimes they also take part in
the leisure activities that the students plan for each other, but then
they no longer have such an obvious reason for being present. Lars
points out the opportunities arising in connection with the organisation of everyday life on the "Valuable Competencies" course. He
feels that this course gives the teachers different opportunities for
talking to the students. During my observations I noticed that on the
January course the students worked in project groups. This meant that
they worked with each other a great deal, thereby releasing the teachers from their more conventional teaching commitments. Instead, the
teachers assumed the role of project supervisors in relation to the
learning processes of the project groups and the individuals concerned. This meant that the teachers had more time to mix with the

9

students and join in with their group work without being required to fulfil their more traditional role. They were available to answer the students' questions not only about the project work, but also about any other thoughts that the students wished to discuss. Releasing the teachers from their traditional role may also mean a shift in focus: instead of communicating to a group they could focus on the learning processes, participation in the community and general interests of the individuals concerned. So the career guidance provided at the folk high school did not only depend on the form and community in which it is provided, as described by Kofod it was also influenced by the architecture of the school, the way in which everyday teaching and leisure were organised, the availability of the teachers, and the school's perception of career guidance.

9.4.2 Analytical perspectives – career guidance space at the folk high school

A study of the physical space in which career guidance takes place leads to consideration of the way in which this physical space influences the students' possibilities for participation. In interaction with the school's organisation of career guidance, the long corridors and the movement of teachers and students between classrooms, cafeteria and other rooms is significant. They produce greater possibilities for participation. The students can walk alongside the teachers to ask them questions, and the teachers can approach the students and follow up on questions regarding conversations they have had previously. Studying the possibilities for participation offered by physical spaces also makes it possible to consider the concrete availability of career guidance; it becomes clear that organising career guidance based on the office of a career guidance practitioner in another building must result in very different possibilities for participation. But as was pointed out by Peter in the section above on "Career guidance at the folk high school", the fact that career guidance can take place anywhere, any time and with anyone may make it difficult for the students to decide what career guidance is. This resembles the dilemma at the company, where a number of the employees did not

9

think that they had received any career guidance even though they had talked to Ulla. For both institutional arrangements, individual sessions were possible side by side with a form of organisation that interacted with everyday life. When career guidance practice is no longer recognised as such by the participants, it becomes part of everyday life without anyone noticing that this has happened. But when Peter explains that he does not think there is much career guidance, it may be necessary (in order to provide documentation) to identify the possibilities for participation in order to show that the school does in fact provide the level of career guidance required under Danish law. During one teachers' meeting, some of the teachers expressed concern as to whether or not they actually talked to all the students as they are required to do. They discussed whether they could start a special system of registration so they could be more certain that they were indeed in contact with all the students during the time spent at the school. The need to distinguish career guidance as a separate practice seems to be linked to the legal requirement for offering the students career guidance and describing this career guidance on the school's homepage. On the other hand, incorporating career guidance into the everyday life of the school provides entirely different possibilities for participation because the students can then ask spontaneous questions as they arise in connection with discussions during the teaching or when talking to the other students.

9.5 The importance of community

9

At the folk high school career guidance is far from being individual. The community is used and has a practical impact in particular ways. This section focuses on the perspectives of the students on the importance of community, and includes a teacher's perspective on the importance of community as well.

During the student interviews a number of the students described their own communities as important to their individual decision-making process. They emphasised the importance of these communities in relation to both their choice of further education and their awareness of their own competences. Their decision-making process was not limited to dialogues with the teachers, but occurred in all kinds of places in their community, and this was a process to which career guidance could contribute. In the statement below, Mads stresses that the students talk to each other a lot about their choices of further education.

MADS: You probably need to emphasise the social network you've built up a bit more, (Laughs) Just to use one of the fancy words we're learned here. You get loads of friends here who also want to study medicine. About half of our last group was interested in medicine. So you hear their thoughts and hopes, and you hear about what they're doing to get in. You talk it over and discuss it. If they've got any good ideas they let you know, and if you've got any you pass them on too. I think this is what really helps.

The questions he mentions that the students discuss can be characterised as thoughts which might also occur in a career guidance situation, such as: What are they doing to get in? What kind of thoughts and doubts have they had? What will they do if they don't get in? The next statement is by Tine, who refers to the possibility of expressing your uncertainty and distinguishes between the folk high school community and the community of her friends back home. She feels that expressing your uncertainty gets a positive response in the folk high school community.

RIE: Well … In what kind of situations do you get the chance to talk about it at the school?

TINE: We do it all the time (laughs).

RIE: (Laughs). You talk about it all the time?

TINE: We spend a lot of time on it during the lessons on our special subject. When you say something, ask a question, and then they ask you a specific thing like what if you did that when you finish your time at the school – so in one way we talk about it all the time. So we've had career guidance all the time – writing applications and what you're supposed to do. I didn't know whether I should apply this year or not. I talk-

ed it over with some of the other students and some of the
teachers. You can hear us talk about it even at breakfast. I think
it's great actually. There's a really relaxed atmosphere about it.
When we had to send in our applications you could tell that
people were a bit stressed and touchy, and there was nobody
in the school because everyone was on their computers. But
we can't do any more now, so we just have to wait, so we're
still all in the same boat in one way.

Tine attributes great importance to the community and to the fact
that she can ask the teachers and her fellow students questions. She
feels that dialogue with the others helps her and she goes in search of
them at breakfast time in order to air her thoughts about when to apply for further education. She emphasises that it is good to have such
a relaxed approach to the issue. For the individual student, the fact
that the community is included in this kind of dialogue about educational choices means that they can ask questions at any time, which
means that these questions become part of a discussion involving
a number of people. The fact that several people are involved in such
discussions means that each individual is in a situation very different
from that of a career guidance intervention with a career guidance
practitioner, to which nobody else can contribute. In such one-to-
one career guidance interventions the thoughts of each individual
will constantly be the focus for follow-up questions asked by the
practitioner, and the practitioner will start with the expectation or
hope that the discussion will lead to a decision or even action. Even
after the students have applied for further education they are still in
the same boat: they are still uncertain as to whether their applications
will be successful. The personal problem of choosing a course of further education partly becomes a shared problem. It is still a personal
problem, but the students are facing it together. By contrast with
Peter, who found it hard to say when career guidance was actually
going on and wanted the chance to defend his choices, Tine felt that
career guidance was available to her anywhere and any time, and she
liked the opportunity to express her uncertainty.

9

9.5.1 Creating cross-communities

The teachers at the folk high school are aware of the sense of community prevailing among the students. In the extracts below we switch to the perspective of the teachers with regard to the importance of community to career guidance. The quotation below is taken from an interview with the teacher responsible for career guidance at the folk high school. She has her own office and represents the school in a variety of contexts including the Study Choice Centre. She also takes part in supplementary training courses. In this quotation she underlines the importance of community: a wish that the students should use each other as a resource in their decision-making. Trine tries to encourage this by establishing links between the students. She includes both current and previous students of the school. In the first quotation she explains how the school works with career guidance:

TRINE: Career guidance is dealt with mostly in the special subjects that the students have chosen in preparation for further education, and in a subject called "Study Choices". We try to give them a sense of the subject they are thinking of studying; but we also try to give them some insight into the life of a student by contacting previous students of ours who are now studying various subjects. We've got a really good, broad group of previous students who are happy to give us some input. We have a database of these previous students who allow us to contact them by phone or email; and sometimes we can tell current students to contact them direct – they can then arrange to meet up at a café in town and talk things over. And the previous students might even offer to show them round their college or university.

Trine explains that career guidance is provided both in the special subjects the students have chosen and in a subject focusing specifically on study choices. She distinguishes between trying to give the students insight into the subject they want to study, and insight into the life of a student on the course they are considering. For Trine career guidance is closely connected to gaining concrete experience of specific subjects. It is not merely a question of giving information about subjects – she also wants the students to gain a real "sense" of the subject of their choice. But career guidance involves more than specific subjects. Trine also stresses that the students should gain insight into the life of a student at the specific college or university that they are considering – and this insight cannot be achieved by talking about it. She encourages the students to contact previous students of the folk high school and meet them at a café or college. In the quotation below, Trine explains why she encourages the students to meet previous students at colleges or universities.

RIE: Why is it a good idea for them to meet up with previous students?

TRINE: It's to give them the chance to ask all the questions that they can't ask a student counsellor.

RIE: What kind of questions are those?

TRINE: Questions about the study environment, what it's like to be a student at a particular college. One of the things I try to remember is that it's not enough for them to study the academic regulations of the courses they are considering – they also need to learn what it's actually like to be a student on these courses. So I tell them to walk into the lunch room at the Department of Law, for instance, and then try to sense whether they think the general atmosphere would suit them … do I belong here? Do I look like the rest of them – because this is what I will look like if I decide to study law. Obviously it's not quite that simple, but it does tell them something about whether they will feel at home here, and it's a good idea to actually have a chat with someone who is actually studying law and get a sense of what the course is like: what are the hard parts, what are the good bits, what kind of support will you be given if you get stuck? How do they organise their study groups? Do you find them yourself, or are they found for you? So they're prepared if they do decide to study law, for instance, so they know they will have to find their own study groups if that's how it's done.

9

RIE: How important is this knowledge in your view?

TRINE: ... I hope they get a broader all-round knowledge of the course they're considering. A wide range of research confirms that when people drop out of courses of further education, the reason is often nothing to do with the actual subject they are studying – there are all kinds of other reasons.

Trine encourages the current students to contact previous students so they can find out about a number of issues that are not mentioned in the academic regulations. She wants them to experience the environment and meet some of their potential fellow students; and she wants them to learn more about the way in which the courses of their choice are organised. What will they be responsible for themselves? For instance, will they need to form their own study groups, or will the department organise these groups for them? Trine does not attend these meetings between previous and current students, but she plays a vital role in ensuring that such meetings can take place. In this way Trine creates the conditions needed for interaction between different practices, and for the meeting between different people in their everyday lives. The fact that she creates these conditions reflects her belief that career guidance is a practice which interacts with other practices which may help young people to choose the right course of further education. In this case what is involved is a discussion based on the understanding that your physical presence in a particular location gives you more information (and different information) about this location than simply talking about it would do. Tangible entities are meaningful, the idea being that the decision-making process should be contextualised and situated.

Trine connects her perception of the decision-making process with one of the political goals of career guidance: reducing the drop-out rate from further education. She points out that studies show that people often drop out of further education for reasons not connected to the subject they are studying. So she limks her reasons for regarding tangible entities as meaningful to the political reasons for providing career guidance as an institutional arrangement. Trine's description of her task reflects her recognition of some of the limitations of

190

her career guidance practice: there are some questions that she does not expect the students to ask her, for instance, what it is actually like to study a particular course. In this respect her expectations match Peter's view that the teachers cannot answer questions about what it is like to study medicine. Based on this acknowledgement, she tries to make it possible for her students to ask this question elsewhere. It is Trine who develops and maintains a community involving both previous and current students at the folk high school. Many of the previous students are happy for the current students to contact them, and happy to tell them about the courses they are studying. Trine's efforts will only succeed if they have the support of both previous and current students. Both groups must be willing to participate, because otherwise the conditions on which this community depends cannot be maintained. In this way she contributes to a community of previous and current folk high school students by allowing their current or previous participation at the folk high school to form the basis for contact regarding choices of further education.

9.5.2 Abandoning privacy

Trine seeks to facilitate not only a community with previous students, but also a community among present students. Prior to the quotation below, we had just been talking about how the students are included in the planning of the teaching and other activities at the folk high school.

RIE: Are they (the students) also included in aspects of career guidance?

TRINE: ... Yes – in some ways. For instance, when they don't have the required grades and need to justify their applications in order to gain extra credits, we encourage them to consult each other instead of only using us. We're always happy to read their applications and give them some input about what they've written, but we want them to use each other too. And the same when they go for interviews – they talk about it a lot then ... And then there are the concrete aspects as well.

9

191

And I'm sure they talk a lot about what life's going to be like after their time here. This is sort of an abstract level: what am I going to do, and what will my life look like in 15 years' time? But it could be concrete things as well … for instance when they come and ask me about totally specific things, I tell them that I know some of the others have found out about them already and have already asked. So if they can't find a student counsellor at the college or university, they can always ask someone else who has already made inquiries.

In this way Trine includes the opportunities in the community that can support the students in the task of giving reasons for their choices and making up their minds about their academic futures. She tries to create links between the students. This will only work if the individuals concerned accept that they should indeed help each other (instead of regarding each other as competitors), and on the assumption that any questions already asked by individual students are regarded not as private issues but as issues of general concern. The issues are not individualised because Trine's efforts to connect the students raises them (and also her support for them) from the private, individualised sphere into the shared, communal sphere. But this also runs counter to the confidentiality stipulated in Ethical Standards – a dilemma which is discussed in section 10.3 ("Ethics and confidentiality"). For the students, the attraction of sharing their experiences with each other may be that the issues with which they are faced can then be turned into shared, communal issues. Sharing such issues means that individuals do not have to perceive themselves as weak and unable to handle their problems. Instead, they can see that the other students are also trying to handle similar problems. Sharing the issues confronting the students gives them access to each other's experiences, allowing them to hope that something that is possible for one person in certain conditions may also be possible for someone else in similar conditions.

9.5.3 Analytical perspectives – the importance of community

The students use each other as resources in relation to discussions and thoughts about their choices of further education and their experiences of submitting applications. The possibility of regarding each other as resources is supported by the practice of the career guidance practitioner or teachers, who encourage contact between students who are facing similar problems and thoughts. This results in such issues being raised from the individual and personal sphere into the general sphere, which in turn allows the students to perceive dilemmas from a shared perspective rather than potentially regarding themselves as particularly weak, difficult or confused.

From the perspective of the teachers, Trine seeks to use the community actively by creating connections between present and previous students. In this way she creates the conditions required to ensure that discussions between these students can take place. In order to create these conditions, career guidance questions must be regarded not as private but rather as shared, general questions facing a number of people – questions to which more than one person can therefore seek the answers. In addition, Trine must acknowledge the limitations of her career guidance practice and appreciate the potential benefits of cooperating with participants in other practices. Viewed against this background, it will be interesting to discuss the conditions of community in the form of ethical dilemmas relating to questions of whether similar conditions for possibilities for participation in communities can be created elsewhere. This will be discussed later in sections 10.2 and 10.3.

9

10 **Discussion**

This book explores the everyday lives of groups of participants at a Danish folk high school and company, as well as their encounter with career guidance in those settings. The analysis has shown that the participants in both settings live in and relate to communities, and that this has an influence on their actions, self-understanding and navigation through the possibilities offered by their lives and their options with regard to changing these possibilities. The discussion connects a participant perspective, which is given space in the empirical analysis, with the particular social history and changing issues of which career guidance is part.

10.1 **Career guidance from a participant perspective**

At the company it was difficult for Ulla to do her job as long as she tried to employ a form of organisation that was based on individual activities. Similarily, the career guidance practitioner at the folk high school, Trine, reported that the students rarely came looking for her in her office. This does not mean that the students at the folk high school and the employees at the company did not value the support that career guidance could offer them in connection with their thoughts about the situation in which they found themselves. However, it does mean that career guidance must interact with the everyday lives of both sets of participants in different ways. At the folk high school and company, where career guidance interacted with practice, the career guidance practitioner and the teachers did not exclude the possibility of participants having one-to-one sessions with a practitioner. However, my observations and interviews indicate that very few participants wanted their career guidance activities to be organised in this way. They rarely availed themselves of this opportunity. They were interested in one-to-one activities with a career guidance practitioner when they wanted concrete help in reading through their applications, entering their CVs into the Jobnet database and other tasks. The thoughts of each individual regarding educational and vocational opportunities seem to be of a general, shared nature rather than being private; it does not seem to be the case that individual sessions are regarded as being particularly important among the participants in the practices I have studied. However, perhaps such sessions are important in the sense that the empty career guidance offices reflect the fact that the participants reject the individualisation of educational and vocational issues and seek to cope with these issues in a more collective fashion instead. Career guidance can be seen as a way of coping with these issues, with the participants helping to change the nature of career guidance so that the coping strategy used matches the problem as they see it: a societal and collective problem rather than an individual one. This change in career guidance is also important in terms of the allocation of responsibility for the situation. Career guidance is not only reorganised; the responsibility for the situation is also allocated in new ways. When career guidance interacts with the places and community where it is practiced, the responsibility is allocated differently: the problem is dealt with through the community instead of by individuals in relation to their own attitudes and wishes.

10.2 Other people's experiences as a resource

For Tine the uncertainty and mistakes of the other students with regard to educational choices were a resource for the community as a whole. When the students share their different experiences, they gain shared insight into the reasons for and results of their decisions as well as their mistakes. This is information and insight which cannot necessarily be obtained anywhere else, since institutions of education only tend to report success stories regarding students who made the right choices. The reasons why a particular course of further education might be the wrong one for an individual to choose seem to be just as highly valued at the folk high school as the reasons

10

why it might be the right one. The analysis of the folk high school revealed that Tine regarded the experiences of her fellow students as resources. Career guidance as a collective phenomenon makes it possible to adopt a variety of participant positions, which help people to understand previous experiences of education and the interaction of education with everyday life in cases when the wrong decision had been made as a valuable form of insight. Mistaken decisions and changes of mind are turned into insight for the community instead of being simply mistakes made by the individual.

Krøjer and Hutters' critique of career guidance concerned the fact that responsibility or commitment is a central element in neo-liberal regulation, and that individual young people have become central actors in the political government and control of educational choices (Krøjer and Hutters, 2008). However, in the concrete practices in which career guidance takes place as a context for action at the folk high school and company studied here, and in which it seeks to gain a connection with the communities already in existence in these places, the situation with regard to responsibility looks a little different. At the folk high school and at the company, people are interested in each other and in the way other people cope with their situations. This interest in other people's choices and wellbeing means that problems are dealt with as a shared challenge. When problems are seen as a shared challenge, it is no longer the individual's responsibility that he is facing potential unemployment because he has failed to develop his own competences or lacked the motivation required to attend supplementary training courses, for instance. In the introduction to this book we considered the way in which Poul gave Flemming various suggestions for jobs which he thought might be relevant for him. The analysis of material from the folk high school also indicated that the students accepted the idea of sharing any knowledge gained when one of them called a student counsellor to find the answer to some of the questions which they were all facing. When career guidance interacts with existing communities, the free choice which is the individual's responsibility may be institutionalised to a lesser extent. Career guidance in interaction with communities should be seen as connected to a shared situation, the goal being to connect people and their experiences, problems and wishes with the links these problems and wishes have to societal conditions.

10

196

10.3 **Ethics and confidentiality**

However, when career guidance takes place in interaction with the everyday life of communities, this has an influence on on career guidance practitioners consideration of ethics and confidentiality. The analysis shows that the employees of the company help to change career guidance from an individual practice into a communal practice, and that this transition can be seen as the opposite of individualising societal problems through career guidance. The analysis also shows that the efforts of the school career guidance practitioner (Trine) to maintain contact between the students raise the issues (and thereby also the support provided for them) from the private, individual sphere into the shared, common sphere. Trine's efforts can be understood in the light of various ways of perceiving problems. The idea that problems are individual and (for instance) existential may result in a particular form of organisation focusing on the way each individual makes decisions in relation to their own values, whereas the idea that problems are social in nature results in a form of organisation that provides opportunities for joining forces to explore a variety of positions in relation to such problems.

These changes are important in a discussion of perceptions of confidentiality, trust and ethics. In my discussions with career guidance practitioners regarding the analysis contained in this book, trust, confidentiality and ethics were a focal point in terms of the limitations on the practice of career guidance in communities.[19] Some practitioners expressed scepticism as to whether people would talk about their problems if several other people were present, and they were also sceptical as to whether practitioners could arrange for people with similar problems to contact each other without this being regarded as a breach of the confidentiality and trust which individuals had shown them. In these discussions with practitioners, confidentiality seemed to be linked to understanding problems as private and thus to the idea that solutions are confidential and should only involve the practitioner and the participant. The conditions required to achieve confidentiality seem to be linked to the fact that individuals can talk to practitioners alone, and that the information discussed is not communicated to anybody else.

10

The perception of these practitioners with regard to the conditions required for confidentiality makes career guidance resemble therapy in some respects. This is not an unknown phenomenon within career guidance research. Lovén (1995) shows how career guidance can be placed between psychotherapy and teaching/information, his aim being to demonstrate that career guidance is not therapy.

Psychotherapy	Career guidance	Teaching/information

Figure 6. Therapy and career guidance (Lovén, 1995, p. 63).

Lovén emphasises that the objectives of career guidance and therapy are different, pointing out that whereas the main goal of therapy is to change the way people perceive themselves, the objective of career guidance is to assist people to find employment in the best possible way (Lovén, 1995, p. 65). He stresses the societal goal of career guid-ance practice with a view to distinguishing career guidance from ther-apy. His discus-sion should be seen as an attempt to problematise methods of career guidance that focus on life stories or living space (Peavy, 2004 is one example of a method that focuses on descriptions of living space). In other words, Lovén points out that the aim of ca-reer guidance is to influence the lives of participants in a particular direction, and he criticises career guidance for tending towards ther-apy when it loses sight of this direction. When career guidance is con-ceptualised as an institutional arrangement, it becomes possible to include the direction in which this arrangement is intended to influ-ence the participants. Dreier writes that the aim of institutional ar-rangements is to give a particular direction to the lives of participants (Dreier, 2008). It is this sense of direction that distinguishes career guidance from therapy.

In my discussions with career guidance practitioners, it was impor-tant for them to emphasise that there may be things that individuals wish to talk to a practitioner about in confidence. So this option needs to be available, and thus far I am happy to agree: practitioners cannot know in advance how the thoughts of individuals regarding educa-tional or vocational choices are connected to other aspects of their lives. But nor can practitioners know in advance whether individuals perceive these connections as private or problematic. The analysis contained in this book supports the idea that differences of perception regarding the focus of career guidance lead to different forms of organisation and consequently different perceptions of usefulness and relevance. As I have demonstrated previously, the way in which problems are experienced is also linked to the way in which career guidance is organised, with individual sessions being criticised for supporting a sense of frustration, stress and powerlessness (Krøjer & Hutters, 2008; Usher, 2005). It is worth pointing out that the extreme poles may also reflect extremes in relation to the organisation of career guidance as a primarily individual or collective experience; psychotherapy is generally practised individually, and teaching/information often involves a number of participants at the same time.

Lovén describes the interests of society in career guidance as a potential problem for practitioners in relation to the creation of trust in their practice (Lovén, 1995). An attempt is made to solve this dilemma in various ways in ethical standards, one of the aims of which is to ensure that individuals can place trust in the career guidance process. One solution indicated by these ethical standards involves the practitioner explaining that career guidance practice is embedded in the interests of society. Another solution proposed is that the practitioner should not allow the interests of society to influence the career guidance process, but should solely protect the interests of the individual. Both proposals stand side by side in the international and Danish ethical standards for career guidance (FUE, 2006; IAEVG, 1995). The argument presented in this book is that when career guidance is conceptualised as an institutional arrangement, the distinction between the interests of society and those of the individual can be transcended because career guidance always corresponds with the political reasons on which institutional arrangements are based. But this transcendence also indicates that there is a need for new ethical standpoints because this understanding makes it impossible for practitioners to prevent the interests of society from having an influence on their practice. These interests are always present anyway, and are never solely represented by the individual participants.

10

199

In the light of this point, it is interesting to focus on the way in which practitioners perceive the interests of society in relation to their practice. Gunnel Lindh's doctoral dissertation explores career guidance interviews with 9th-grade students. The objective of this study was to gain greater understanding of what happens in such interviews, and the dilemma of the interests that are involved also seems to play a role here. Among other things, Lindh concludes that career guidance practitioners face a difficult problem in trying to balance the needs of society with those of the individual (Lindh, 2000, p. 305). Lindh's research also demonstrates that individual interviews are dominated by practitioners in various ways, and that these practitioners do find it difficult to balance the needs of society and the individual (Lindh, 2000). When the basic problem is divided into two different interests which are perceived as being in conflict with each other, and when there are also two participants in an individual session, it is easy to attribute one of the two interests to each participant. The practitioner is regarded as the person protecting the interests of society, and the participant as the person protecting their own interests. In this division the interests of the individual and society are distinguished from each other. In contrast with this view, the individual can also be regarded as embedded in society as a participant in a social and communal process involving the conduct of life (Holzkamp, 1989). This is the perception on which this book is based: the interests involved change and are subject to influence, as well as being inseparable. In this view, the interests of society are always present in career guidance, but not in either of the participants concerned.

When career guidance is practised in interaction with communities, a number of participants are involved – making it more likely that fellow students at the folk high school or colleagues at the company will see the situation from my perspective. People are aware that their friends or colleagues know them through different relationships and in different contexts, and these fellow students and colleagues may also know how they conduct their lives and how they spend their leisure time outside the company or folk high school. The practitioner has to navigate through a field of interests that is connected to career guidance as an institutional arrangement with all the objectives

10

and interests of society on which the state funding of career guidance is based. The feedback that people receive from their colleagues regarding the reactions and recommendations they receive from practitioners may add perspective to these recommendations. And in this way career guidance in communities may help to change the traditional perception of career guidance as being a bipolar affair involving a conflict of interests. Practising career guidance in a community can therefore be seen as a strength in relation to the ethics of career guidance and trust in career guidance practitioners.

It is worth pointing out that in his study of group guidance at Danish job centres, Bauer concludes that participants in group guidance had a more positive impression of these job centres than participants in individual guidance (Bauer, 1984). At the same time, it must be emphasised that the awareness of practitioners and participants regarding the embedded nature of institutional guidance is not necessarily a way to break existing power structures, in which a bipolar perception helps to individualise the responsibility for the problems of society. According to Osterkamp, the challenge lies in understanding the social/communicative nature of personal attitudes. Osterkamp points out that the failure to comprehend the social/communicative nature of personal attitudes such as discipline, commitment and trust means that however hard we try to overcome the contrast between individual and society, we will automatically resort to a dualistic form of thinking – thereby confirming the confusion of cause and effect of suppression that is a central aspect of the ideological assurance of existing power relations, instead of conquering it (Osterkamp, 2000, p. 19).

The confusion of cause and effect can be explained as follows: when practitioners interpret personal problems as a private matter, they are helping to conceal the connection between these problems and social contexts – from both the participant and themselves. In the analysis above it was clear that the feeling of a lack of competence with regard to producing a CV arose as an interaction between being fired, a change in conditions and the company's demand that a CV had to be produced. It was only then that the employees discover problems to do with actually writing their CVs on a computer and describing and documenting their competences. The initial cause of the problem facing the employees was that they had been made re-

10

dundant, but the suppressive effect arose when they were placed in a position of deficit owing to their lack of specific competences.

In relation to the issues of confidentiality, ethics and trust, the practice of career guidance seems to face several difficulties. These difficulties can be associated with the expectation that confidentiality and trust depend on the way career guidance is organised, which I have discussed above. It is important to emphasise that abandoning individualisation is not only a question of organisation but also one of content. What should the goal of establishing specific career guidance practices be? Like therapy (see Dreier, 2002; Højholt, 1999), career guidance can target either individuals, own life competences, or conditions and societal problems. This book argues that *career guidance should target the dialectical relationship between the individual and societal conditions and possibilities.*

The empirical evidence contained in this book indicates that previous career guidance at the company regarding possibilities for attending courses of supplementary training had targeted the individual by focusing on the concept of their motivation for attending such courses.

10.4 **Motivation and realism**

Before the company fired its employees, it tried to motivate them to take part in supplementary training courses. The analysis above shows that their motivation to participate was linked to far more concrete conditions for participation – so it could not be encouraged in each individual, but had to involve changes in these concrete conditions instead. Seen in this light, it was perhaps not completely mistaken of 13 Centres for Adult Education and Continuing Training (see The Danish Agency for Universities and Internationalisation, 2012) to focus on the company as the primary target instead of individual employees. The situation of the folk high school students was different. Most of the young people had chosen to study at the school because they felt it might improve their chances of being admitted to their chosen courses of further education. They were highly motivated with regard to starting emphasise courses – but they also had

10

to prepare themselves for the possibility that they might be rejected. They felt that they were expected to start further education after their time at folk high school, and it therefore seems that their expectations and those of the politicians and business community in terms of further education were divided by nothing more than a few credits. This situation arises because the education system wants more applicants on the one hand, but functions as a grading system in relation to privileges in society on the other (Mathiesen, 2000). As a result, no matter how highly motivated they are, some of the young people will be rejected. In order to provide a legitimate reason for this rejection, the suitability of young people for admission to courses of further education is normally determined on the basis of the subjects studied and grades achieved at upper-secondary school – instead of being based concretely on the likelihood that they will be motivated to complete the courses they choose. The likelihood of completion is understood in essential terms, individually and statically – not in relation to social practice. Seen in this light, it does not make any sense to work on the motivation of these particular people to participate in further education, because they are already highly motivated to do so. On the other hand, other forms of encouragement may be relevant: encouraging young people to be realistic in their choices, or encouraging some of them to lower their expectations and find a course for which the grades they have achieved at upper-secondary school are sufficient.

In her dissertation Lindh introduces the concept of "adapting to reality", which she defines as the information provided by the practitioner which does not match what the young persons deems to be realistic or necessary (Lindh, 2000, p. 306). According to Lindh, the goal of information that is adapted to reality is to encourage young people to apply for several courses of further education at the same time, enabling practitioners to cater for the needs of both the individual and society. The young people still make their own choices based on their own interests, but practitioners increase the likelihood that they will be admitted and that they will actually start studying, thereby helping to reduce the admission costs defrayed by society (Lindh, 2000). Lindh uses the concept of adapting to reality to criticise the way in which practitioners deal with the targeted nature of career guidance (pushing individuals in the direction of education

10

or employment). This criticism should be seen in the light of Lindh's limits to career guidance: she denounces career guidance whose purpose is to find people for specific positions (Lindh, 2000). Her point is that career guidance can be carried out on the terms of the individual alone – but in saying this she fails to consider that career guidance is an institutional arrangement designed to deal with specific challenges facing the education system and labour market. She seems to offer career guidance practitioners a position in which the interests of the individuals are the sole concern. But this book argues that the wish for such a position is a result of the dualistic presentation of the basic dilemma of career guidance – and is therefore only a theoretical possibility as long as the dualistic understanding of this basic dilemma is maintained.

The strength of considering two different study settings becomes evident in relation to this discussion: it is clear that adults and young people require different career guidance in terms of content. Realism is not a concrete theme for the employees at the company, and motivation to participate in further education is not a theme for the young people at the folk high school. These ways of understanding the task of career guidance must therefore be seen in interaction with the conditions in which career guidance has to function. The fact that career guidance needs to focus on individual motivation or realism is an answer to the changing historical problems and challenges connected to the use of the education system as a grading mechanism; it is also an answer to the difficulties of predicting society's need for a labour force in the future. Motivation and realism turn structural challenges in the education system and labour market into career guidance questions by relocating these challenges in the individual. This means that through career guidance individuals are encouraged to work on themselves and their own understandings of their situation, instead of working together on structural problems in relation to the admissions system, education policy or labour market development, for instance.

10

10.5 Understanding wishes as an "internal" affair

The analysis shows that the motivation of the company employees to participate in supplementary training courses did not change as the result of discussions with a career guidance practitioner, or as the result of society's discourses regarding the benefits of lifelong learning. The possibilities for participation in and the relevance of training courses seem to be tied to the concrete conditions, which changed when the employees were fired. This change in concrete conditions also results in a change in the way the employees understand their own participation in training activities. When people's actions are based on the meaning that each individual attributes to social structures and conditions, the reasons given by each individual change in interaction with changes in structures and conditions. Societal changes take place all the time, so the same thing is true of people's views of themselves and their own possibilities. Human development is linked to historical development because people are in a continuous, dialectical relationship with their surroundings and will therefore perceive new needs and wishes with regard to their participation in society alongside other people (Holzkamp, 1989).

The analysis represented in this book shows that folk high school students connect their decision-making process to participation in concrete activities such as visits to institutions of education or meetings with current university/college students. This gives us the opportunity to challenge career guidance theories and methods which understand and deal with participants' wishes as internal wishes which must be identified or tackled to form the basis of future choices. If choices are understood in the light of dialectical materialism, wishes are created by participation in practices. In other words, my participation and my perception of myself in this participation have an influence on my wishes for the future. But these are not internal wishes because they are connected to the idea of "wishing something for the future". They are connected to the possibilities I experience and to my understanding of what are possible and acceptable "wishes for the future". Each time I participate in something with other

10

people, we jointly produce and reproduce our shared understanding of wishes, needs and possibilities.

In contrast with the idea of individuals "discovering their inner wishes", there is the idea of finding a way to participate. These two different ways of understanding decision-making may result in different ways of organising career guidance practice. The notion that wishes are internal may result in career guidance practitioners creating opportunities for individuals to 'look inside themselves' and reflect on their values to try to find out which choices would match these values. The idea that wishes are created through participation focuses on the fact that career guidance practitioners create opportunities for people to participate in various practices with a view to studying their possibilities for participation. For instance, at the folk high school and the employees at the company were encouraged to visit institutions of education and workplaces, respectively.

Other studies also indicate the importance of participation. For instance, one Youth Guidance Centre in Aalborg has studied the importance of bridge-building activities. As pointed out by the Danish Minister for Education Bertel Haarder (Haarder, 2008, p.4), in Aalborg the effect of bridge-building activities on the choices of further education by young people is evident: the systematic evaluation of career guidance activities including bridge-building shows that 1/3 of the students involved changed their educational wishes after participating in bridge-building activities. In other words, career guidance practice is not unaccustomed to working with various forms of organisation involving concrete participation – although there has been little development of methods for this compared with the development of methods for individual sessions.

10

10.6 Making career guidance relevant

The analysis underlines that participation in career guidance is only one of many contexts for thoughts about education and work and that these thought are not reserved for the context of guidance solely. One folk high school student described precisely her wish that the career guidance practitioner should give her feedback about what he thought would be a good choice for her. He, on the other hand, underlined that the student had to work this out for herself. She said that she only regarded his opinion as one of many. The reluctance of the practitioner to say what he thought may reflect the fact that he felt his opinion might determine and control the student's choice. However, this was not the case. The analysis shows that the student also participates in other contexts, is also influenced by other people.

The analysis gives good reason to emphasise that the participants do not regard career guidance as omnipotent in relation to the choices they make, and that they do not all regard career guidance as being equally important in solving the problems they face. As Frans at the company said: "Just give us a job! We don't need career guidance, we need a job". The analysis shows that career guidance is sometimes regarded as one of a number of annoying stages that actually seem to prevent the individual from getting a job (job centres and electronic applications on the internet being two more of these stages). The example from the empirical evidence presented here shows that some of the employees at the company regarded career guidance as superfluous to their needs. What they needed was to find a new job, to have some help in finding a new job, or to have someone else find a new job for them. Career guidance was not perceived as unconditionally good, attractive or relevant. The analysis shows that some people made objections to career guidance and to participating in it. Career guidance practitioners cannot simply assume that all participants will necessarily think that they need career guidance. It is therefore not possible for practitioners to decide in advance who needs what. But the analysis also shows that thanks to some movement in relation to the resistance which practice encountered in the company, career

10

guidance can interact with the everyday life of the company and become a practice which is perceived by the participants as relevant and useful. There may be good reason to offer career guidance in many different forms, thereby making a variety of participant positions possible. At the same time, career guidance can also be changed in response to the kind of resistance it may encounter among company employees in particular – a resistance based on the idea that career guidance will not solve their problem.

When career guidance takes place in a community, the analysis shows that it can be made relevant by focusing on concrete dilemmas in the practice in question. At the company a lack of experience in writing a CV was perceived as a concrete and practical problem, and the employees appreciated any help given with a view to solving this problem. The lack of competences that were needed to write a CV was a problem that the employees experienced in a concrete situation – but it was also a problem that they had not created themselves which only arose because the career guidance process demanded that they should write a CV. So career guidance was part of the problem as well as being part of the solution. Career guidance made special demands on the employees in terms of their participation in society: they were expected to find a new job. The solution was to use career guidance as an activity to help them identify their competences, apply for jobs and enter their CVs on the Jobnet database, thereby equipping them to solve their problem themselves and take responsibility for it as well. The work involved in producing a CV can therefore be criticised for turning a societal problem (collective dismissals owing to changes in the demand for unskilled labour) into an individual problem (the lack or absence of qualifications and competences).

The analysis shows that working with various documents in career guidance has an influence on whether or not career guidance is perceived as relevant – but it also has an influence on the concrete possibilities for participation of the individual. The work involved in giving reasons for their applications among some of the folk high school students has an influence on the kind of thoughts they have about their futures. These are the students whose grades are not sufficient to grant them access to their chosen course of further educa-

10

tion. Peter did not face this demand because his grades were sufficient in themselves without requiring him to justify his choice. This leads Peter to look for career guidance that does challenge his choice. So the students have to deal with different conditions, which is why their views on the value of certain career guidance activities differ. But these different conditions also mean that their possibilities for participation differ. Working with various documents plays a role in relation to the possibilities for participation available to each individual, it is therefore possible to acquire knowledge about potential possibilities for participation in career guidance practices by studying the documents that are used. This is an analysis strategy that is also used in institutional ethnography, and it is based on the assumption that analysing documents that are used in a social practice generates knowledge of how this practice is mediated by "relations of ruling", a term which means that texts mediate what is said and done in practice (see Devault & McCoy, 2006, p. 35). The work involved in producing a CV at the company and the work involved in justifying choices of further education at the folk high school can also be discussed as relations of ruling. At first sight the two documents involved are very different, but they are connected to the same task: influencing and giving a direction to people's paths to the labour market. The analysis here indicates that future research into career guidance might find it interesting to focus on the documents that participants in various career guidance practices encounter. The task of producing a CV made the employees at the company aware of the fact that they lacked the competences required to do this, and the fact that the CVs had to be uploaded to the net made them realise that they also lacked computer skills. The production of a CV led to a focus on other problems as well, problems linked to the tools used by the career guidance practitioner. This shows that the documents used are not just "harmless". They have a role to play as co-creators of both self-understanding and possibilities for participation.

10

10.7 **The importance of place**

The analysis shows the importance of place when career guidance takes place in communities. Career guidance cannot be expected to take place in the same way in all possible places. The place in which it is practised and the people who are already participants at this place have an influence on practice. This draws our attention to the importance of place in relation to analysing possibilities for participation in interaction with the practice of career guidance in a concrete place.

The place in which career guidance is practised also has an influence on the way participants perceive career guidance. The analysis of the career guidance corner at the company showed that the participants had a hand in moving this corner and creating a career guidance wall in the lunch room instead, which can be analysed as a movement from the private and personal sphere to the shared, collective sphere – and thus towards a form of career guidance which the employees perceived as more relevant and useful. This movement of practice was only possible because the career guidance practitioner allowed her career guidance to take place in a situated fashion and in interaction with the participants and the physical surroundings. She could have stuck with her original form of organisation and stayed in the office which she had been allocated originally – and if she had done this it is highly probable that very little career guidance would have occurred. This indicates that if career guidance practice fails to work, it might be important to consider the importance of place in connection with didactic considerations concerning the way career guidance is organised. Career guidance space at the folk high school seems to be quite unique simply because the availability of teachers (and remember that career guidance is a shared reponsibility between all teachers) gives students an opportunity to ask questions whilst engaging in various activities during their daily routine at school. Teachers' availability is also connected to the way in which career guidance is designed didactically. This is important because the students do not need to consider whether the questions they want to ask are career guidance questions, or whether their questions are im-

10

210

portant enough to justify asking for a more formal interview. It also means that the career guidance practised by the teachers can interact with the everyday lives of the students and their current thoughts about their educational choices and futures.

11 Conclusion

The aim of this book is to contribute knowledge about how we can understand the meaning of career guidance from a participant perspective, based on a study of two different institutional arrangements for career guidance.

The conclusion is divided into three parts. The first section summarises the points made in the book in relation to career guidance as a collective phenomenon. The second section presents a discussion of whether career guidance can be conceptualised as a governing technology.The third section presents proposals for developing practice based on the points made in book, including some ideas about the significance of community in relation to possibilities for participation. The conclusion ends with a proposal for a reinterpretation of the basic purpose of career guidance.

11.1 Career guidance as a collective phenomenon

The study on which this book is based provides insight into the significance of our understanding of what career guidance should seek to achieve. The empirical material indicates that the participants move career guidance from the private towards the public sphere, from being organised in the form of individual sessions towards being organised more collectively; and that the collective forms of organisation interact with the concrete places, communities and participants to open a path leading to new possibilities for participation. The study also demonstrates that the place in which career guidance is practised and the documents that are used in a career guidance context contribute towards the creation of the conditions of practice and of the problems on which the participants focus. The documents that

11

are used in practice may help to shift the focus of the problem – for instance the focus can be placed on a lack of competences and computer skills instead of on unemployment. The book also discusses the significance of the career guidance practitioner's understanding of ethics and confidentiality to the organisation of career guidance, and indicates that this understanding is also connected to the perception of what career guidance should seek to achieve. If decision-making is regarded as an "internal" process, career guidance must create opportunities for individuals to reflect on their own wishes and express what they want; whereas if decision-making is understood as being created through participation, career guidance should perhaps be organised in the form of concrete participation in various educational and vocational contexts with a view to reaching decisions via such participation. Seen in the light of my efforts to work dialectically, the answer is probably not either/or but both/and.

When career guidance is studied from a participant perspective, its partiality becomes clear. This raises the question of how it can become a relevant context for participation in the lives of individuals, since the experience of relevance has an influence on whether and how participants participate in career guidance. The results presented here indicate that career guidance practitioners, researchers and politicians cannot assume that career guidance will be perceived as relevant and useful by everyone; but they also indicate that career guidance may be relevant if it provides a context for action in which participants can join forces with career guidance practitioners to analyse and create opportunities to find their way in a situation calling for particular thoughts and choices in relation to their future educational or vocational participation in society. Career guidance has the potential to be a context for action in which people can join forces to deal with problems and the conditions associated with these problems.

When career guidance is conceptualised as an institutional arrangement, it can be identified as an answer to the structural challenges (both historical and social) which our society is currently facing. In concrete practices these challenges relate to the composition of the workforce and the way in which companies handle redundancies in a manner which ensures that the individuals being fired are not left feeling that they are responsible for a situation which was beyond their

11

control from the outset. Career guidance is just one way of meeting these challenges in a social context. It is one of several societal solutions, which it why it is important to view career guidance in interaction with other measures designed to address the same problems.

Career guidance also has a limited influence on the way the participants conduct their lives. It is one of many contexts for action, so it is not omnipotent with regard to persuading individuals to take particular actions. If we want to understand the task of career guidance, we need to explore its interaction with the conditions under which it functions. These conditions, under which individuals make their choices, also reveal that various choices are only *possibilities* for action and not *necessary* actions for the individual. In this light it makes little sense to conceptualise career guidance as a governing technology – in fact such a conceptualisation may even help to support the idea that career guidance is omnipotent, a discussion which is rounded off in section 11.2. Career guidance is not a goal in itself, but a means to achieve something concrete: educational or vocational participation in society. When career guidance is limited to the competences needed to apply for jobs or the idea of helping participants to help themselves, the focus is removed from concrete problems which practitioners and participants can help each other to solve; and the goal of helping yourself becomes the goal of career guidance in itself. The question of whether something is a possibility or a necessity depends on the perspective from which it is perceived with regard to the way individuals conduct their lives. For instance, some of the employees at the company needed to find a job, others regarded finding a job as only one of several possibilities for the future, while yet others saw retirement as an option.

11.2 Career guidance understood as a governing technology

The analysis shows that the participants seek to change the career guidance that is offered to them. In the concrete interaction in practice and between practices, the analysis shows that the participants did not merely accept career guidance as a governing technology; they did not do what they were expected to do. For instance, they did not turn up for individual interviews. They also stressed that they had not participated in career guidance. They said that they did not need it, and in various ways they dealt with the individualisation and shifting of responsibility which career guidance on a governing technology basis is criticised for accentuating to. All the options for reshaping and tackling career guidance in concrete interaction mean that it seems reductionist to conceptualise career guidance as a governing technology, and that this conceptualisation could be seen as a result of the study method that has been used. Power according to Foucault "… seems to be historically specific but contextually unspecific. It is an apochal theory of power. Governing through the conduct of autonomous individuals is a general logic of power that is all over and nowhere in particular in neoliberal societies" (Dreier, 2008, p. 28). In extension of this point, Dreier also argues in favour of a more contextual understanding of power which acknowledges that power and influence must be characterised differently in different social contexts (Dreier, 2008). If an analysis is only interested in career guidance in the sense of something that happens in only one context, for instance in a room designed for the purpose, or something that is described in official documents and descriptions of method (see for instance Otto, 2001; Usher, 2005), and is not interested in what happens to career guidance subsequently, it is tempting to assume that individuals will do what is suggested by the career guidance they are given. But the decentred analysis presented in this book demonstrates that this is not the case; we have seen that career guidance comes into existence through participation and is created by the participants jointly in concrete practices.

11.3 Opportunities for the development of practice and further research

In extension of the theoretical and methodological inspiration from practice research presented here, my ambition is that this book should also provide some opportunities for the development of practice. This process has already been launched thanks to the co-researchers who have contributed to the book along the way, and since research is not an omnipotent practice in relation to other practices either, this section simply presents a number of opportunities for developing practice as I see them. These opportunities are divided into two themes: organisation and method, and the significance of communities.

11.3.1 Organisation and method

The discussion and conclusion of this book do not evaluate specific career guidance methods. Instead, two opportunities are presented that appear when career guidance is regarded as being in interaction with everyday life in concrete practices. When career guidance looks for interaction, this may provide a reason for testing various methodological possibilities ranging from individual career guidance interviews to group career guidance and career guidance walls, and to storytelling workshops. None of these methods in itself can be said to support the organisation of career guidance in interaction with communities, the goal of which should be that the participants connect their problems to the conditions shaped by society. For instance, group career guidance can easily be practised in isolation from everyday life, without the need for career guidance practitioners to create opportunities for the participants to explore together the collective and social conditions to which they feel these problems are connected (see for instance Bauer, 1984, 1985; Borgen, 1988). If practitioners want to use collective career guidance with a view to creating awareness of social conditions, the method known as "storytelling workshops" seems suitable; this is its emancipatory goal (Krøjer & Hutters, 2006, 2008). However, I should like to emphasise that the empirical evidence shows that any organisation which cooperates with the community (the career guidance wall and the career guidance space at the folk high school, for instance) has the chance to let participants know that they are not alone – there are others with similar thoughts and experiences. This is seen as a relief, a positive state that can generate practical knowledge.

The results presented here also indicate that the decision-making process involves practical participation, which is why the task of the

11

career guidance practitioner must include arranging possibilities for participation. This conclusion is supported by a Danish study entitled *Unges veje mod ungdomsuddannelserne* ("The paths of young people towards youth education programmes"), which concludes that young people attach particular importance to participation in placement activities with a view to finding out what such programmes actually feel like (Katznelson & Pless, 2007, p. 104). It would be interesting if future research could discover whether the same thing is true of adult decision-making processes with regard to supplementary training courses and job changes, as indicated by the findings presented in this book.

11.3.2 Possibilities when participating in a community

The analysis of the everyday lives of the participants shows that when career guidance is practised in communities it does have an influence on the possibilities for participation that it offers. When career guidance takes place next to the career guidance wall in the lunch room at the company or in the folk high school hallways, it differs from individual sessions with only two participants in that it can provide different possibilities for participation.

These include possibilities to:

- Listen
- Hear and see the answers given to other people
- Get ideas for your own questions
- Other people offering concrete solutions or problems in relation to the questions you ask
- Other people adding perspectives to your perception of the situation based on their own experiences
- Refer to each other based on the questions and dialogues you have heard
- Discuss previous questions and dialogues with others who have also heard what has been said
- Gain new understanding of obstacles and your options in maneuvering around them

11

Opportunities for developing practice may involve organising projects aimed at developing knowledge about the importance of making these opportunities available and gaining experience of how they might work. At the moment there is no overall description or systematic analysis of Danish development projects and experiences of group career guidance, and other collective forms of organisation in connection with career guidance. Bauer's study of group career guidance at Danish job centres indicates that the participants preferred group career guidance to individual career guidance (Bauer, 1984, p. 64), while UNI-C's study of upper-secondary school students and their use of career guidance indicates that 88% of the respondents knew about the possibility of individual career guidance, but that only 34% of them had used it (UNI-C, 2008). This may reveal that this is not a form of career guidance that most people deem to be attractive and relevant. Internationally speaking it would be useful to carry out comparative analyses of group/individual career guidance, for instance, one hypothesis being that group career guidance provides the best results in relation to both the use of resources and its effect (Brown & Krane, 2000).

A company called Rambøll has carried out a financial analysis for the Danish Education Committee of educational and vocational guidance in the education sector. Their recommendations were: define your target groups clearly; distinguish between transitional guidance and study-completion guidance; define your career guidance tools; differentiate your efforts; use the internet more; and use the experiences and knowledge of the participants more (Rambøll, 2008, p. 8). To summarise, it seems true to say that these recommendations propose that the resources invested should be targeted more precisely, and that the problems of particular groups in relation to the education system should be dealt with more carefully. These are problems which may very well be linked to structural conditions in the education system (a paucity or total lack of possibilities in this system). If these recommendations are followed, the result might be that career guidance will continue to contribute to the individualisation of problems which could be solved better by remembering that problems are not just problems for individuals – they are connected to structural conditions which also need to be addressed and changed.

11

218

However, the report by Rambøll also supports an increase in the inclusion of the experiences and knowledge of participants. This book proposes that if the resources of a community are utilised in interaction with the resources of career guidance, then career guidance is more likely to be perceived as useful and relevant by the participants in the community in question.

11.4 Reinterpreting career guidance objectives

This book demonstrates that the politicians in Denmark expect career guidance to take place with due regard for the needs and interests of the individual and society, and this has been conceptualised as "the basic dilemma of career guidance". This basic dilemma arises a division into societal and individual interests which makes it easy to attribute particular interests to one of the participants involved. The career guidance practitioner is typically seen as the person protecting the interests of society, while individuals protect their own interests. An alternative to this division is based on a dialectical understanding of the interests of individuals and society in which these interests are inseparable, changing and subject to influence. According to Lave (2011), a binary division makes it possible to separate particular groups and regard them as having particular or extended needs for career guidance, for instance, because it is implicit in the binary division into societal and individual interests that some choices are in accordance with both individual and societal interests, and that some choices are not. This approach helps to legitimise the segregation of anyone who makes choices that are not in accordance with the interests of society. Such individuals are regarded as needing more, better or different forms of career guidance so that they can make choices that are in accordance with the needs of society/the labour market as well as their own. This distinction is particularly evident in relation to young people who risk not getting any form of further education or training. This group is described as being in special need of career guidance. The distinction is also relevant for folk high school students, who have not yet chosen a course of further education, and who are therefore entitled to career guidance under Danish law. It is relevant for the un-

11

employed, who need to make new choices and who can be helped by career guidance to re-enter the labour market. And it is relevant for people with little or no further training, a group which is also categorised as being in special need of career guidance efforts to increase their motivation to participate in training courses and to remove any barriers preventing them from doing so. The distinction has a concrete significance for both the folk high school students and the company employees studied here because they all encounter career guidance. Career guidance presents them with special expectations regarding their participation in society, and it gives them responsibility for complying with the needs of society. However, the needs of society are difficult to predict (Sultana 2011), which is why it must be assumed that career guidance practitioners provide career guidance to match the society they know and the needs with which they are presented by various players. There is therefore a danger that this binary division contributes to the creation of a stagnant society rather than one under development, as discussed in chapter 3.

Chapter 4 pointed out that these dualisms help to produce a form of rhetoric that justifies the stigmatisation and marginalisation of social problems rather than criticising political suppression. The goal of reinterpreting the purpose of career guidance is to indicate a potential space in which career guidance and career guidance practitioners can manoeuvre with a view to connecting the problems of the individual with relevant structural conditions, and to identify opportunities for, as well as the need to support, any changes in restrictive structures (the education system, for instance). A study of career guidance in the Danish city of Roskilde gives us a glimpse of the kind of frustration experienced by career guidance practitioners in relation to social conditions when they are forced to point out that there are no educational possibilities for young people who are unable to complete any of the youth education schemes on offer (Katznelson, 2004). When the knowledge of career guidance practitioners is not used to create structural changes, there is a risk that career guidance will instead help to support systems that actually increase drop-out rates and exclusion. Other researchers have pointed out that career guidance practitioners have a special opportunity to exploit their encounter with participants (both individuals and groups) with a view to giving critical feedback at the structural level (cf. Mignot, 2000). This is also addressed by the academic network Network for Innovation in Career Guidance & Counselling in Europe (NICE), and conceptualised as one of six core competences under the heading "social system interventions".

On the basis of this conceptualisation the purpose of career guidance is reinterpreted as follows: career guidance can function as a framework for exploring and creating new possibilities in connection with transitional situations. The knowledge contributed by this book makes it apparent that there are times in the complex social lives of human beings when their conditions change and become uncertain, creating the need for a common practice to explore or create new possibilities together. These times can be described as transitions characterised by major changes in the structures of communities. Describing and understanding the purpose of career guidance as *the creation of new possibilities in relation to the participation of individuals in education and the labour market during periods of transition and change* is in many ways different from focusing on the categorisation of distinct groups of individuals using a dualistic understanding of the basic dilemma of career guidance.

This reinterpretation creates the basis for underlining reasons for practice other than those associated with catering for the interests of individuals and society, which result in the need to identify people who have a need for special career guidance efforts. There is a difference between saying that the problem is you (establishing a practice in which the focus is placed on the motivation of the individual), and saying that the problem is societal (establishing a practice for the joint analysis of possibilities). This joint analysis on an awareness that other people are experiencing similar situations which have different meanings for them. A focus on *creating possibilities* intensifies our awareness of the way in which career guidance can contribute knowledge about the need for structural changes in relation to the problems which career guidance can solve. Creating possibilities should consequently be understood dialectically, with the task of the practitioner involving helping individuals to analyse their possibilities as well as appreciating the relevant or irrelevant influence of social conditions on these possibilities and encouraging discussions of this influence.

11

In Sweden during the 1970s a similar goal was defined, described as "compensatory counselling": "The guidance counsellors should contribute to greater equality and try to change patterns related to social background and gender" (Lovén, 2003, p. 126). It seems that this rhetoric bore little relation to reality, however Lovén continues by pointing out that "In practice, guidance counsellors were mainly occupied with information giving and the researchers could see few signs of the guidance counsellor as an agent of social change" (ibid.).

One even earlier attempt to use career guidance as a modus for social change can be seen in the work of Frank Parsons, who is described as the father of educational and vocational guidance. In 1909 Parsons described a "Society of Mutualism" in which individuals identified their own abilities and matched them with corresponding vocational demands, after which they made rational choices (Plant, 1994). The fact that this can be regarded as an argument for social change should be seen in connection with the times in which it was written. In 1909 Parsons felt that rational choices should apply to everyone irrespective of their social class. The abilities of each individual would therefore form the point of departure for a rational choice of education whose rationality also required the privileged classes to appreciate that important resources would be lost if everyone was not given the chance to utilise their abilities to the greatest possible extent.

Today it is widely felt that people should have a free choice of education and that it is possible for everyone, when given professional career guidance, to make choices in accordance with their abilities and wishes. Even so, the education system is still criticised constantly for reproducing the same social patterns (Hansen, 2003). The idea that career guidance can function as a social lever should therefore be seen in the light of the fact that making choices is not the same as graduating with an examination certificate. Young people also need to be able to complete the courses that they start to allow themselves to find a relevant occupation.

The main objective of such reinterpretation is to focus on how career guidance practitioners can best add their knowledge to political discussions and policy-making and in such a way that enhances individuals' potential to contribute to just those societal and structural changes that career guidance is deeply committed to in the first place.

11.4.1 A contribution to research in career guidance

As shown in chapter 4, career guidance research typically contributes knowledge at various levels in relation to its field of study: the societal level, the institutional level, the concrete level of practice, the target group level (understood as various target groups for career guidance), or the professional level. The scientific/philosophical approach adopted by researchers to their field of study helps to decide the level which is made the object of study, and the perspective from which the study is carried out. Lindh and Lundahl point out that career guidance research rarely unites a structural and an actor perspective on career guidance (Lindh & Lundahl, 2007). The research contribution of this book is characterised by the fact that it contains empirical analyses of the connections between several levels; the use of the categories of critical psychology has made it possible to carry out analyses which (from the perspective of the participants) indicate connections between these levels.

Chapter 1 described a political interest in user-driven development of the field of career guidance. This book contributes insight into the perspectives of the participants on career guidance, and shows that the participants seek to change change career guidance with a view to making it more relevant and useful for themselves. This indicates the need for methodological consideration of how we can continue to work with the user-driven development of career guidance practice. For instance, in my interviews a number of the employees at the company said that they had not participated in career guidance at all. In my study I could have accepted this explanation and then used this to indicate a number of development opportunities for career guidance practice. However, my observations revealed that the employees did in fact discuss career-related issues with the career guidance practitioner and each other while standing at the career guidance wall in the lunch room. They referred to this as discussing their thoughts about finding new jobs. This led me to consider the way that career guidance was organised and made me wonder why the employees did not regard what they were doing as career guidance. This realisation is important when designing studies of user-driven development. Knowledge of the needs of users with regard to development can be

11

created in many different ways: by evaluation forms, interviews, observations, development projects or practice research (like this study), for instance. Questions can be asked about the wishes of users in many different ways, too: What do they use? What would be useful to them? And, finally, observations can also be carried out in many different ways: One might focus on practice as it currently appears, or consider it as a developing practice while being aware of the direction in which the users influence practice.

12 **Perspectives**

The perspectives outlined in this final section consider practice research as a modus for the development of career guidance practice, and indicate how this book can contribute to the development of critical psychology.

12.1 **Practice research as a modus for development**

Practice research has proven useful and relevant as a modus for career guidance research in several areas. Firstly, because the decentred perspective makes it possible to understand the way in which career guidance can have significance for people in their everyday lives, by studying how career guidance is either regarded as relevant or rejected, changed and turned into something that is more significant. And secondly, it challenges what is presented as the basic dilemma of career guidance by offering analytical categories which, in a Danish context, have productively helped to challenge the distinction between the interests of the individual and those of society. We now have new opportunities for developing of our understanding of the purpose of career guidance.

The typical interaction of practice research between interviews and observation from a participant perspective introduces researchers to a variety of practices, and has proven to be particularly productive to appreciating that career guidance is not just given by a career guidance practitioner as an institutional practice but also influenced and changed by the place in which it is practised and by the participants at that place.

There is one other Danish study focusing on career guidance as a field of study in the form of practice research, as it is understood in

12

225

a critical psychological framework. This study was carried out by *Videncenter for Uddannelses- og Erhvervsvejledning* (the Knowledge Centre for Educational and Vocational Guidance), focusing on parental inclusion in career guidance (Buhl, Day & Harck, 2008).

I should like to translate a sequence from Buhl and Harck's interviews with the career guidance practitioners who functioned as co-researchers in their study in order to illustrate two important points about practice research as a modus for the development of career guidance practice. Buhl and Harck ask "How do you think the partnership between the Youth Guidance Centre and the Knowledge Centre could be developed and qualified more thoroughly?". The answer from the practitioners who took part as co-researchers was: "As a method for cooperation, practice research is really good at getting processes launched. We have often been involved in projects in which everything stops when the project stops. But with this method it's something we're already doing and something we will continue to do. Just in a more reflected and qualified manner. That's also why we don't feel we've spent any extra time on it. It's not a project on top of everything else, but part of what we do in our job. We know what we've got out of it. But what about you? Have you got anything out of our partnership?" (Buhl & Harck, 2008, p. 26; author's translation).

The goal of practice research is to study an existing or developing practice by entering into a partnership with the participants in this practice. One indication that Buhl and Harck's project succeeded is the practitioners' comment "It's not a project on top of everything else, but part of what we do in our job". But practice research also aims to contribute to the development of practice, a development which can be traced in the quotation above when the practitioners say that the method is really good at getting processes launched. They will continue to do their job in future, but they will do so in a more reflected and qualified manner. And more importantly than anything else, they do not feel that the research project simply studied their practice and then disappeared again. In conclusion, the question that the practitioners asked the researchers demonstrates that efforts to democratise the process had succeeded. The practitioners do not only see themselves as informants; they understand that they are contributing to the learning process of the researchers and changes in their

12

226

practice when they ask "But what about you? Have you got anything out of our partnership?".

The time frame allowed for the work involved in this book did not permit me to study developments in relation to my partnerships with the co-researchers settings. This is why I have included the example above: to illustrate the experiences of other career guidance practitioners/co-researchers with regard to this form of cooperation in relation to development work and research into career guidance. The example shows that practice research is a potential and attractive option in terms of the organisation of research into career guidance.

12.2 Contribution to critical psychology

In previous chapters I have pointed out a number of development opportunities in relation to understanding various critical psychological categories. These are:

- Understanding how researchers can work across contexts
- Research as knowledge sharing – also throughout the process
- Adding more detail to categories, which are given content by exploring them in relation to a new field of study: career guidance

12.2.1 Across contexts and actions

When Dreier argues that studying individuals in a single context is not sufficient (Dreier, 2008), I should like to add that this challenge can be approached in various ways. Researchers can physically move from one concrete location to another; but it is also possible to work in a context-sensitive manner in the research process, with researchers being aware of howparticipants are connected to other contexts and asking about these connections. The participation of researchers in one context also provides access to knowledge about other contexts in which individuals participate. This can be done by asking a particular type of question to examine the connections between contexts: *You were talking about your family life. Can you tell me more about the influence of your family life on your working situation? Or: You*

12

mentioned your old school friends. Can you tell me more about the connection between them and the community of which you are now a part?

12.2.2 Research as knowledge sharing
– also throughout the process

Practice research is research carried out in cooperation with participants in practice. This cooperation is largely based on sharing knowledge. But this does not only involve the participants in practice sharing their knowledge with researchers. On several occasions I was asked what I had seen, what I saw, and what I thought about it. This can be regarded as a natural reaction when your ambition is that your participants should join you as co-researchers into the issue in question. At first it was difficult not to occupy the role of a researcher who was not part of the practice concerned but who visited this practice, observed it, but did not influence it: a position that clearly contrasted with my theoretical and methodological ambition to achieve a democratic research process. Consequently, it was important to maintain that I was *cooperating* with the participants in studying particular issues. This meant that I also had to contribute my knowledge when asked, and share my thoughts in the same way that my co-researchers were asked to share their everyday thoughts and experiences with me. Regarding my research as a process of exchange which did not simply involve me taking what I wanted, but in which the participants also had expectations about what I ought to be contributing, made it clear to me that it was important to think about the expectations I wanted to live up to. This was done with least difficulty in relation to the teacher and career guidance practitioner. The questions they asked often focused on my view of the development opportunities for practice, in extension of our shared exploration of the issues concerned.

The situation was slightly different for the folk high school students. Their expectations focused more on approaching me as if I were a career guidance practitioner, at which point other thoughts became relevant. One classical but relevant discussion concerns the similarities between the therapeutic interview and the research in-

terview; this underlines the importance of ensuring that the researcher does not cross the line into the therapeutic area, where the goal of
discussion is that participants should change themselves and their life
situation (Kvale, 1997).

In this book I have demonstrated that therapy and career guidance
can be distinguished by the fact that career guidance has a clear institutional goal in working with the educational and vocational thoughts
of participants. I have also shown that career guidance and career
guidance practitioners cannot be regarded as omnipotent in relation
to the choices of participants, and that educational and vocational
thoughts are not reserved to any one context for action. So when
I entered into a discussion with Peter about his educational choices
(as described in section 7.3.5 "Interviews and career guidance are
closely connected"), and interpreted this discussion as career guidance, my interpretation may be due more to the fact that I have a background as a career guidance practitioner which enabled me to carry
out a practice-centred interpretation – rather than the fact that Peter
felt I had put on my "career guidance practitioner" hat. Another possible interpretation is that we were involved in a form of exchange in
which he helped me with my interview and allowed me to observe
him for a few days – after which it was my turn to give him something, which is why he asked me for my opinion about his choice.

Højholt has some fascinating thoughts about the relationship
between researchers and co-researchers. She points out that this is
not a relationship of assistance or exchange, but a form of partnership in which both parties contribute to the study of the common
third: the issue which is the focus of the research concerned (Højholt,
2005, pp. 76 ff.) This indicates the need to ensure that the research
issue at stake contains both general and shared interests. My co-
researchers were very interested in helping to develop a career guidance practice which was more relevant for them and for anyone coming after them. So this is not only a question of exchange; exploration
is part of my research practice, but it is also part of career guidance
practice. My exploration of general aspects of the significance of career guidance practice is connected to Peter's personal exploration of
his possibilities for action and his reasons for his actions. The latter
interpretation is in contrast to an understanding of research that does

12

not influence practice, and an understanding of the researcher as someone who can step into and out of different roles. I argue that being a researcher does not mean being present in a role, but being present as a participant in practice alongside other participants and practices.

12.2.3 New angles via a new field of study

Critical psychology categories and practice research as a procedure have been used in a wide range of fields of study including health issues, studies of children, social studies and education studies (Kousholt & Thomsen, 2012). Many of these studies share the researcher's sense of surprise at the level of responsibility given to individuals in relation to the situation in which they find themselves. In this book this process has been described as transferring the problem from society to the individual, resulting in individualisation and categorising certain groups as having special needs. This book adds a number of new angles to the analytical categories considered by seeking to apply these categories to a new field of study: career guidance. The empirical work, analysis and discussion contained in these pages have made it possible to challenge the idea that the individual should be regarded as the natural point of departure for the process of career guidance. Career guidance can also contribute the basis for dealing with social structures which prevent the achievement of the goals of society with regard to career guidance in various ways. This can be done by using the knowledge that career guidance practitioners gain of the connections between personal problems and structures in the education system as well as of changes in the structure of the labour market.

Postscript

By way of introduction to this book, I quoted the final point made by Paul Willis in his book, *Learning to Labour*, in which he says that reflections on everyday life deprive it of its innocense and congeal reflection with guilt. He explains this by saying that ethnographic descriptions communicate knowledge at a vital level of experience and a level of human activity that is often overlooked or suppressed – but which becomes increasingly important for other levels of the social whole (Willis, 1981). I hope that the detailed descriptions of participants' experiences with regard to career guidance contained in this book will give rise to concrete actions that can create better career guidance regarding the interaction of people in society at large.

Willis' point about innocence and guilt draws my attention to the fact that my reflections on how career guidance can become part of the lives of participants do not necessarily create opportunities for social changes. These reflections can be used to organise career guidance so that individuals are still held to be responsible for social changes and are not made aware of the connection between their own situation and the social conditions, and are therefore prevented from seeing that social conditions could be different and can be changed.

Even if this book has stolen the innocence of career guidance, I have also tried to identify opportunities for a form of career guidance that is is guilty neither of suppression nor the continuation of those social problems that it seeks to change.

Notes

1. Folk high schools are residential schools providing general and non-formal education. The length of courses vary – from one week to up to almost a year – and are attended by adults of all ages. They are non-qualifying courses meant to broaden general, social and democratic competencies. Danish Agency for International Education (2010, p. 11).

2. Transcripts from interviews and quotations from theoretical works in Danish have been translated into English.

3. For a historical survey of the development of guidance in Denmark 1896-2008, see Plant 1996, 2009.

4. *Bekendtgørelse af lov om folkehøjskoler, efterskoler, husholdningsskoler og håndarbejdsskoler* no. 285 of 18/07/2008.

5. See www.ug.dk.

6. A.G. Watts is frequently used as a consultant by multinational institutions interested in career guidance (the OECD, for instance).

7. The registry includes research that has been completed or begun up until 2004.

8. In Sultana's report reports were made available from 29 countries.

9. British Journal of Guidance & Counselling, vol. 33, no. 3, August 2005 is an issue focusing specifically on post-structuralism and the impact of the work of Michel Foucault on counselling and guidance.

10. Following a presentation of the provisional results of the dissertation on which this book is based, on 20 December 2007 I received an email from Karen Raunkjær, Manager of the Study Choice Centre for Mid- and West-Jutland, in which she informed me that her centre was experimenting with group career guidance.

11. The term "theoretically informed analysis" is used here to indicate that critical psychological categories drew my attention to the research question and informed my awareness of the empirical study in dialectic interaction with the concrete connections that are studied.

12. Introductions to Danish critical psychology can be found in Nissen 2000 and Mørch & Huniche 2006.

13. See www.praksisforskning-iudvikling.dk.

14. The Munich Group: the group of researchers behind the project "Flexibilising working conditions and the organisation of the individual conduct of everyday life", cf. Holzkamp, 1998.

15. See, for example, Urban, 25 June 2008, p. 7.

16. Jobnet is an internet-based tool operated by the Danish job centres, Public Employment Services (PES), and available to applicants and employers all over the country. The job centres refer to the Danish National Labour Market Authority and the municipalities.

17. www.herninghfogvuc.dk/sw7957.asp.

18. This evaluation was part of an EU project called "Workplace Guidance". See www.gla.ac.uk/wg for more information.

19. Ethics and confidentiality were discussed, for instance, in connection with a presentation given to municipal and national career guidance practitioners on 5 December 2007 and a presentation given to student counsellors at the University of Copenhagen on 13 June 2008.

Bibliography

Axel, E. (2002). *Regulation as Productive Tool Use. Participatory Observation in the Control Room of a District Heating System.* Roskilde: Roskilde University Press.

Andersen, I. (1999). *Den skinbarlige virkelighed: om valg af samfundsvidenskabelige metoder.* Frederiksberg: Samfundslitteratur.

Bauer, D. (1984). *Værdien af aktiverende gruppevejledning.* Copenhagen: Arbejdsdirektoratet Psykologisk Tjeneste.

Bauer, D. (1985). *Værdien af gruppevejledning for forskellige målgrupper – sammenfatningsrapport.* Arbejdsdirektoratet.

Bimrose, J., S.A. Barnes & J. Brown (2005). *A Systematic Literature Review of Research into Career-Related Interventions for Higher Education: HECSU.* Manchester & Institute for Employment Research, University of Warwick.

Borg, T. (2002). *Livsførelse i hverdagen under rehabilitering – et socialpsykologisk studie. Ålborg: Institut for Sociale Forhold og Organisation.* Ålborg Universitet.

Borgen, W.A. (1998). *Gruppevejledning teori og metode.* Copenhagen: Rådet for Uddannelses- og Erhvervsvejledning.

Borgen, W. A., P. Diane, N. Amundso & M. Westwood (1989). *Employment Groups: The counselling Connection.* Canada: Minister of Supply and Services Canada.

Brown, S.D. & N.E.R. Krane (2000). Four (or Five) Sessions and a Cloud of Dust: Old Assumptions and New Observations about Career Counseling. In S.D. Brown & R.W. Lent (eds.), *Handbook of counseling psychology.* New York: Wiley.

Buhl, J. & J. Flindt Pedersen (2007). *Den ægte dialog – i vejledning og rådgivning.* Copenhagen: Hans Reitzel.

Buhl, R., B. Day & T. Harck (2008). *Vejleder-forældre-samarbejde – at udvide begrebet om forældreinddragelse i vejledningen.* Vejle: Videncenter for uddannelsesog erhvervsvejledning.

Buhl, R. & T. Harck (2008). Erfaringer fra samarbejde mellem UU og VUE. *Nyhedsbrev Videncenter for Uddannelses- og Erhvervsvejledning,* 2008(3), 209.

Baagøe Nielsen, S. & A. Rieck Sørensen (2004). *Unges valg af uddannelse og job. Udfordringer og veje til det kønsopdelte arbejdsmarked.* Roskilde: Center for Ligestillingsforskning, Roskilde Universitetscenter.

Callesen, M.M., J. Jensen, S. Roesen & R. Thomsen (2003). *Vejledning – et moderne projekt.* Unpubl. report. Roskilde Universitet.

Callesen, M.M. & R. Thomsen (2005a). *Er vejledningen Omnipotent?* Unpubl. MA dissertation. Roskilde Universitet.

Callesen, M.M. & R. Thomsen (2005b). Refleksion – en tom betegnelse?, p. 13 in P. Plant (ed.), *Vejbred: en antologi om vejledning.* Copenhagen: Danmarks Pædagogiske Universitets Forlag.

Casey, S.E. (1996). How to Get from Space to Place in a Fairly Short Stretch of Time. In S. Feld & K.H. Basso (eds.), *Senses of place.* Santa Fe, NM: School of American Research Press.

Christensen, G. (2003). *Psykologiens videnskabsteori – en introduktion.* Frederiksberg: Roskilde Universitetsforlag.

Christensen, L. (1997). *Travle, halv-gamle mænd i uddannelsessamfundet: en undersøgelse af nogle 40-60-årige mænds motivation og barrierer i forhold til deltagelse i voksen-uddannelse.* Copenhagen: Undervisningsministeriet.

Clayton, P.H., S. Greco & M. Persson (2007). *Guidance for Life Working and Learning in the Third Age.* Milan: FrancoAngeli.

Costall, A. & O. Dreier (2006). *Doing Things with Things – The Design and Use of Everyday Objects.* Aldershot, Hampshire: Ashgate.

Council of the European Union (2004). *Draft resolution of the Council and of the representatives of the Member States meeting within the Council on strengthening policies, systems and practices in the field of guidance throughout life in Europe.* Brussels: Council of the European Union, 2004.

Council of the European Union (2008). *Better Integrating Lifelong Guidance into Lifelong Learning Strategies.* 2905th Education, Youth and Culture Council meeting, Brussels, 21 November 2008.

Devault, L. M. & L. McCoy (2006). Institutional Ethnography: Using Interviews to Investigate Ruling Relations. In D.E. Smith (ed.), *Institutional Ethnography as Practice* 1. Oxford: Rowman & Littlefield Publishers, Inc.

Dreier, O. (1993). Re-Searching Psychotherapeutic Practice. In S. Chaiklin & J. Lave (eds.), *Understanding practice.* Cambridge: Cambridge University Press.

Dreier, O. (1996). Ændring af professionel praksis på sundhedsområdet gennem praksisforskning. In *Forskelle og forandringer – bidrag til humanistisk sundhedsforskning.* Philosophia.

Dreier, O. (1999a). Læring som ændring af personlig deltagelse i sociale kontekster. In K. Nielsen & S. Kvale (eds.), *Mesterlære.* Copenhagen: Hans Reitzels Forlag.

Dreier, O. (1999b). *Personal Trajectories of Participation across Contexts of Social Practice. Outlines,* (1), 5.

Dreier, O. (2002). *Psykosocial behandling – en teori om et praksisområde* (2. ed.). Copenhagen: Dansk Psykologisk Forlag.

Dreier, O. (2006). Imod abstraktionen af struktur. *Nordiske Udkast,* 34(1), 3.

Dreier, O. (2008). *Psychotherapy in Everyday life. Learning in Doing: Social, Cognitive & Computational Perspectives.* Cambridge University Press.

Dreier, O. (2009). Persons in Structures of Social Practice. *Theory & Psychology,* 19(2), 193-212.

Engeström, Y. (1993). Developmental studies of work as a testbench of activity theory. In S. Chaiklin & J. Lave (eds.), *Understanding Practice.* Cambridge: Cambridge University Press.

EVA (2007). *Vejledning om valg af uddannelse og erhverv.* Copenhagen: Danmarks Evalueringsinstitut.

Euroguidance Denmark. (2012). Guidance in Education – The Educational Guidance System in Denmark (3. ed.). Copenhagen: Euroguidance Denmark, The Danish Agency for Universities and Internationalisation. www.eng.uvm.dk/Education/Education-and-vocational-guidance.

Forchhammer, H.B. (2001). Interviewet som handlesammenhæng. *Nordiske Udkast,* 29(1).

FUE (2006). Etiske retningslinier. www1.sdu.dk [FUE + etiske retningslinjer]

Gruenewald, D.A. (2003). Foundations of Place: A Multidisciplinary Framework for Place-Conscious Education. *American Educational Research Journal,* 40(3).

Hansen, E.J. (2003). *Uddannelsessystemerne i sociologisk perspektiv.* Copenhagen: Hans Reitzels Forlag.

Hansen, L. (1999). (Nogle) voksnes lærings- og undervisningsbegreber. In Undervisningsministeriet (ed.), *Hvad tænder? Et debatskrift om voksenundervisning,* 13. Copenhagen: Undervisningsministeriet.

Holsbo, A.o.N. & L. Mærsk (2005). *Analyseopgave vedrørende voksen-, efter- og videreuddannelse (VEU). Delanalyse 3: Deltagelse i VEU – motivation og barrierer for ansatte.* Aarhus: Teknologisk Institut, Arbejdsliv.

Holzkamp, K. (1983). *Grundlegung der Psychologie.* Frankfurt: Campus.

Holzkamp, K. (1985). *Mennesket som subjekt for videnskabelig metodik.* Kommunistiske studenter på Psykologi ved Københavns Universitet.

Holzkamp, K. (1989). Menneskets samfundsmæssige natur – om forholdet mellem den total-samfundsmæssige proces og den individuelle livsproces. *Forum,* 5.

Holzkamp, K. (1991). Societal and Individual Life Processes. In C. W. Tolman & W. Maiers eds.), *Critical Psychology. Contributions to an Historical Science of the Subject* (pp. 50-65). Cambridge: Cambridge University Press.

Holzkamp, K. (1993). *Lernen. Subjektwissenschaftliche Grundlegung.* Frankfurt/Main: Campus.

Holzkamp, K. (1998). Daglig livsførelse som subjektvidenskabeligt grundkoncept. *Nordiske Udkast,* 26(2).

236

Hughes, D., J. Bimrose, A.A. Barnes, L. Bowes & M. Orton (2005). *A Systematic Literature Review: Career Development Interventions in the Workplace*. Sheffield: Department for Education & Skills.

Hutters, C. (2004). *Mellem lyst og nødvendighed. En analyse af unges valg af videregående uddannelse*. Unpubl. PhD dissertation, Roskilde: Forskerskolen i livslang læring, Roskilde Universitetscenter.

Højdal, L. & L. Poulsen (2007). *Karrierevalg – teorier om valg og valgprocesser*. Fredensborg: Studie og Erhverv.

Højholt, C. (1993). *Brugerperspektiver – forældres, læreres og psykologers erfaringer med psykosocialt arbejde*. Copenhagen: Dansk Psykologisk Forlag.

Højholt, C. (1999). *Samarbejde om børns udvikling – subjekter i praksisser*. Unpubl. PhD dissertation, Københavns Universitet Amager, Institut for Psykologi.

Højholt, C. (2001). *Samarbejde om børns udvikling*. Copenhagen: Gyldendal.

Højholt, C. (2005). *Forældresamarbejde: forskning i fællesskab*. Virum: Dansk Psykologisk Forlag.

Højholt, C. (2006). Knowledge and professionalism – from the perspectives of children? *International journal of Critical Psychology*, 81.

Højmark Jensen, U. (2005). Unge uden uddannelse: Hvem er de og hvordan kan de vejledes? In P. Plant (ed.), *Vejbred: en antologi om vejledning*. København: Danmarks Pædagogiske Universitet.

Haarder, B. (2008). *Kvalitet i vejledningen*, Åbningstale til konferencen Kvalitet i Vejledningen. www.uvm. dk/vejl/documents/KvalitetivejledningenMtale.doc.

IAEVG (1995). *Ethical Standards*. www.iaevg.org/iaevg/nav. cfm?lang=2&menu=1&submenu=2.

Jartoft, V. (1996). Den Kritiske Psykologi – en videnskab med fokus på subjektivitet og handling. In *Skolelivets socialpsykologi – Nyere socialpsykologiske teorier og perspektiver*. Virum: Unge Pædagoger.

Jensen, T.I. (2008). *Voksenvejledningsnetværk i støbeskeen*. Via Vejledning, undervisningsministeriet, 14.

Katznelson, N. (2004). *Vejledning på tværs*. Roskilde: Center for Ungdomsforskning, KL, UVM.

Katznelson, N. & M. Pless (2007). *Unges veje mod ungdomsuddannelserne. Tredje rapport om unges uddannelsesvalg og overgang fra grundskole til ungdomsuddannelse og arbejde*. Copenhagen: Center for Ungdomsforskning, LLD.

Kofod, A. (2004). Vejledningens betydning på højskolerne – unges afklaring af uddannelsesvalg. *Ungdomsforskning*, 3(3/4).

Kousholt, D. (2006). *Familieliv fra et børneperspektiv*. Unpubl. PhD dissertation. Roskilde Universitetscenter, Institut for Psykologi, Roskilde.

Kousholt, K. & R. Thomsen (2012; forthcoming). Dialectics in recent danish critical psychology. *Annual Review of Critical Psychology*.

Krøjer, J. & C. Hutters (2006). *Metodehåndbog i fortælleværk-steder*. Copenhagen: FFD.

Krøjer, J. & C. Hutters (2008). Kollektivet som korrektiv: Fortælle-værksteder som kritik af neoliberalt selvarbejde. *Tidsskrift for arbejdsliv*, 10(1).

Kvale, S. (1997). *Interview: En intro-duktion til det kvalitative forsknings-interview*. Copenhagen: Hans Reitzels Forlag.

Kvale, S. & J. Lave (2003). Hvad er antropologisk forskning? In J. Lave & E. Wenger (eds.), *Situeret læring og andre tekster*. Copenhagen: Hans Reitzels Forlag.

Lave, J. (1993). The Practice of Learning. In S. Chaiklin & J. Lave (eds.), *Under-standing practice*. Cambridge: Cambridge University Press.

Lave, J. (2011). *Apprenticeship in Critical Ethnograhic Practice*. Chicago Univer-sity Press.

Lave, J. & E. Wenger (2007). *Situeret læring – og andre tekster*. Copen-hagen: Hans Reitzels Forlag.

Lave, J. & E. Wenger (1991). *Situated Learning, Legitimate Peripheral Participation*. New York: Cambridge University Press.

LBK 630 af 200608 C.F.R. (2008). *Bekendtgørelse af Lov om vejledning om valg af uddannelse og erhverv.* 214

LBK 785 af 180708 C.F.R. (2008). *Bekendtgørelse af Lov om folkehøj-skoler, efterskoler, husholdningsskoler og håndarbejdsskoler (frie kostskoler)*

Lindh, G. (2000). *Samtalen: et værktøj i uddannelses- og erhvervsvalgspro-cessen*. Copenhagen: Rådet for Ud-dannelses- og Erhvervsvejledning.

Lindh, G. & L. Lundahl (2007). *Den resandes ensak?* http:sherwood. lh.umu.se/fkvv.

Lov om realkompetencevurdering (Udbygning af anerkendelse af re-alkompetence på voksen- og efter-uddannelsesområdet m.v.), LOV 556 af 060607 C.F.R. (2007).

Lovén, A. (1995). *Vejledning i nær-billede. En analyse af den individuelle vejlednings forudsætninger, vilkår og indhold*. Copenhagen: Rådet for Uddannelses- og Erhvervsvejledning.

Lovén, A. (2003). The Paradigm Shift – Rhetoric or Reality? *International Journal for Educational and Voca-tional Guidance*, 3.

Lund, L.S. (2003). *Vejledning og rea-lisering af handlingsplaner – i et bio-grafisk perspektiv*. Unpubl. PhD dis-sertation. Copenhagen: Danmarks Pædagogiske Universitet.

Løve, T. (2005). *Vejledning ansigt til ansigt. Teorier og metoder i den individuelle vejledning*. Fredensborg: Studie og Erhverv.

Mathiesen, A. (2000). *Uddannelsernes sociologi*. København: Pædagogisk Forum. Christian Ejlers Forlag.

Mignot, P. (2000). Metaphor: A Para-digm for Practice-Based Research into 'Career'. *British Journal of Guidance & Counselling*, 28(4).

Morin, A. (2007). *Børns deltagelse og læring. På tværs af almen- og specialpædagogiske lærearrangementer.* Unpubl. PhD dissertation. Copenhagen: Danmarks Pædagogiske Universitet.

Mørck, L.L. (1995). Praksisforskning som metode, teori og praksis. Refleksion over praksisforskerens positionering i og mellem handlesammenhænge. *Nordiske Udkast*, 23(1).

Mørck, L.L. (2003). *Læring og overskridelse af marginalisering. Studie af unge mænd med etnisk minoritetsbaggrund.* Danmarks Pædagogiske Universitet, København.

Mørck, L. L., & L. Huniche (2006). Critical Psychology in a Danish Context. *Annual Review of Critical Psychology*(5).

Mørck, L.L. & M. Nissen (2001). Vilde forskningsprocesser: kritik, metoder og læring i socialt arbejde. *Nordiske Udkast*, 29(1).

Nissen, M. (2000). Practice Research. Critical Psychology in and through Practices. *Annual Review of Critical Psychology*, 2, 145-179.

Nissen, M. (2001). *Projekt Gadebørn. Et forsøg med dialogisk, bevægelig og lokalkulturel socialpædagogik med de mest udsatte unge.* Frederikshavn: Dafolo.

Nissen, M. (2002). Det kritiske subjekt. *Psyke & logos*, 23(1).

OECD (2004). *Career Guidance and Public Policy; Bridging The Gap.* Luxembourg: OECD.

Olsen, H. (2002). *Dansk kvalitativ interviewforskning: kvalitet eller kvaler?* København: Socialforskningsinstituttet.

Osterkamp, U. (2000). Livsførelse som subjektvidenskabelig problematik. *Nordiske Udkast*, 28.

Otto, L. (2001). Livshistorier og biografisk subjektivitet. *Dansk Pædagogisk Tidsskrift*, 1(3).

Peavy, V. (2004). *Sociodynamic Counselling. A Practical Approach to Meaning Making.* Ohio: Taos Institute Publications.

Plant, P. (1994). *Et sikkert fodfæste.* Unpubl. PhD dissertation. Danmarks Lærerhøjskole, Copenhagen.

Plant, P. (1996). *Fodfæste. Dansk uddannelses- og erhvervsvejledning 1886-1976.* Copenhagen: Rådet for Uddannelses- og Erhvervsvejledning.

Plant, P. (1998). Danish preface in A.G. Watts (ed.), *Uddannelses og erhvervsvejledning. Teori og praksis.* Copenhagen: Studie og Erhverv.

Plant, P. (2002). *Vocational Guidance for low-paid workers in Denmark.* www.gla.ac.uk/wg/dan_rep2.htm.

Plant, P. (2007a). Nordic research in Educational and Vocational Guidance. In P. Plant (ed.), *Ways.* København: Danish University of Education Press.

Plant, P. (2007b). On the shopfloor: Guidance in the workplace. In J. Athanasou & R.V. Esbroek (eds.), *International Handbook of Career Guidance.* London: Springer.

Plant, P. (2009). *Fæste. Dansk uddannelses- og erhvervsvejledning, 1886-2008.* Fredensborg: Studie og Erhverv.

Preisler, M. (2008). Mange vælger den forkerte uddannelse. *Ugebrevet A4*, 2008(27).

Rambøll. (2008). *Analyse af ud-dannelses- og erhvervsvejledning i Uddannelsessektoren.* Copenhagen: Finansministeriet, Undervisningsministeriet.

Rasmussen, O.V. (2003). Viden i praksis – om forskning som prak-sisudviklingsforskning. *Nordiske Udkast* (1).

Rogers, C.R. (1961). *On Becoming a Person: A Therapist's View of Psychotherapy.* Boston.

Schedin, G. (2007). *Expectations and Experiences of Career Counselling: An Exploration of Interpersonal Behaviour.* Unpubl. PhD dissertation. Umeå University, Umeå.

Schwartz, I. (2007). *Børneliv på døgninstitution – Socialpædagogik på tværs af børns livssammenhænge.* Unpubl. PhD dissertation, Syddansk Universitet, Institut for Filosofi, Pædagogik og Religionsstudier.

Spradley, J.P. (1980). *Participant Observation.* New York: Holt, Rinehart and Winston.

Sultana, R.G. (2004). *Guidance Policies in the Knowledge Society Trends, Challenges and Responses across Europe.* Luxembourg: Office for Official Publications of the European Communities.

Sultana, R.G. (2011). On Being a Boundary Person: Mediating Between the Local and the Global in Career Guidance Policy Learning. *Globalisation, Societies and Education,* 9(2), 265-283.

Sørensen, E. (2006). Politics of Things. In A. Costall & O. Dreier (Eds.), *Doing Things with Things – The Design and Use of Everyday Objects.* Aldershot, Hampshire: Ashgate.

The Danish Agency for Universities and Internationalisation (2012). *Guidance in Education – The Educational Guidance System in Denmark.* Copenhagen: Euroguidance Denmark, The Danish Agency for Universities and Internationalisation.

Thomsen, R. (2007). Reflection – An Empty Category? In P. Plant (ed.), *Ways* (1). Copenhagen: DPUs Forlag.

Thomsen, R. (2008). *Realkompetence-processen: Identifikation og afklaring.* VejledningsIntermezzo, FUE, 1.

Thomsen, R. & P. Plant (2012, forthc.). Guidance and Counselling in Denmark. In T. Hohenshill, N.E. Amundson & S. Niles, (eds.), *American Psychological Association International Counseling Book.*

Tolman, C.W. (1991). Critical Psychology: An Overview. In C.W. Tolman & W. Maiers (eds.), *Critical Psychology. Contributions to an Historical Science of the Subject* (pp. 1-22). Cambridge: Cambridge University Press.

Trepartsudvalget (2006). *Livslang opkvalificering og uddannelse for alle på arbejdsmarkede. Vol. 1: Den fremtidige voksen- og efteruddannelsesindsats.* Copenhagen: Finansministeriet, Center for arbejdsmarkedsforhold, fordeling og overførselsindkomster.

UNI-C (2008). *Undersøgelse af gymnasieelevers udbytte af Studievalgscentrenes vejledende indsats.* Copenhagen: UNI-C.

Usher, R. (2005). Subjects, Networks and Positions: Thinking Educational Guidance Differently. *British Journal of Guidance & Counselling*, 33(3).

UVM (2004). *Guidance in Education – A New Guidance System in Denmark*. pub.uvm.dk/2004/guidance/hel.pdf

UVM (2007). *FAKTAARK – Bedre vejledning og rådgivning*. www.vejledning.net/Sider/Videndeling/Dokumenter/Faktaark_vejledning+raadgivning.pdf.

Vejledning om a-kasses pligt til at vejlede, VEJ nr. 15 af 190207 C.F.R. (2007).

VUS-Kontakt (2005). *Årsrapport*. www.vuskontakt.dk.

Watts, A.G. (1998). *Uddannelses- og erhvervsvejledning. Teori og praksis*. Fredensborg: Studie og Erhverv.

Watts, A.G. (2004). Career Guidance Policies in 37 Countries: Contrasts and Common Themes. *International Journal for Educational and Vocational Guidance*, 4(2).

Wenger, E. (1998). *Communities of Practice: Learning, Meaning, and Identity*. Cambridge: Cambridge University Press.

Wenger, E. (2004). *Praksisfællesskaber. Læring, mening og identitet*. Copenhagen: Hans Reitzels Forlag.

Willis, P.E. (1981). *Learning to Labour. How Working Class Kids Get Working Class Jobs*. Aldershot, Hampshire: Gower.

Ziehe, T. (2005). *Øer af intensitet i et hav af rutine: nye tekster om ungdom, skole og kultur*. Copenhagen: Gyldendals Bogklubber.

Appendices

APPENDIX 1

Interview guide for folk high school students

A piece of A3 paper was lying on the table between myself and my interviewee. I explained that we could both use this, and that I hoped we could explore the issues arising together. I also explained that the interview was anonymous.

Background and goal of studying at folk high school	– Why did you decide to study at a folk high school? – Have you thought about what you wanted to learn at folk high school? – What are the goals of your time here? Why are these your goals? – Will your time at the school help you to achieve these goals? – What are the activities at the school that influence your opportunities after leaving? – Have you thought about what to do when you leave? If so, what thoughts have you had? What will you be doing in three years' and five years' time, and do you have any alternative plans?
Career guidance/ the participant's perspective	– How do the students here tackle the choice of further education? – How and in what situations are you given the opportunity to talk about your choice of further education? – What is career guidance in your view? Have you received any career guidance in the past? – Have you worked with educational and vocational guidance at the folk high school? – Is there a difference between the career guidance you are given here and the career guidance you have received in the past? Has any one thing made a particular difference for you? – What is good career guidance in your view? What are your wishes regarding activities? – The folk high school organises plenty of opportunities for participation. How would you describe the elements of your time here that have helped you to make your decision?

– Previous students say that their time at folk high school helped them to make their decision. Why do you think this is so?
– The drop-out rate of students who have been to folk high school is lower than that of students who have not. Why do you think this is so?

Competences and identifying competences	– What were your thoughts when you registered for the January course called "Valuable Competencies"?
	– Have you thought about what you will learn on this course?
	– What does identifying your competences involve in your view?
	– What made you realise that you had new competences?
	– Has your time at folk high school made you more aware of your competences?
	– What do you think helped to make this happen?
	– What activities have helped you to realise your own competences?
	– How can identifying your competences help your educational future?
	– Has your time at the school changed you, or taught you anything that you think will influence your life in general?
Formal, informal and non-formal learning systems	– Can you describe a good folk high school student for me?
	– How do the students help each other's learning processes?
	– How would you describe the relationship between teachers and students at this school? In relation to demands, expectations etc.
	– How would you describe the difference between teaching at this folk high school and teaching at upper-secondary school level?
	– Is there a difference between learning at this school and learning in more formal learning contexts such as upper-secondary school? Can you describe the difference?
	– Is there a difference between how you learn at this school and how you learn in other contexts?
	– Can you describe the difference?
	– How do you think other people view the time you spend at folk high school?
	– Have you learnt anything elsewhere which has been important for you? When and how?
Evaluation	Is there anything I haven't asked you about in the interview or while we were walking around together that you thought we would be talking about?
	What were your thoughts when you agreed to participate in this research project?

APPENDIX 2

Interview guide for teachers

A piece of A3 paper was lying on the table between myself and my interviewee. I explained that we could both use this, and that I hoped we could explore the issues arising together.

Background	– Tell me a bit about what it's like to be a folk high school teacher.
Competences and identifying competences	– What was your thinking when you planned this course called Valuable Competencies? – Have you thought about what you wanted the students to learn on this course? Why do you want them to learn this? – What does identifying competences mean in your view? – How are the students included in identifying their competences at this school? – In your view, what are the indicators showing that students have identified their competences? – How can identifying competences help the students in their educational futures?
Career guidance	– How do the students here tackle the choice of further education? – How and in what situations are the students given the opportunity to talk about their choice of further education? – The folk high school organises plenty of opportunities for participation. How would you describe the elements of the school that help students to make their decision? – What is career guidance in your view? – How do you work with educational and vocational guidance at the folk high school? – How are the students included in career guidance? How would you describe the relationship between the teachers and students at the folk high school?
The participant perspective	– Many previous students say that their time at folk high school helped them to make their decision. Why do you think this is so? – The drop-out rate of students who have been to folk high school is lower than that of students who have not. Why do you think this is so?

244

Formal, informal and non-formal learning systems	– We have already discussed your goals with regard to the students. Do these goals influence the way you organise and carry out your teaching or discussions? – Is there a difference between learning at this school and learning in more formal learning contexts such as upper-secondary school? – Do the students talk about what they have learned elsewhere while they are at this folk high school? – What is the importance of previous learning (formal and informal) at this folk high school? – How would you describe a good folk high school student? – How do the students affect each other's learning processes?
Evaluation	– Is there anything I haven't asked you about in the interview or while we were walking around together that you thought we would be talking about? – What were your thoughts when the folk high school agreed to participate in this research project?

APPENDIX 3

Interview guide for company employees

Background	– Tell me a bit about what it's like to be an employee at this company.
	– What are your thoughts in connection with the closure of the company?
	– Have you thought about how to find another job? What will you be doing in three years' and five years' time, and do you have any alternative plans?
Career guidance/the participant perspective	– How have the company employees tackled the loss of their jobs?
	– Who do you talk to about being fired?
	– How and in what situations are you given the opportunity to talk about applying for other jobs?
	– What is career guidance in your view? Have you received any career guidance in the past?
	– Have you had any sessions with Ulla? What did you talk about?
	– If you could organise a course for the employees of a company that was closing down, what would you do?
	– What is good career guidance in your view? What are your wishes for activities?
	– Has your participation in career guidance (discussions with Ulla) changed you or taught you anything you think will influence your life in general?
Competences and identifying competences	– What do employers regard as important when hiring people for a job like yours?
	– Do you like writing applications?
	– If an employer sees a description of your job, does he know what you can do?
	– What would you emphasise if you were asked about your competences at a job interview?
	– What does identifying your competences involve in your view?
	– What made you realise that you had new competences?
	– Has career guidance or supplementary training made you more aware of your competences? What do you think helped to make this happen?
	– What activities have helped you to realise your own competences?
	– How can identifying your competences help your future working life?
	– What makes people motivated to take supplementary training courses?

Formal, informal and non-formal learning systems	– Have you learned anything new while working here? – Can you describe a good labourer for me? – How would you describe the relationship between the employer and employees at this company? – Is there a difference between the way you learn things at this company and the way you learn things in other learning contexts? Can you describe this difference? – Have you learned things elsewhere that have been important for you? – What, when and how?
Evaluation	– Is there anything I haven't asked you about in the interview or while we were walking around together that you thought we would be talking about? – What were your thoughts when you were told you'd be participating in this research project?

APPENDIX 4

Interview guide for VUS Kontakt practitioner/HR at the company

Background	– Tell me a bit about what it's like to be a VUS Kontakt practitioner. What is the role? How many of you are there? Tell me a bit about what it's like to work with HR at the company, what are the tasks involved, etc.
Competences and identifying competences	– What was your thinking when you planned the process at this company? Who was involved in the process? – What was your thinking about what you wanted the employees to get out of the process? Why did you want them to learn these things? – You talked about competences on the job application course. What does identifying your competences mean in your view? – How are the employees included in identifying their competences at the company? – In your view, what are the indicators showing that employees have identified their competences? Can you describe a situation in which this happened? What activities do you use? – How can identifying competences help the employees in their future working lives? – How do you work with identifying competences at VUS?
Career guidance	– How have the employees tackled the loss of their jobs? How and in what situations are they given the opportunity to talk about being fired and new job opportunities? – Have you been a practitioner in other companies that have fired people? How do you think this company has handled the situation? Satisfaction/dissatisfaction among the employees. What are the wishes of the employees regarding the process? – Do you think that the employees use each other? How and for what? – Observation: On the job application course the employees talked to each other about what they could do (competences) and what jobs they could apply for. (Ulla: You can use each other – you're good at that!). What are your views on this?

248

The participant perspective	– How are the employees included in planning the process? (Wishes for courses, etc.). How would you describe the relationship between the employees and management at the company? What influence do the employees have on the career guidance process?
Formal, informal and non-formal learning systems	– We have already discussed what you want the employees to get out of the process. Does this influence the way you plan and carry out your teaching or discussions? – Is there a difference between the way people learn things at this company and the way they learn things in other learning contexts (courses, job applications etc.)? – Do the employees discuss what they have learned elsewhere – for instance when you're talking about CVs? – A lot of employees talk indirectly about what they have learned at the company, where work sharing and responsibility seem to be important for the development of their competences. – What is the importance of things they have learned elsewhere for their job opportunities?
Evaluation	– Is there anything I haven't asked you about in the interview or while we were walking around together that you thought we would be talking about? – What were your thoughts when VUS agreed to participate in this research project?

APPENDIX 5
Notice at folk high school

Research project

Dear teachers and students
In collaboration with the teachers and students at XX folk high school, this spring I am carrying out a PhD research project about career guidance and identifying competences.

In the spring of 2006:
– You can meet me at the school
– You may be asked about the activities you participate in at the school
– You may see me jotting down my thoughts for subsequent analysis

FAQs
Will I be quoted on what I say? No – at least not word for word. And your input will be anonymous.
Can I refuse to participate? Yes – no problem at all.
Can I discuss things with you? Yes. What I am doing is called participatory observation, which means that I'll be talking to everyone at the school and taking part in what goes on here.

Who will be involved?
Basically everybody. But I'd like to observe about five of you for two days. Please use the short questionnaire which will be distributed on 16-18 January 2006 to say whether you want to be involved. You will be informed as soon as possible.

Rie Thomsen
PhD student
Danish School of Education

APPENDIX 6
Questionnaire for folk high school students

Dear teachers and students
In collaboration with the teachers and students at XX folk high school, this spring I am carrying out a PhD research project about career guidance and identifying competences. I hope you will spend five minutes completing this questionnaire, in which I also ask you whether you want to be observed during the project.

Please tick

Gender: ☐ Man ☐ Woman Age ....

Special subject at the school:

☐ Travel ☐ Journalism ☐ Social education ☐ Nursing/medicine

Why did you decide to go to folk high school?

....

....

What do you expect to get out of your time here?

....

....

Can Rie Thomsen follow you around for two days?	☐ Yes	☐ No
Can she interview you for about an hour afterwards?	☐ Yes	☐ No
Are you prepared to participate in a focus group interview about six months after leaving the school?	☐ Yes	☐ No

If yes, please complete the following:

Name: ....

Cell phone no.: ....

Email address: ....

Contact address: ....

APPENDIX 7
The Danish Educational System

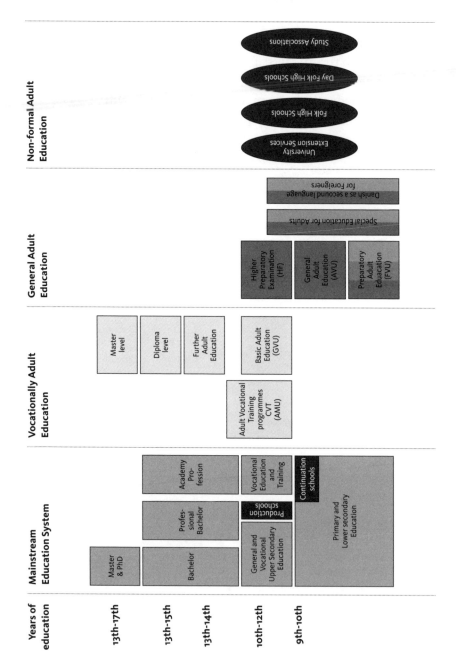

Ill. 1: Adult education and continuing training. Levels can not be indicated precisely. The model only shows levels not extent of activity
(Euroguidance Denmark, 2012, p. 10)

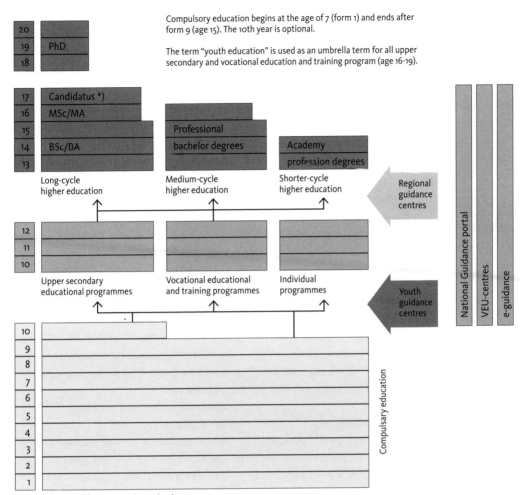

Compulsory education begins at the age of 7 (form 1) and ends after form 9 (age 15). The 10th year is optional.

The term "youth education" is used as an umbrella term for all upper secondary and vocational education and training program (age 16-19).

Primary and lower secondary school

*) Some programs last more than 2 years

Ill. 2: Guidance in Education in Denmark.
(*Euroguidance Denmark*, 2012)

Regional Guidance Centres

7 regional guidance centres are responsible for guidance related to the transition from youth education programmes to higher education, provision of quality information on all higher education programmes in Denmark and provision of quality information on the possible occupations or professions that higher education programmes may lead to

Youth Guidance Centres

45 municipal youth guidance centres provide guidance services for young people up to the age of 25 years. The 45 centres cover the 98 municipalities in Denmark, each centre covering a "sustainable" area in terms of the number and variety of youth education institutions as well as geographical distance. The youth guidance centres focus on guidance related to the transition from compulsory school to youth education or, alternatively, to the labour market. The main target groups are:

- Pupils in primary and lower secondary school – forms 6 to 9 (10)
- Young people under the age of 25 who are not involved in education, training or employment.

The centres provide outreach services for these groups as they are obliged to establish contact with these young people and help them get back into education and training or employment

National guidance portal

A national guidance portal – the "Education Guide": www.ug.dk – provides comprehensive information on education and training possibilities at all levels, professions, labour market conditions and statistics.

e-guidance

A national e-guidance centre provides users with online guidance service seven days a week. It is established in relation to www.ug.dk Danish Agency for International Education.

VEU-centres

13 centres for adult education and continuing training offer guidance related to a wide range of education programs to adults. At the centres guidance counselors provide career guidance to companies as well as individuals.

Index

254